Competitive Intelligence

A FRAMEWORK FOR WEB-BASED ANALYSIS AND DECISION MAKING

CONOR VIBERT
Acadia University

Australia · Canada · Mexico · Singapore · Spain · United Kingdom · United States

THOMSON

SOUTH-WESTERN

Competitive Intelligence: A Framework for Web-Based Analysis and Decision Making
Conor Vibert

VP/Editorial Director:
Jack Calhoun

VP/Editor-in-Chief:
Dave Shaut

Acquisition Editor:
Steve Momper

Channel Manager, Retail:
Chris McNamee

Channel Manager, Professional:
Mark Linton

Production Manager:
Tricia Matthews Boies

Editor:
Kim Kusnerak

Sr. Print Buyer:
Charlene Taylor

Production House:
electro-publishing

Copyeditor:
Elaine Langlois

Sr. Design Project Manager:
Michelle Kunkler

Cover Designer:
R. Alcorn

Cover Image:
© Digital Vision

Printer:
Phoenix Book Technology
Hagerstown, MD

International Division List

ASIA (Including India):
Thomson Learning
60 Albert Street, #15-01
Albert Complex
Singapore 189969
Tel 65 336-6411
Fax 65 336-7411

AUSTRALIA/NEW ZEALAND:
Nelson
102 Dodds Street
South Melbourne
Victoria 3205
Australia
Tel 61 (0)3 9685-4111
Fax 61 (0)3 9685-4199

LATIN AMERICA:
Thomson Learning
Seneca 53
Colonia Polanco
11560 Mexico, D.F. Mexico
Tel (525) 281-2906
Fax (525) 281-2656

CANADA:
Nelson
1120 Birchmount Road
Toronto, Ontario
Canada M1K 5G4
Tel (416) 752-9100
Fax (416) 752-8102

UK/EUROPE/MIDDLE EAST/AFRICA:
Thomson Learning
Berkshire House
168-173 High Holborn
London WC1V 7AA
United Kingdom
Tel 44 (0)20 497-1422
Fax 44 (0)20 497-1426

SPAIN (Includes Portugal):
Paraninfo
Calle Magallanes 25
28015 Madrid
España
Tel 34 (0)91 446-3350
Fax 34 (0)91 445-6218

Acknowledgments

In 1997, I started this project with an aim of writing an organization theory manuscript suitable for instructional use in an electronic undergraduate teaching environment. Soon it became evident that the manuscript would be of interest to a far broader audience that included academics, graduate and undergraduate students, business analysts, and competitive intelligence (CI) professionals. This book is the outcome of that effort. I would like to acknowledge a number of individuals who have supported this initiative.

My wife, Sonia, and our children, Colin, Brendan, Jennifer, and Sean, are my true inspiration. Sonia's support and understanding coupled with the children's love kept this project moving over four years. The encouragement of my parents, Doreen and Bert, my brother, Dermot, and the entire D'Angelo clan also helped to keep the fire burning.

I owe a debt of gratitude to Steve Momper and Thomson South-Western for publishing this book and to my editor, Eric Valentine. Also deserving of thanks are Dianne MacPhee, Jonathan Campbell, Hope Corkum, and Kendra Carmichael for their editing and support. I'd like to recognize my professional colleagues who contributed chapters to this endeavor. These include John Prescott, Craig Fleisher, Danny Silver, David Campbell, Jennifer Richards, Carolyn Vella, John McGonagle, and Tanja Harrison. I would also like to mention Heather Ongo and Erin Burke, undergraduate business students at Acadia University, who contributed to the case material in Chapter 10.

Finally, this book was funded in part by the Fred C. Manning School of Business of Acadia University and a McConnell Foundation grant administered by the Strategy in the Real World Program of the Schulich School of Business of York University.

Conor Vibert
Wolfville, Nova Scotia
2003

TABLE OF CONTENTS

Introduction

CONOR VIBERT

Competitive intelligence (CI) is the process of monitoring the competitive environment, one that includes general business trends and competitor activities. This process involves individuals or teams who collect data, compile it, develop information, analyze it to create knowledge, and then communicate it to decision makers who in turn take action that leads to results ("What Is," 2001). CI concerns itself with tasks such as identifying emerging competitors, understanding the behavior of existing adversaries and their impact on a company, building awareness of the competitive opportunities represented by the creation of new markets, seeking out the alterations that are occurring to the existing operating environment, uncovering new technologies that are on the horizon, and identifying new legislation that is being developed as well as its potential impact on the existing competitive landscape. As a field informed by practice, CI has roots that are diverse. They are also well entrenched in organization theory.

CI is a practice whose time has arrived. One need only ponder the symbolisms associated with Enron, Nortel Networks, Global Crossing, and the dot-com era to understand why. Interestingly, in the minds of many, these four topics all share one thing in common. Analysts who sought to understand the competitive and internal dynamics associated with each got it wrong. They were unable to make sense of what was really going on until it was too late.

This book is a response to that concern. It mixes the theoretical with the practical, the timely with the timeless, skills enhancement with mental models, and the Internet with paper and pen. Our readers are academics, business analysts, corporate trainers, students, online researchers, and the curious. Upon completion, readers will note an increase in their abilities to offer critical insight and make sense of the competitive and environmental complexity facing organizations as they grapple with the realities of operating in an Internet-enabled world. This book offers tools and ideas that will help readers use the free information resources of the World Wide Web to improve their ability to reason. Its major contribution is the presentation of a series of innovative Web-enhanced analytical approaches useful for students, researchers, and professional analysts in their day-to-day activities. It does not, however, replace the human qualities that support decision making. At best, it lays a foundation stone in the lifelong quest for knowledge.

Competitive intelligence. The term conjures up different meanings for different people. For some, the CIA and industrial espionage come to mind. Whether it be rumors of electronic listening devices on European jetliners, satellite photos of industrial manufacturing facilities, minivans equipped with high-resolution cameras and dark curtains, trained interrogators posing as trade show employees, or the arrest of shady characters in garbage dumpsters, the topic is of interest to many.

As it happens, these activities have nothing at all to do with CI. Increasingly, executives are realizing that just as money laundering is not considered a legitimate pursuit by your typical chartered accountant, and spin doctoring is unacceptable to serious journalists, illegal and unethical conduct is not condoned by professional CI practitioners. What CI is about is analysis and processes for understanding the competitive environment.

Throughout this book, reference will be made to the *practice* of CI. The assumption underlying this term is that competitive intelligence is something that organizations or individuals do. How they do it often differs by individual or entity. Larger corporations may practice CI with sophisticated intranets, highly cultivated networks of experts, fee-based online information services such as LexisNexis or Infomart, and customized reports from companies such as Forrester Research or Yankee Group (Metayer, 1999). They may also make use of carefully chosen teams of highly skilled analysts who are formally embedded in the corporate hierarchy to allow decision makers quick access to information (Metayer, 1999). Unfortunately, many analysts or researchers do not have access to these specialized services.

Instead, they may make use of free, public resources available on the World Wide Web. Interestingly, these resources are often similar to those used by their multinational counterparts, such as corporate regulatory filings from the U.S. Securities and Exchange Commission Web site, industry reports from Strategis, patent summaries from the U.S. Patent and Trademark office, share price trends from BigCharts and company profiles from CorporateInformation. To organize their data, these practitioners may use the book-marking feature of their browser along with folders available in Microsoft® Outlook® [messaging software] or [IBM®] Lotus Notes® [messaging and collaboration software]. They may also cultivate a network of experts that may include university librarians and academics, fellow industry association members (i.e. those of the Society of Competitive Intelligence Professionals (SCIP)), members of government support organizations, university alumni, stockbrokers, and others. (Vibert, 2001)

Whether they work with many or few resources, CI professionals and researchers have come to recognize the important role that an ever-changing Internet may play in their efforts to understand the competitive environment and the behavior of large-scale organizations. Harnessing the power of the Internet is itself a challenge. Many academics are in the forefront of helping users make sense of this vast library of information.

This book offers a set of chapters that suggest how researchers, CI practitioners, managers, analysts, academics, and students may combine insights from the field of organization theory with the online resources of the Internet to improve business analysis. Its main argument is as follows. Simplified, CI is really an alternative style of research. Organization theory is a body of insight that explains how companies act, why some are more successful than others, why they look as they do, and how they compete. CI is a process that is enhanced by access to online information sources. Organization theory is content. The benefit to CI professionals and researchers of exposure to this combination of content and process is improved analysis. Researchers who practice Web-based CI and who incorporate insights from this body of knowledge will gain a competitive advantage over their peers.

ABOUT ORGANIZATION THEORY

Competitive Intelligence: A Framework for Web-based Analysis & Decision Making incorporates thinking from the practitioner-oriented field of competitive intelligence, the academic discipline of organization theory, and researchers and practitioners seeking to improve the means by which online research is conducted. It presents a series of well-established theories of organization and economic theories of the firm. For each of these perspectives, analytical frameworks are presented that incorporate Web-based commercial, regulatory, and educational information sources. The result is a body of theoretically informed online research processes or missions that are situated within an educational research stream developed originally to incorporate the Internet into K–12 education. To support this application of theory, essays are offered that enhance the reader's ability to use the Internet effectively to undertake meaningful analysis. Together, these components allow readers to improve their understanding of why corporations and other large entities act as they do while introducing them to leading-edge thinking from the nascent field of competitive intelligence.

Why are companies such as General Electric, Cisco®, and IBM so successful? Responses to this question often depend on the viewpoint of the respondent. Contributors to the fields of organization theory and strategic management address issues of this nature. As theorists and researchers, these individuals are primarily concerned with explaining why organizations look and act as they do and why they are effective. As with many other areas of scholarly activity, no one response or perspective accurately reflects current thinking in these fields. The result is a healthy body of scholarly thought that offers informed readers numerous alternative approaches to understanding the behavior of our major corporations and institutions. Indeed, few areas of research have been as active in recent years as the field of management inquiry.

A number of common themes tie together the disparate group of frameworks and perspectives that cumulatively form the body of insight known as organization theory. Among the most of important of these themes is the idea that efforts to improve the corporate bottom line do not always drive the behavior of large organizations. Despite the popular conception among many lay observers and commentators that profit is the sole motivator of corporate activity, evidence suggests strong roles for objectives other than improvements to the bottom line. Organization theory is the intellectual platform for this book. Ideas are added to it that cross the line from theory to practice and find a home under the heading of competitive intelligence.

ABOUT EDUCATIONAL APPROACHES
TO ONLINE RESEARCH

The Internet's role in liberating information is no longer a novelty. As with government and commercial enterprises, its incorporation into traditional fields of academic endeavor is still in its infancy. This relative newness presents an opportunity to increase the timeliness and relevance to practitioners of academic perspectives that have traditionally been viewed as bounded by the constraints of theory.

Interestingly, a growing body of literature can be found in the domain of educational researchers concerned with improving K–12 pedagogy through effective use of the Internet. Faced with a constraint of limited teaching time and the frustrations associated with undirected Web surfing, teachers, academics, and theorists are developing Web-supported, inquiry-oriented activities. One successful example of these initiatives, known as a WebQuest, suggests a series of clear steps for students to follow when undertaking research on the Internet (Dodge, 1999). WebQuests are research processes that offer an introduction to set the stage, a task that is doable, a defined set of online information sources to complete the task, a description of the process students should follow to accomplish the task, guidance on how to organize the acquired information, and a conclusion.

Although not the topic of this book, WebQuests offer useful insight. When combined with the academic insight of organization theorists and the practice of competitive intelligence, structured Web-enabled processes offer individuals a powerful set of analytical tools for resolving some of our most important business concerns.

OVERVIEW OF THE BOOK

This book is divided into three sections. The theme of Section I is competitive intelligence in an online world, or how Web-based CI is practiced. The chapters in this section address issues such as the role of competitive intelligence, the challenges of online research, the questionable reliability of many online information sources, and strategies for protecting organizations from Web-based CI.

The theme of Section II is linking management thought and analysis with the online world. Along with a discussion of the importance of analysis, chapter topics include an overview of management thinking regarding corporate behavior and its relationship to CI, a discussion of how organization theory can improve Web-based CI, an exploration of a number of research missions that demonstrate how useful established management approaches can be to analysts when online information is incorporated, and a series of case studies. This section concludes with a discussion about knowledge management. In short, analysis is explained, organization theory's incorporation into CI is justified, its link with Web-based CI is introduced, research applications are illustrated, case examples are presented, and knowledge management is highlighted.

Section III is titled "Web-Based CI in Corporate and Academic Classrooms." Its chapters explore the teaching and training side of Web-based CI. The first of these chapters supports the incorporation of managerial insight with online information sources, arguing that the practice of competitive intelligence can only be improved. The second describes an innovative teaching environment, the electronic classroom, one that can improve the effectiveness of corporate training initiatives and academic teaching endeavors. The third chapter in this section presents a case example with an alternative approach to the online research missions described in the previous section.

Section I

In Chapter 2, David Campbell, vice president of research and CI services with ShiftCentral, offers readers a primer on competitive intelligence and suggests quite strongly that solid analysis lies at the heart of effective inquiry. Even with an awareness of how to search the Web effectively and an ability to distinguish good information from bad, researchers often fall short in sorting through the vast quantity of information available to them and placing it in context.

Interestingly, large entities are also challenged by the awesome power of the Internet. With no shortage of information and often hundreds or occasionally thousands of exceptional analysts in their employ, large corporations are increasingly faced with the difficult task of making sense of large volumes of information and making it available in a manner meaningful to decisions makers. These issues are in the domain of CI, a practice that seeks to aid analysts and their employers in their quest to make sense of the competitive environment and its inherent information.

Effective practice of CI assumes a basic understanding of online information sources and their origins. The importance of this assumption becomes even more apparent if we take into account the continued phenomenal pace of growth of the Internet. As if information overload were not enough, online researchers also need to consider one new obstacle—the invisible Web. This refers to online information that persists in eluding even the most advanced search engine spiders. While the Web offers countless opportunities for organizations to gain competitive intelligence, strategy and logic are needed to tap it and use it to its full potential.

In Chapter 3, Tanja Harrison, an academic librarian at the Vaughan Memorial Library of Acadia University, looks at current Web issues and explores the new generation of search engines that sift through the myriad of information for real results. Harrison also explores the role of the Web for gaining an edge on competitors, offers insight into the gathering of timely, reliable information from an array of sources, and takes a look at the future agenda of the serious Web researcher.

In Chapter 4, Academic Librarian Jennifer Richard, also of Acadia University, addresses the topic of how to differentiate good online information from bad. The issues surrounding the evaluation of accurate scholarly materials, whether in print or in newer media formats like television or the Internet, have always existed. Similar techniques that scholars, researchers, and librarians have used to critique printed sources can now be applied to determine the usefulness of information found on the Web.

Some consider that the Internet has caused a proliferation of hoaxes and misinformation. However, the Internet also provides a forum to correct these inaccuracies. Specific questions addressed in this chapter include the following: How timely is the information at a particular Web site? Is it reliable? How might reliability be quickly assessed? Are some online sources better than others?

For many organizations, easy online access to information has become a double-edged sword. While the Internet has helped to build an awareness among customers and stakeholders of available products and services, in many instances it has also opened an unwanted flow of information to competitors. The relative newness of online information access poses a challenge to most organizations. How much information should be made available to the public, and how should that information be presented? In Chapter 5, John McGonagle and Carolyn Vella, partners in The Helicon Group, discuss how companies can protect themselves against Web-based CI.

Section I offers readers a portrait of the role and challenges of online information for the practice of competitive intelligence. Section II moves to the next step with a series of chapters that explain why analysis matters and how CI practitioners might borrow insights from the field of organization theory to improve the effectiveness of their online research, as well as their understanding of the competitive environment.

Section II

The author of Chapter 6 is Craig Fleisher, Ph.D., the Odette research chair in business and professor of business strategy and entrepreneurship at the Odette School of Business of the University of Windsor. In it he discusses the importance of analysis for CI practitioners. In particular, he focuses on what analysis is, why it matters, how it is performed, the challenges facing analysts, and what the future may hold.

Chapter 7 introduces the body of knowledge known as organization theory. It argues that CI analysis can be improved when researchers incorporate concepts from this body of knowledge. It also highlights a number of issues to justify this claim.

Chapter 8 links organization theory to Web-based CI. It provides an overview of current management thought regarding why and how companies behave as they do. Brief summaries of profit-driven economic theories of the firm are presented side by side with effectiveness-driven theories of organization. These theories are grouped according to some of the themes that they address. These include growth and profitability, safety in the workplace, the dehumanizing nature of organizations, protection, behavior, and sustainability. Suggestions as to how these ideas might complement online research are explored. The remaining chapters in this section provide context to support these positions and suggest how readers may apply these ideas.

Chapter 9 presents readers with a series of research missions that explore and explain how the information resources of the Internet can be used to apply established management insight to contemporary situations. These specific applications seek to couple theory with real-time information in a manner that improves analysis (Vibert, 2000). Research missions are search processes that include a statement of context, a mission statement, guides for online searching, suggested online information sources, and a customized rationale for the use and display of the information. Effective use of research missions assumes that the reader possesses a basic knowledge of how to efficiently search the Internet and identify relevant information.

Chapter 10 offers four case studies of research missions. These missions illustrate the role that four different perspectives may play in improving analytical insight. The first case study examines the online music distributor MP3.com, while the latter three case studies use the diversified media industry as a setting.

In Chapter 11, you will find a discussion of knowledge management. CI is a subset of this larger area of nascent research. In this chapter, Daniel Silver, an assistant professor in the Jodrey School of Computer Science at Acadia University, explores the differences between an individual's and an organization's ability to manage knowledge and provides justification for current areas of research and application. Based on two perspectives, the major challenges facing practitioners in this field in the coming years are explored.

Section III

John Prescott, Ph.D., professor of business administration at the Katz Graduate School of Business at the University of Pittsburgh, is the author of Chapter 12. Dr. Prescott makes the case that, in the not-too-distant future, business academics will have no choice but to incorporate online information sources and Web-based CI into their teaching. The cost associated with not altering their style of instruction will be a perception of irrelevance in the eyes of students and other stakeholders. Comments are also offered on the importance of incorporating management concepts into CI instructional initiatives and the role of CI in academia.

Chapter 13 describes how laptop-friendly, fully wired electronic classrooms can support the teaching of online research missions and serve as intellectual platforms for effectively training students in the art of competitive intelligence. The chapter illustrates how specific technologies can be used to simulate the operating environments of CI practitioners. It also describes the challenges facing trainers and academics using electronic classrooms for instructional purposes and offers a series of teaching tips.

Although in its infancy, the practice of Web-based analysis is dramatically altering the way corporations approach the discipline of competitive intelligence. Chapter 14 outlines an innovative approach to case instruction that will be useful to corporate trainers and academics and that also serves as an alternative to the online research mission method described in Chapter 9. Using the online music distributor MP3.com as an example, the chapter illustrates how a combination of Web-based online evidence and management concepts can be presented in a manner that improves decision making.

Finally, the book concludes with Chapter 15 and some thoughts on the field of CI by Bonnie Hohhof, editor of *Competitive Intelligence Magazine* (*http://www.scip.org*), and Ian Smith, editor of *Competia Magazine* (*http://www.competia.com*).

Competitive Intelligence in an Online World

2

A Primer on Competitive Intelligence[1]

DAVID CAMPBELL

Competitive intelligence is the formalized process of monitoring the competitive environment. The Society of Competitive Intelligence Professionals (SCIP) defines CI as "a continuous process involving the legal and ethical collection of information, analysis that doesn't avoid unwelcome conclusions, and controlled dissemination of actionable intelligence to decision makers" ("What Is," 2003). Unlike the ad hoc nature of traditional market research (as you need it), competitive intelligence involves establishing a systematic program for collecting, analyzing, and disseminating key competitor and market information at regular intervals. Most industry practitioners now believe that in the current context of rapidly evolving markets, developing a real-time or on-the-fly approach to CI is the only way to effectively cope and keep ahead of the competition. In addition, CI is at its greatest value when it is tied to and feeds strategy.

Although the CI process is multifaceted, a robust CI methodology encompasses at least these five key components:

1. **Design and setup.** This initial phase of the CI process is arguably the most critical. It involves determining the requirements for intelligence within the organization. In the past, CI was considered a strategic activity, and the results were shared only among senior management and key staff. The emerging mindset around CI is that it can be used by all levels of the organization to enhance competitive advantage. This point was emphasized by Tom Peters as

---

[1] David Campbell—ShiftCentral

early as 1986, when he admonished corporations to "get everyone involved—educate the factory team, the MIS bunch, the product designers and sales persons about the best competitors' ways of doing things" (Peters, 1986).

2. **Information collection.** After determining the requirements, an effective CI program establishes a methodology around the collection and archiving of key information. This market and competitor information is collected in a legal and ethical manner.

3. **Analysis.** The real value of CI is in the strategic analysis of key informational variables. A good system will compile and archive information, but a vital next step is transforming that raw data into strategic knowledge, including benchmarking, product/service reengineering, trend identification, strategic positioning, etc. In fact, a recent study found that the success of a competitive intelligence program within an organization is tied to its role in developing and implementing strategy (Best Practices, 2002).

4. **Dissemination.** Highly tailored analysis is then presented to decision makers throughout the organization based on their individual requirements.

5. **Feedback/system reset.** The Internet has opened up whole new models for CI collection, analysis, dissemination, and archiving. With any CI program, it is important to constantly monitor the environment for CI itself to adopt leading industry methods and tools. It is also critical to integrate any feedback on the CI program from staff, as they are the ultimate users. A recent report by Best Practices, LLC, found that company-wide support for the competitive intelligence function is critical to its success (Best Practices, 2002).

THE ROLE OF COMPETITIVE INTELLIGENCE

Competitive intelligence methodologies provide the bridge between the vast amount of unstructured but potentially important information and empowered business strategies and action. Figure 2.1 (ShiftCentral Inc., 2002) illustrates how CI is used to turn unstructured information (content) into business action, particularly in light of emerging Web-based research tools.

The first stage, *content generation,* involves the creation of primary information that may or may not be relevant in a particular competitive intelligence context. The sources of this content range from magazines and trade journals to company Web sites to high-end analyst reports and market research. They can also include chat rooms, message boards, and other informal information sources, especially when the goal is to better understand consumer markets.

Better-known primary content generators would include census agencies such as Statistics Canada, magazines such as *Time* and *Newsweek,* newswire services such as PR Newswire and Business Wire, and newspapers such as *The New York Times* and *USA TODAY.* Many of these sources have much (if not all) of their content available on the Web and can be searched either directly at the source or through a major search engine such as the Google, AltaVista®, or HotBot® search engines. For the most part, the content generation industry is mature; however, the Web has revolutionized how this created content reaches users by opening up whole new cost-effective distribution channels and methods.

Figure 2.1 Competitive Intelligence: The Bridge Between Information and Action

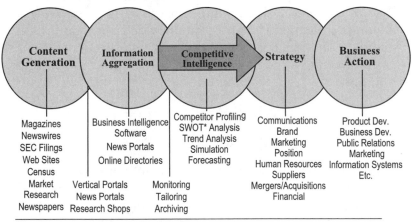

*Strengths, weaknesses, opportunities, & threats
From ShiftCentral Inc., 2002 (*http://www.shiftcentral.com*).

The second phase, *information aggregation,* is the process of compiling primary information (content) in various formats. Information aggregation is becoming a major industry in and of itself. Outsell, Inc., estimates the total content aggregation and distribution market is worth some $8 billion U.S. (Outsell, Inc., 2001). Factiva, a joint venture between Dow Jones and Reuters, is a good example of an information aggregator. The company compiles information from more than 8,000 global information sources ranging from newspapers to magazines to technical information databases. Factiva then provides custom content in various formats (e-mail, PDAs, etc.) to users based on their individual preferences.

There can be an overlap between content generation and information aggregation. This occurs when an organization creates its own primary information but also aggregates information from other sources. News portals such as CNN.com are good examples of this category.

The third phase, *competitive intelligence*, uses information from primary content sources and information aggregators to develop a comprehensive monitoring system. The CI analyst then employs tools to tailor, analyze, and archive the intelligence (detailed below). There can be overlap between information aggregation and competitive intelligence, and in fact, many of the information aggregators (Factiva, NewsEdge, Lexis-Nexis, etc.) are starting to provide more value-added services rather than just content, realizing that the real value is not embedded in the primary information per se but in its analysis.

The fourth phase, *strategy*, involves turning the gathering and analysis of competitive intelligence into strategies that are based firmly on the competitive landscape in which an organization is positioned. The final phase, *business action*, occurs when the organization turns good strategy into empowered business action.

CATEGORIES OF CI

A popular misconception of competitive intelligence is that it is actually "competitor" intelligence and involves only the detailed analysis of direct competitor moves. In reality, a strong competitive intelligence program includes monitoring and analysis of all information that can affect a company's strategic positioning within its market. There are at least five broad categories of CI:

- **Market intelligence** includes industry-level information on trends, government regulation, geopolitical issues, and so on.
- **Partner intelligence** involves monitoring the activities of a company's major suppliers and strategic partners. This keeps the company abreast of any trends that may negatively affect it down the road—and allows it to take action.

- **Competitor intelligence** involves detailed monitoring and analysis of key competitors, high-level scans of other competitors, and the ongoing identification of new entrants into the market.
- **Technical intelligence** is emerging as a major component of a robust CI program. Technical intelligence involves monitoring advancements of a technical nature that may affect a company's business model (internal and external).
- **Customer/prospect intelligence** is an especially important tool for products and services that have a longer and more intensive sales cycle. It involves determining and monitoring key internal influences, budget cycles, key focus areas, and the like.

USES OF CI

To facilitate strategic direction.   This is the traditional use of CI. By tabulating and analyzing key competitor and market information, senior management can make well-informed and rapid decisions. CI can be used to benchmark a product or service, to assist in the identification of a merger and acquisition candidate, and to stimulate wholesale changes to management direction. A recent article in *Fast Company* (Fuller, 1993) outlined the view of CEOs on why companies fail: (1) They have the right information but can't get it to the right place, (2) they get information to the right place but don't take the appropriate action, and (3) they don't act quickly enough.   A robust CI program can help companies avoid these three pitfalls.

For new product/service development. By effectively monitoring its competitors' product development activities, patent databases, and trade journals, a company can determine the best-of-breed components of a wide variety of competitors and build those functionalities into its product or service.

Within the sales process. Increasingly, having a strong CI program for the frontline sales team is becoming a key strategic advantage. Traditionally, the sales force is closest to the market and typically has a fairly good read on it. However, in a time of many new entrants, mergers/consolidation, foreign competition, and wholesale technological advancements, even frontline staff cannot keep up.

To assist with marketing/communications/public relations. There is no more important role for competitive intelligence than in the development and conveyance of the corporate brand and image in the marketplace. The link between these functions and competitive intelligence is becoming more visible. In 2001, there were at least seven partnerships between major marketing/PR agencies and competitive intelligence providers, culminating in the partnership between Fleishman-Hillard, one of the largest public relations firms, and Fuld & Company, a leading provider of CI services. Under their agreement, Fleishman-Hillard offers its clients access to Fuld & Company's competitive intelligence services, while Fuld provides its clients access to Fleishman-Hillard's communications services ("F-H," 2001).

For HR and recruiting. Using Internet-based CI, companies can monitor the job descriptions and in many cases the pay scales of their competition. In addition, U.S. Securities and Exchange Commission (SEC) filings and other public-disclosure documents provide insight into senior management and executive-level salaries as well as benefits such as stock options.

SOURCES OF CI

Just a few short years ago, collecting a wide range of market and competitor information was a very expensive and laborious process. However, the advent of the Internet has opened up a wealth of information sources that can be exploited for competitive intelligence purposes. Upwards of 90 percent of relevant competitive information is in the public domain. Some examples of sources include the following:

Corporate Web sites. The Web sites of the competition tend to be an excellent source of information about a company's products and services and its approach to brands and marketing. Company Web sites also typically include financial information if the company is publicly traded. Most companies tend to brag about their major clients, providing valuable information for CI analysis. On a cautionary note, corporate Web sites tend to have a marketing focus and not to reveal any direct weaknesses.

News aggregators. A relatively new phenomenon, these are companies that aggregate information in real time from thousands of different sources, including newswires, newspapers, trade journals, general interest magazines, industry portals, etc. The information can then be searched by keyword or by category. In most cases the companies have free and premium service offerings. A list of major news aggregators appears in Figure 2.2.

Figure 2.2 Major News Aggregators

COMPANY/SERVICE	URL
bizjournals.com	*http://www.bizjournals.com*
FT.com	*http://news.ft.com*
Hoover's Online	*http://www.hoovers.com*
NewsHub	*http://www.newshub.com*
NewsNow	*http://www.newsnow.co.uk*
RocketNews	*http://www.rocketnews.com*
Yahoo! Finance	*http://finance.yahoo.com*

Public company disclosure information. All publicly traded companies in the United States and Canada (and a number of other countries) are required to make detailed information about the company's financial situation and future plans available so that shareholders can have a clear picture of the company they are investing in. This information, submitted to the SEC, is invaluable to the CI analyst. However, plowing through hundred-page filings with a fine-tooth comb can be cumbersome. Fortunately, there are tools available to help analyze these documents.

Vertical portals. In recent years, Web sites have emerged that provide detailed information on a specific industry vertical. Called vertical portals, these sites can be advertising- or subscription-based and include a wide variety of industry-specific information. Typically, industry directories, research reports, and industry-specific news and analysis can be found within vertical portals.

Analyst reports. Most of the major investment management companies provide detailed analysis of specific companies and industries. This information tends to be well thought out and valuable to the CI process. However, since the dot-com meltdown, these analysts have come under increased scrutiny as their so-called unbiased analysis has tended to favor companies they have invested in.

Newsgroups and chat forums. Newsgroups and chat forums have become a convenient way to interact with various industry experts and glean valuable intelligence. In many cases, first contact with an expert can be facilitated through an online discussion group, but deeper analysis will come at a price.

Surveys and interviews. This old-fashioned CI collection method continues to be an important way to extract competitive information. This is not misrepresentation or interviewing under false pretenses: it involves interviewing legitimate sources with intentions stated up front.

INFORMATION OVERLOAD: THE IMPORTANCE OF A STRUCTURED CI PROGRAM

There are at least 2.1 billion unique URLs (Internet pages) that are publicly available through the Internet (Google's, 2001). In addition, millions of new pages are added on a daily basis. For example, it is estimated that there are some 10,000 global newspapers that post content on the Internet (Campbell, 2002). There is also an emerging trend towards premium content sources that are not indexed by the major search engines (the hidden Internet) and are only accessible through a fee-based service.

To provide a sense of scope, Figure 2.3 displays the results of a simple search on various keywords related to the telecommunications industry. The search was completed using the Hot-Bot®/Lycos® search engine, which date-codes new URLs as they are added to its database, allowing for date-sensitive searching. In the two-week period preceding this search, HotBot® had indexed 34,900 new URLs in which the word *telecommunications* appeared. Over the past three months, there were more than 1.3 million new URLs added with the word *telecommunications* included somewhere on the page. The sources of these URLs include magazine articles, research reports, press releases, corporate Web sites, etc.

Figure 2.3 URLs Added to a Search Engine

SEARCH TERM	URLS ADDED LAST 2 WEEKS	URLS ADDED PAST 3 MONTHS
telecommunications	34,900	1,300,000
Nortel	5,100	190,500
virtual private network (VPN)	3,200	216,400
Lucent	5,000	250,200
broadband	17,200	848,500
satellite	31,500	1,200,000

From HotBot®/Lycos®. Search run on April 8, 2002.

For any particular competitive intelligence program, only a very small fraction of the information is required. It is vitally important, then, for the CI analyst to put in place a robust and targeted monitoring, gathering, analysis, and archiving program that will scan the widest possible array of information sources but will pull back highly targeted results.

THE WEB-BASED TOOLS OF CI

Given the vastness of the information on the Web and its exponential growth, a variety of tools and services have been developed to assist companies in the monitoring, gathering, analysis, and archiving of intelligence. Some examples include the following:

Web search and meta-search engines. Web search engines are essential for today's competitive intelligence professional. Essentially, Web search engines act as the indexing system for the Web. They operate by sending out automated search agents that prowl around the Web and index all of the Web pages they find. Most search engines then categorize the information in some fashion to assist users in targeting their searches.

Because of the sheer volume of information and multiple formats available on the Web, this indexing process faces significant challenges. For example, most of these engines claim to re-index the Web every three to six months. However, independent studies have found significant gaps in this process (Brantford, 2001). Generally speaking, given the monumental task, many of the major search engines have done a reasonably good job, and there are other methods (detailed below) to capture information not indexed in the major search engines.

There are dozens of major search engines. The most used are shown in Figure 2.4 (Search, 2002). Most of these search engines offer unique functions such as date-sensitive searching and on-the-fly language translation. The example of Google, the most-used Internet searching tool, is detailed in this chapter.

Figure 2.4 Major Web Search Engines

SEARCH ENGINE	URL
AlltheWeb.com	*http://www.alltheweb.com*
AltaVista	*http://www.altavista.com*
AOL Search	*http://search.aol.com*
Ask Jeeves	*http://www.ask.com*
Google	*http://www.google.com*
HotBot®	*http://www.hotbot.com*
iWon	*http://home.iwon.com*
LookSmart	*http://www.looksmart.com*
Lycos®	*http://www.lycos.com*
MSN® Search	*http://search.msn.com*
Netscape Search	*http://channels.netscape.com/ns/search*
Open Directory Project	*http://dmoz.org*
Teoma	*http://www.teoma.com*
Yahoo!	*http://www.yahoo.com*

From Search, 2002 (*http://www.searchenginewatch.com*).

Web surveillance software. These are software agents that can be given specific tasks and set up to monitor various Internet URLs at preset intervals. While there are dozens on the market, there are very few that are powerful enough to overcome specific challenges around different databases, platforms, and content management tools.

Alerts. A number of companies now offer alerts. With these systems, a person enters in URLs and keywords to be monitored, and when there is a change, they are notified in real time. Like Web surveillance software, alerts have some technical hurdles to overcome, and the best services are pay-for-use.

Third-party monitoring services. Despite the advancements in technology, there is still no substitute for human intervention. A new group of CI companies is emerging that offers a blended solution encompassing the best of Web surveillance techniques. With these services, human analysts pore over the raw data to tailor it to the needs of a specific client.

Analysis software. A recent survey conducted by Fuld & Company found that the lack of good CI analysis software is a major issue among CI practitioners (Fuld & Company, 2000). While attempts have been made to develop software that will perform some CI functions within the system (e.g., trend identification and scenario development), the results have been less than spectacular. As more and more raw data become available, the ability to have an intelligent tool to analyze and make expert decisions will become increasingly important.

ADVANCED WEB SEARCHING: THE GOOGLE EXAMPLE

As noted earlier in the chapter, the vast amount of information available via the Internet and the volume of new information regularly added make the task of pinpointing relevant sources and information very challenging. Google, the most widely used search engine, has been adding new features periodically to assist in this process. Google's advanced search capabilities include the following:

1. **Phrase searches.** The user can search for specific phrases and concepts instead of only keywords. In addition, the user can conduct either/or searches (retrieving pages containing either or both of two terms) as well as keyword exclusions,

which return search results without specific words or phrases.

2. **Specific language searches.** Google allows users to restrict a search to one of more than 30 different languages. Google also has a robust translation tool (see the discussion of multilingual CI later in the chapter).

3. **Specific country searches.** Google indexes URLs based on their country of origin, allowing users to limit a search to specific geographic regions.

4. **Multiformat searches.** In addition to standard web formats such as Hypertext Markup Language (HTML) and Active Server Page (ASP), Google also indexes Adobe® Acrobat® (.pdf), Adobe® PostScript® (.ps), Rich Text Format (.rtf), Microsoft® Word (.doc), Microsoft® PowerPoint® presentation graphics program (.ppt), and Microsoft® Excel (.xls) formats.

5. **Date-sensitive searches.** Google allows the user to search Web pages added to its index with specific date parameters. None of the major search engines has effectively conquered this problem. Date-sensitive searches are based on the most recent time that a given Web page has changed. For example, a page posted in 1997 that has a date code that updates every day will be indexed as a new page every time the search engine reindexes the URL.

6. **Occurrence in the page.** Users can restrict searches to specific areas of the Web page such as the title, URL, and main body.

7. **Domain search.** Google allows the user to search only in specific domains. Doing a Google search on a specific domain is sometimes more effective than using the search engine employed by the actual Web site. For example, many people find that Strategis, Industry Canada's business portal, does not have an overly effective search tool built into its site. By using Google's advanced functions and specifying, for Domain, "strategis.ic.gc.ca," the user can do highly targeted searches not available via Strategis's internal search tool.

This method has two drawbacks. First, there is no way of knowing when Google last indexed Strategis (although within the last three months is a good estimate), and second, there is no way of knowing the extent of Google's index of Strategis's database.

8. **News search.** Google has added a News search function that searches various news media it has indexed. Google indexes news sites on a daily basis, allowing access to up-to-date information.

9. **Image search.** One of the more interesting search functions Google has introduced is the Image Search. Google indexes graphics files found on the Web, and users can search for specific images. This function is particularly useful to the CI analyst who is looking for charts, graphs, and tables. For example, a search on "GDP growth" yields more than a thousand charts, graphs, and tables that the CI analyst can plow through for relevant information.

10. **Groups search.** Google also allows users to search through Usenet newsgroup postings that are updated daily. This is particularly helpful if the CI analyst is looking to evaluate public opinion or find any informal scuttlebutt about a specific topic of interest.

MULTILINGUAL COMPETITIVE INTELLIGENCE

CI professionals are no longer constrained by language in their competitive intelligence-gathering activities. New online language translation tools allow researchers to translate documents quickly and easily between multiple languages, and in most cases, this service is free (see Figure 2.5).

Figure 2.5 Online Translation Tools

TOOL	URL
AltaVista's Babel Fish	http://babelfish.altavista.com
Dictionary.com/Translator	http://translator.dictionary.com
FreeTranslation	http://www.freetranslation.com
Google	http://www.google.com (choose Language Tools)

Google, for example, translates Web pages from English to German, Spanish, French, Italian, and Portuguese, as well as from some of these languages to others. Google will also translate on the fly, meaning that when it detects that a search term in a Web page is not in the user's preferred language, it provides a "translate" option that the user can click to translate immediately. Google then continues to translate pages as the user clicks through the Web site. The AltaVista search engine offers an even more expansive list of languages, including Japanese, Korean, and Chinese.

On a cautionary note, these language tools are still not very advanced and tend to conduct literal, word-for-word translations. Therefore, the translated text is to be used with caution but typically can provide the essence of what the researcher is looking for.

COMPETITIVE INTELLIGENCE ON PUBLICLY TRADED COMPANIES

Since the Securities Act of 1933, U.S.-based publicly traded companies have been required to disclose detailed information on their financial situation to their shareholders. Specifically, the act "require[s] that investors receive financial and other significant information concerning securities being offered for public sale; and prohibit[s] deceit, misrepresentations, and other fraud in the sale of securities" ("The Laws That," 2003).

The Securities and Exchange Commission is the governing agency for all U.S. securities regulation. All companies publicly traded on U.S.-based stock exchanges are required to file company documents with the SEC, and since 1995, the Commission has provided this information to the public at no charge via its Web site, *http://www.sec.gov.*

Of specific interest to the CI researcher are the 10-K and 10-Q filings, which are the annual and quarterly filings to the SEC, respectively. In the filings is a wealth of intelligence, including the following:

- Detailed financial information
- A review of product and service offerings
- Mergers and acquisitions
- Geographic markets
- Any outstanding legal proceedings against the company
- The company's market risk factors

In addition, the CI researcher can use these SEC filings and others for a number of specific CI functions, including identifying power holders in an organization; performing a social responsibility audit on an organization; and completing a due diligence process for a potential merger, acquisition, or new partner (Vibert, 2000).

Other countries have different legislation, policies, and procedures governing disclosure of public company information. Many European countries, for example, do not require disclosure at anywhere near the level that the SEC mandates. Other countries, such as Canada, have similar reporting requirements. SEDAR is the public filings Web site for the Canadian Depository for Securities, the agency governing publicly traded companies in Canada.

There are two potentially significant challenges facing CI analysts with the use of public company SEC filings. First, if the company they are analyzing is not publicly traded (or is foreign), access to this information is much more difficult. However, it has been shown that most of the information required to properly analyze a company from a CI perspective (i.e., competitive threat) can be found in public information sources. Second, a number of high-profile companies recently have not followed the spirit of the Securities Act of 1933 and have filed false or misleading information. Therefore, CI analysts must examine information from a variety of sources to uncover anomalies that may not be evident from using just one information source.

THE CI PRACTITIONER

Who performs the CI function? Typically, a good CI professional has a strong business background with one or more specific industry strengths. The person also has strong research skills and a good understanding of technology.

Finally, and of vital importance, the best CI practitioners have very strong analysis and writing/communication skills. The graph in Figure 2.6 shows a breakdown of CI professionals by area of expertise. It is based on the membership of the Society of Competitive Intelligence Professionals ("Membership," 2001). CI practitioners can be found in a variety of functional areas within organizations.

Figure 2.6 CI Practitioners Job Functions and Areas of Work

From Membership Survey, SCIP, 2001 (*http://www.scip.org*).

EXAMPLE OF USING CI METHODS TO COLLECT AND ANALYZE COMPETITOR FINANCIAL DATA

At the time of this writing, there had been a lot of discussion about the firing of Ford's CEO and the financial troubles that faced the company. Implementing a formalized and systematic approach to analyzing the competition's financial position in a relative fashion can be a valuable tool in developing and maintaining a competitive advantage.

Figure 2.7 provides a financial snapshot of Ford against three of its major competitors right before the firing of the CEO. Set within a proper CI program, senior management would review these figures on at least a quarterly basis.

For Ford, the numbers reveal some interesting facts. While their employee-to-revenue ratio and gross profit margins are as good as or better than those of their competition, bottom-line profits and the profit trend are noticeably down relative to at least two of their competitors. In addition, their leverage and debt-to-equity ratios are out of line, which indicates the company has too much debt, undermining its ability to grow. The current and quick ratios are both significantly lower than their competitors' and indicate real structural problems within the company.

Closely monitoring and analyzing financial performance is a key feature of a robust competitive intelligence program.

Figure 2.7 Competitive Landscape Review

	FORD	DAIMLER-CHRYSLER	GENERAL MOTORS	TOYOTA
Annual Sales ($mil.)	170,064	152,446	184,632	106,030
Employees	345,991	416,501	386,000	215,648
Market Value ($mil.)	29,369	36,841	61,187	92,954
Profitability				
Gross Profit Margin	24.4%	24.3%	27.6%	24.9%
Pretax Profit Margin	2.2%	-1.4%	1.6%	9.2%
Net Profit Margin	0.4%	-0.9%	0.9%	5.1%
Return on Equity	5.0%	—	5.5%	9.5%
Return on Assets	0.2%	-0.7%	0.5%	4.0%
Return on Invested Capital	0.4%	-1.1%	1.0%	6.6%
Operations				
Days of Sales Outstanding	10.7	—	266.9	89.4
Inventory Turnover	18.4	6.7	11.3	11.0
Days COGS in Inventory	20.0	—	32.0	33.3
Assets Turnover	0.6	0.8	0.6	0.7
Effective Tax Rate	34.5%	—	42.2%	43.3%
Financial				
Current Ratio	0.88	2.77	3.26	1.24
Quick Ratio	0.50	2.30	2.40	0.90
Leverage Ratio	21.05	5.37	10.24	2.40
Total Debt/Equity	12.66	2.38	4.86	0.74
Interest Coverage	1.30	(15.20)	1.30	30.30
Growth				
12-Month Revenue Growth	-4.7%	-1.7%	0.1%	-11.4%
12-Month Net Income Growth	-83.5%	-100.0%	-70.6%	20.0%
12-Month EPS Growth	-89.5%	-100.0%	-72.9%	20.7%
12-Month Dividend Growth	-40.0%	-6.3%	8.1%	32.4%

From Media General Financial Services, SEC filings, annual reports.

COMPETITIVE INTELLIGENCE IN GOVERNMENT

Traditionally, techniques for competitive intelligence gathering and analysis have been employed primarily in the private sector, particularly in highly competitive markets or markets with a high rate of technical change. In recent years, however, governments and other public sector and quasi-public sector organizations have begun to understand the importance of competitive intelligence. Although government departments or agencies may not be competing in a traditional sense, they are competing in many other ways, including the following:

- With other jurisdictions and countries
- With other government departments and functions for increasingly scarce public funds
- For public support of their activities
- To attract and retain key staff

A good CI program can provide critical information to assist in fulfilling a government mandate. Because most government functions do not have a profit motive or other market drivers, the value of their services has become increasingly subjective in the minds of elected officials and the public at large. Competitive intelligence can provide insight on a variety of themes, such as the following:

- Best practices in government service delivery
- Developing public policy in the context of a global economy
- Developing legislation and regulation
- Best practices and methods for global economic development
- Taxation issues
- Environmental issues

EXAMPLES OF COMPETITIVE INTELLIGENCE USE IN THE PUBLIC SECTOR

In recent years the competition for new business investments among states, provinces, and even countries has reached a fevered pitch as governments have realized the economic impact that this activity can have in their jurisdictions. High-profile expansions such as the Mercedes-Benz plant in Alabama and the BMW plant in South Carolina have forced governments to hone their value proposition, marketing techniques, and approach to financial incentives. The Michigan Economic Development Corporation (MEDC) is using innovative competitive intelligence techniques to assist with lead generation activities for investment attraction (Blake, 2002). MEDC developed a comprehensive database of companies headquartered outside Michigan and uses competitive intelligence techniques to determine linkages with the state that will help it target its business development activities. MEDC's assumption is that if a company has a solid linkage to the Michigan economy, it is more likely to establish a business function in the state. Using CI, MEDC ranks companies within the database in the following ways:

- **Products**—are they made with a Michigan resource?
- **Present location**—do they have a need for additional capacity in the U.S. Midwest region?
- **Customers**—do they have major customers in Michigan?
- **Growth projection**—will they have to expand anytime soon?
- **Proximity needs**—would it be advantageous to be located near a major supplier based in Michigan?

By using a systematic and formalized CI model, MEDC is able to target companies that have a higher probability of locating in Michigan. As a result, it can be much more focused in its business development activities. Does this approach work? Michigan was among the top ten U.S. states for new and expanded facilities during 1997–2000.

Another government example is the Alberta Agriculture, Food and Rural Development Department (Blake, 2002). In 1996, the department established a competitive intelligence unit mandated to collect and analyze critical market information that would help Alberta-based farmers and agri-food producers compete in the global marketplace. The CI unit compiles and analyzes information on a wide variety of topics, including food safety systems, other countries' agriculture biotechnologies development strategies, investment attraction, and the competitiveness of Alberta's industry. It also provides training on competitive intelligence to players within Alberta's agriculture and agri-food industry.

CI IN A GLOBAL ECONOMY

The Internet has opened up tremendous opportunity for the collection of important market and competitor information in the global context. While the requirements for public disclosure of relevant information are highest in the United States, other countries are beginning to demand more accountability from publicly held companies. In addition, the Web has opened up international newswire services, magazines, trade journals, portals, and corporate databases, all of which can provide valuable information on international companies and markets.

THE VALUE OF ANALYSIS

We have outlined the process of good competitive intelligence gathering and have provided a few examples of the implementation of CI in organizations. The true value of CI is in the analysis of data and action on that analysis, not in the process of collection and reading. This section of the chapter provides a summary of some of the specific tools that CI practitioners use to analyze data and then develop accompanying strategies.

Competitor/Company Profiling

Developing detailed information on specific competitors can be very valuable to an organization as it creates strategies for everything from product development to marketing to executive compensation. Constructing detailed profiles of potential clients is equally important, especially in markets offering higher-value goods and services. Understanding a potential client's business model will assist a company in structuring the most appropriate business development process for that individual client.

SWOT Analysis

CI can be very useful when developing a traditional "strengths, weaknesses, opportunities, and threats" (SWOT) analysis for an organization. The research gleaned from the competitive landscape will allow the CI analyst to develop these four quadrants effectively. For example, the strengths and weaknesses of a company can be assessed in the context of a solid analysis of an organization's major competitors. Opportunities can be determined by reviewing industry-level data such as reports and white papers and scanning the general competitive landscape for clues as to what might be on the horizon. Threats to an organization can come from multiple sources, including competitors, suppliers, large customers, and governments. Pulling information from a well-structured CI program can help a company formulate strategies to limit risks.

Trend Analysis

One of the great advantages of implementing a formalized CI program is the long-term capture and archiving of key competitive intelligence. Over time, an organization can map out trends among its competitors, trends in the industry at large, changing consumer preferences, changing cost structures, etc. Instead of starting the research process from scratch each time, with archived intelligence, developing trends becomes a fairly simple process.

Simulation/War Gaming

Simulation uses computer-based tools that enable a company to engineer a strategic game plan and test it in a risk-free environment. Simulation helps ensure that the planning process yields realistic, achievable strategic plans. It assists managers in determining the dynamics of their competitive landscape by allowing them to experiment within a safe environment. Users make decisions, watch indicators, and view competitor actions and reactions as they would in real life. But because of the speed of game play, users can try many different strategies and view many different outcomes—all without risk. The ongoing CI program feeds the simulation process with the required market- and competitor-level intelligence. A recent white paper on the subject of simulation puts it this way:

> [The] safe practice environment levels political tensions, builds consensus among your management team and aligns them with the resulting strategic decision. It also helps define the action plan required to implement the strategic decision. This process builds confidence in the decision since it is based on real industry information and explicit assumptions. (Monitor, 1998)

Forecasting

Related to both simulation and SWOT analysis, a good CI program will provide the information required to forecast sales, the need for new product enhancements, changes in the competitive landscape, etc.

ETHICS IN CI

The perception of competitive intelligence as a mix of illegal and unethical practices to extract internal, private corporate information continues to be a problem for the industry. The association of CI with military intelligence gathering is most likely a major cause of this reputation. In military intelligence practice, activities such as monitoring private communications, infiltrating governments, and spreading disinformation could be considered legitimate (depending on the context). However, in normal business markets, these practices are not only unethical but, in most cases, illegal. A better analogy would depict savvy (and ethical) journalists who are able to ferret out public information that for whatever reason is being deliberately hidden from the public.

The following are some examples of unethical (and, many times, illegal) industrial espionage:

- Hacking into a competitor's Web site to extract confidential information
- "Dumpster diving"—sifting through memos and other confidential documentation (either physical or electronic) to gain access to private intelligence
- Misrepresenting oneself as a potential customer to extract pricing information or other information that the company intends to keep private
- Interviewing (paying) ex-employees of the competition to extract information when the former employees are bound by a nondisclosure agreement
- Deliberately spreading disinformation about a competitor (or even one's own company), especially in the age of the Internet and day trading

In 1999, John Pepper, then chairman of Procter & Gamble, remarked when speaking to the Society of Competitive Intelligence Professionals:

> I can't imagine a time in history when the competencies, skills and knowledge of the men and women in competitive intelligence are more needed and more relevant to a company being able to design a winning strategy and act on it. I can't imagine a company not realizing the fundamental need for this today. (Miller, 2001)

In August 2001, Pepper confessed that P&G managers had implemented an elaborate and unethical spying campaign against a major competitor, Unilever. Procter and Gamble's operation to glean competitive information on its rival's hair-care strategies in order to protect its own important brands of Pantene and Head & Shoulders lasted eight months, cost about $3 million, and involved a CI consultancy ("P&G," 2001). The lesson of this case is that not even the most respected global corporations or CI industry experts are above crossing the line.

Organizations such as the Society of Competitive Intelligence Professionals have taken a strong stance on the ethics of the CI industry. SCIP has developed a detailed Code of Ethics ("SCIP Code," 2002). All members must be in compliance with this code to maintain membership.

Interestingly, most CI practitioners would say that approximately 80 to 90 percent of all useful information is in the public domain anyway and that proper extraction and "filling in the blanks" would yield the same results, in most cases, as gathering the information through unethical and/or illegal activities.

Resisting the temptation to cross the line will continue to be a major challenge facing the industry as it moves forward.

DOES IT WORK?

While the process of CI seems intuitively valid, there has been limited research into the tangible, long-term benefits. One study, however, completed in 1995 at the University of North Texas, found that businesses that used formal CI programs generally outperformed those that did not in three areas: sales, market share, and earnings per share. The study suggested that "there is a positive relationship between emphasis on CI and successful financial performance" (Cappel & Boone, 1995).

STRATEGIC CONSIDERATIONS

There are a number of strategic issues facing the CI industry over the next few years:

Outsourcing versus in-house CI activities. Increasingly, the expertise associated with the CI function itself has become a core competency, and a number of companies are building that expertise and offering it as a service. Because the skill sets, methodologies, and technologies required to develop a strong CI function are quite complex, a blended solution of CI partner(s) complementing a strong internal analysis competency may be the optimal configuration.

Synergies with other business functions. There is a definite overlap between CI and a variety of other business functions such as marketing/communications, traditional R&D, financial analysis, and industry consulting. There will most likely be some merging of those functions over the next few years (e.g., CI as a service of marketing firms or within the Big Five's suite of services).

CONCLUSION

The case for implementing CI within organizations has never been stronger. With the emergence of the Internet and Web-based CI tools, the cost of deploying a robust CI program is within the reach of SMEs (small to medium-sized enterprises) as well as large corporations. A recent survey conducted by The Futures Group found that some 80 percent of large U.S.-based organizations had a formal in-house CI department ("Corporate," 2002). It also found that 60 percent of companies in general utilized some CI functions to assist in the development of their business models (Miller, 2001).

However, just establishing a CI function per se is no guarantee of success in the market. What organizations do with CI (i.e., turning market knowledge into strategic action) is ultimately the true test of its utility as a competitive advantage. An example of problems that can arise when formalizing a competitive information gathering, analyzing, and dissemination program and not acting on the results is demonstrated by the telecom equipment manufacturing industry. The major players (Nortel, Cisco, Alcatel, Lucent Technologies, et al.) were growing at a tremendous rate (primarily through acquisition) and jockeying for position within what was perceived to be an industry with unlimited growth potential. However, from the time that John Roth (former CEO of Nortel) first warned that the company's quarterly revenues would be off significantly, the entire collapse of the sector occurred in less than six months. The industry had shed almost 50 percent of its revenues and employees and had shown record quarterly losses. Paradoxically, the telecom sector had been one of the largest proponents of competitive intelligence, and many of the companies that fell the hardest had been applauded for their competitive intelligence activities (Miller, 2001).

The inability of CI professionals within the telecom equipment manufacturing industry to adequately forecast its meltdown only strengthens the argument that an effective CI program must have more than just a lateral view—i.e., it should not be absorbed by analyzing only the competition. An effective CI program must look upstream at its suppliers to monitor their competitive environment, cost pressures, and legislative issues, and it must look downstream at its customers and keep abreast of their movements. It must also monitor general trends in geopolitics, government regulation, trade policy, and public attitudes, all in the context of a specific business model. Ultimately, it could be argued that it was the telecom equipment manufacturers' preoccupation with each other while ignoring downstream and general economic trends that caused such a hard landing.

Over the next few years, competitive intelligence activities will become even more mainstream as the unit cost of competitive information access will continue to fall and the software tools to aggregate, disseminate, analyze, and archive strategic intelligence will continue to improve. The emphasis going forward will shift from information-gathering models and knowledge management to effective analysis and the resultant strategic action. Successful organizations will be those that have the best knowledge of a broad set of competitive intelligence criteria and that are relentlessly integrating that knowledge into product/service development, marketing/sales, and strategic positioning activities.

Strategically Searching the Web[1]

TANJA HARRISON

The World Wide Web—a more fitting name now than ever before. With millions of Web pages introduced, discarded, moved, and transformed each day, the perplexing task is how to find order in all of this chaos and, more important, how to find the results we need. Further complicating matters is the recent realization that much of the information we seek lies undetectable by current search technology. The fact is, true order is hard to come by on the Web. Surfing used to be fun, but business researchers cannot waste precious time gambling on serendipity. Taking tactical advantage of the eclectic range of current sources and tools to tap useful information is key to effective information gathering. As technological, social, and economic forces continue to shape the Internet, searching efficiently requires strategy, skills, and knowledge of the current search environment.

SEARCH ENGINES: AN EVOLUTION

Before there were search engines, there was absolute disorder on the Web. If you needed to find a site, you had to know the exact address. Knowing the URL of a specific site is still the easiest method to find anything on the Web. However, with the daily proliferation of Web sites, it has become virtually impossible to meet information needs by simply collecting useful Web addresses. In this environment, search engines become essential. The current

[1] Tanja Harrison—Acadia University

industry is saturated with a staggering multiplicity of general search engines, but a revolution is in sight on the search engine horizon. Tools are now being developed that are much more advanced, efficient, and readily customized than those of yesterday (Green, 2000).

Anyone who has used more than one search engine knows that all are not created equal. There is one cardinal rule when searching the Web: If you want to find the best and most complete information on any topic, use more than one engine. Always. Your experiences, good or bad, will be what ultimately form your own judgment about which to use. Because opinions continually shift, depending on new features and the task at hand, outlining the options available in numerous search engines or trying to size them up is not the answer. However, it will be useful to highlight the features of a few favorite general and specialized search tools as well as some notable metasearch newcomers.

THE LITTLE ENGINE THAT CAN

As far as general search engines go, Google has consistently kept pace with the competition. Don't let its clean interface fool you. Google has powerful indexing capabilities and performs sophisticated relevancy ranking. It takes into account the number of times your search terms appear in a Web page and measures link importance. The more links pointing to a particular site, the higher this site will be weighted in your results.

Searchers can take advantage of more advanced options such as date range, domain, field searching, language, and all aspects of Boolean logic, including exact phrase searching. Google's reverse link search allows researchers to seek out affiliations and relationships to a specific Web site. For example, to establish relations to a company home page, simply key *link:http://www.thecompanyinquestion.com* and all URLs pointing to this site will appear in the results list.

Documents surface, are altered dramatically, or even completely disappear on the Web. Can't find a page you found just yesterday? Google's spider program takes a snapshot of every page and archives it in a cache, providing a unique way to redisplay this information. Google's most recent innovation has been its Image Search feature. It is now the only major search engine that lists not only PDF files but also files in Microsoft® Word, the

Microsoft® PowerPoint® presentation graphics program, Microsoft® Excel, Adobe® PostScript®, and Rich Text Format (Sherman, 2001c). Researchers can view the file in its original format or as an HTML file. For those who wish to keep Google close by their side, the Google toolbar is available as an add-on to the Internet Explorer browser.

So far, everything about Google remains free. It is a staple search tool, with a no-nonsense interface and indexing power that brings back results with both speed and accuracy. Google is by far the best general-purpose search tool in the current industry and has become so popular that imitators like WiseNut and Teoma are now emerging onto the search scene.

AN ENTERPRISING SOLUTION

One of the biggest industry innovations is enterprise information portals. These are single-port entry sites to specialized topical information. The market has exploded with vendors offering professional content-enhanced services. Catering to the corporate community, the Northern Light business portal harbors one of the best business search services in the industry. Using a variety of specialized search options, Northern Light sorts retrieved information into customized subject folders to ease the burden of sifting through results. All retrieved information is given a percentage rank corresponding to its relevance to the query.

Portals are a different breed from general search engines in the information they provide. For a long time, the content of Northern Light was either gathered from the Web and viewed for free or pulled from a Special Collection database, including the full text of popular business journals and investment reports written by industry analysts. As one of the first models of half application service provider, half outsourced service provider, Northern Light has recently switched over to a completely fee-based business model.

One service offered by Northern Light to its clients is Rival-Eye. This service gathers data on the Web specifically for tracking competitors. Portals such as Northern Light are designed for instances when a simple Web search won't do because a researcher's information needs include subject analysis and dependable sources. Advanced features and value-added services are going to cost a company money, but Northern Light knows its clients will pay for timely on-demand service and especially for reliable content.

THE POWER OF DIVERSITY

Because any good search depends on using a variety of search tools, metasearch engines were a natural development. Actually, metasearch engines are not, in fact, search engines at all. They are sites designed to search numerous engines at one time. Why use only one search engine when you can use several simultaneously? There is no better way to experience firsthand the vast differences in the way search engines work than by using a metasearch tool for retrieving information from the Web.

Since its arrival in the search world, the metasearch engine Vivísimo has improved. It now has a clean, simply designed interface and provides comprehensive Web coverage using some of the more popular search engines and sources in the current industry. What is different about Vivísimo is its document clustering capability. A search will display collapsible detailed categories of information conveniently placed on one side of the screen, emulating Northern Light's topical results folders.

Vivísimo's system plays to the ideal of "no more tedious lists," addressing the overwhelming task for the user of dealing with reams of information spewing out of popular search engines ("FAQ," 2003). Easily navigated while at the same time offering a sophisticated advanced search syntax, this new-generation search tool is a fast and organized alternative to many of its competitors.

A fairly recent addition to the metasearch scene is SurfWax. Clean and reminiscent of Google, it has customized search settings and anywhere from 250 to more than 1,200 sources to choose from. SurfWax provides access not only to most search engines and directories but also to other Web resources not available or searchable by other metasearch engines.

With SurfWax's My SearchSets, a user can set a relative weight for sources within each set according to selected search criteria. ContextZooming allows the searcher to zoom directly into portions of a Web page document and then use SiteSnap to save a snippet of information. Once we were limited to bookmarking site addresses for the valuable information they contained. Now the actual information can be extracted and saved instead. It can then be sent to an InfoCubby, a personal repository of the gathered information. Web search industry guru Chris Sherman describes InfoCubby as "a collection of bookmarks on steroids" (Sherman, 2001a). Multiple InfoCubby SearchSets may be created for different topics and queries and then either e-mailed to other researchers or placed in a public folder for others to search.

Following the trend of the new-generation search engines, SurfWax offers many of its advanced features with a price tag attached. Free, silver, and gold subscriptions allow for the creation of varying numbers of search sets, and the availability of sources depends on the money the researcher is willing to spend. SurfWax is more than a metasearch engine. It is a search management tool. Far from the simplicity of Google and much more ambitious than Vivísimo, SurfWax's current feature-rich, yet fairly complicated mechanism is not for everyone. Yet its extensive set of tools and variety of sources make SurfWax an interesting new breed of search system that any organizational analyst should consider for ongoing Web research.

LIMITATIONS OF SEARCH ENGINES

Despite the power and flexibility of search engines, they do have limitations. Spider programs that periodically go out and rake the Web for content do not refresh an engine's index as frequently as we would think. How often the index is refreshed is crucial. AltaVista, a former "Big Five" engine, was criticized in a 2001 *Search Engine Report* for its stale index and out-of-date content, major mistakes in the competitive search engine market (Sullivan, 2001b).

The programming of a spider is also extremely important. Search engines have depth and breadth weighted in different ways. While some engines may have spiders index only the surface of sites, such as the main or index pages, others will have spiders dig deep into a site's multiple pages and bring back more information for the searcher (Hock & Berinstein, 1999). Spiders do not work well with frames, and astute designers will always create a no-frames version of their site to ensure their information is included in search engine retrievals (Hock & Berinstein, 1999). For a long time, image files eluded Web spiders, but some search engines, notably Google, are beginning to resolve this problem.

THE INVISIBLE WEB

So you've found a good search engine, one with a fairly current index and spiders programmed to comb Web pages systematically. But still there are places where information hides beneath the surface, beyond detection of general search engines, in the vast and growing Web space. This is the invisible or deep Web. According to a study by BrightPlanet, there is actually 400 to 550 times more public information in the deep Web than in the part of the Web we can readily access (Bergman, 2000).

Much of this hidden information is stored in webbed databases that spiders cannot infiltrate. The invisible Web includes sites requiring registration or subscription login, archives of newspapers or magazines, dynamically created Web pages, and information found with interactive tools. Also included in this elusive information are images. Although, as we have seen, search engines are being developed to index images, they still have a long way to go. Picture a researcher going to a library and discovering it is closed. Although the researcher may be able to give you the location of the building, that person can never bring back the information stored within its walls.

Researchers must now always consider this invisible content that their general-purpose engine's spiders may fail to access. Recently, there have been strategies and tools designed by members of the search industry to tap this information. Gary Price, a reference librarian at George Washington University, has created a site he calls *direct search* (Price, 2002). His advice is to forget about search engines for the moment and instead focus on developing a toolbelt of Web information resources to gain access to invisible sites (Novack, 2001).

Metasearch engines are now actually advertising on their sites that they attempt to infiltrate deep Web content. ProFusion searches more than 1,000 databases on the invisible Web. This site offers interesting ways to choose your search engines, such as the "Fastest 5." ProFusion also allows the researcher to e-mail results and to search Adobe® Acrobat® files. Vivísimo offers researchers the choice of delving into specific database or resource sites such as CNN or U.S. government sites, and Surf-Wax's overwhelming number of searchable sources includes many categorized as on the invisible Web.

Targeting a small area of the Web where you know there is useful information is the best way to penetrate the invisible Web. Just as you would not want to look up the name of a company's

CEO in the *World Book Encyclopedia,* why get lost in a mess of irrelevant results using a general search engine when there are specialized tools and specific collections of information already established to aid you in your task? We all know there are free, accessible, and searchable databases on the Web such as the EDGAR database of Securities and Exchange Commission (SEC) filings. Travel to these sites first to find annual company reports and financials, rather than wasting time with a search engine. Although it is a largely subjective assumption, the deep Web has been reported to frequently offer higher-quality information than the surface Web. And according to the BrightPlanet study, approximately 95 percent of the hidden information is freely accessible to the public, welcome news to the search world (Bergman, 2000).

Chris Sherman and Gary Price, two popular experts on searching the deep Web, have teamed up to publish *The Invisible Web: Uncovering Information Sources Search Engines Can't See.* A Web companion to the publication, the Invisible Web Directory, provides the researcher with access to hundreds of hidden Web resources.

RETHINKING THE WEB

As we learn more about the information that isn't indexed, we realize that no search engine is perfect. A researcher must apply judgment and intuition at all times on the Web. Look at your favorite engine again, this time more closely. Are you taking advantage of any advanced search options and going to the tips or help section to discover how to target your search? Are you choosing unique terms for your query, ones that will retrieve the most relevant results? Are you noting whether AND or OR is the default operator? Does your search engine allow for other Boolean operators, like NOT, to narrow your search? Are you aware that many engines have programmed stop words and that some engines are case-sensitive? Does your engine perform automatic truncation by taking the root of your term and searching all variations? Does it allow for proximity searching and searching within specific fields (Kassler, 2000)? What exactly is the information you are searching for? Becoming aware of the strengths, weaknesses, and content of various search engines will allow you to make strategic choices for the tools you will use.

But perhaps you do not need a search engine at all. Logic should tell you that sometimes choosing an alternative route may be your best bet. For example, suppose you are looking for the newest Environmental Protection Agency (EPA) guidelines for constructing a building near a natural wetland. Governments are huge publishers of information, and they often make this information available on their Web sites. Why waste valuable time and effort with a search engine and risk missing important material when you can go directly to the EPA Web site and access mountains of freely available information? Think about what it is you need to find on the Web. Then choose your search engines or alternative starting points wisely.

KEEPING UP THE PACE

In the ever-changing world of the Web, the serious researcher will want to keep up to date on new features and developments. Search Engine Watch, hosted by the entertaining Danny Sullivan, is a key site to bookmark and monitor. Not enough time in your day for continuous checking? Sign up for *Search Engine Report*, a useful and timely newsletter delivered directly to you by e-mail. The popular Search Engine Showdown, by Greg Notess, a reference librarian and associate professor at Montana State University, is a site where the devoted can compare and analyze the elements, issues, and best practices of the current Web search environment.

FREE VS. FEE

Yesterday, the experts were online. Today, practically everyone in the free world is. Ask information professionals and they will no doubt lecture you on the dangers of the Web and reminisce about the days when they used only traditional, commercial-based databases that offer the speed, precision, and valuable content to do their jobs. But you cannot compare the Web to a subscription database (Kassel, 1999). Each can offer different, unique information. And one resource can often complement the other.

Depending on your budget and resources, there are different approaches to searching the Internet. Key, reliable business information is available from subscription-based online databases by vendors such as Dialog and LexisNexis. There is a reason databases that cost money stay in business. Information found on the Web can be invaluable. It can also be inaccessible, irrelevant, and inaccurate.

Many assume that the information on the Internet is much more current than any commercial database ever was. But commercial products today are increasingly current; the business database ABI/INFORM, from ProQuest, is updated daily. And although the Web can offer recent information, many times it does not go back as far as you would like (McGonagle & Vella, 1999). Consider an example. You are looking for financial information on several U.S. companies over a ten-year period. You find that your first source of choice, CNN's free financial network, does not give you the historical background required. By using Mergent's expensive, yet quality and comprehensive, Mergent Online company database, you are able to gather all information required. Often the Web just does not provide everything you need.

Unless you work at an academic institution or your company or organization has a site license subscription to journal indexes that link to full-text content, it is a tricky business to find newspaper or journal articles online (Harris, 2001). When you do, most of the time there are restrictions on the complete content. However, there are free multidisciplinary sites such as FindArticles.com where companies such as the Gale Group offer free content in the hope that researchers will eventually subscribe to the full database version.

There are also alerting services, many of which are still free, for coverage of the literature. Ingenta provides searchable information from journal publishers such as Academic Press and Wiley. The Scholarly Articles Research Alerting system, SARA, gives access to the tables of contents of academic peer-reviewed journals in many disciplines, including business and management. Each journal will automatically e-mail the table of contents whenever a new issue is published.

There is no service that provides an index to all Web sites and assesses their contents. Although they are not part of the free Web, commercial databases give access to large amounts of business-related quality information from the literature. Primary research tools have not been replaced, but the Web has made secondary research simpler, less expensive, and faster than ever before. Commercial databases, combined with free data on the

Web, can offer the business researcher a variety of valuable, reliable, and distinctive resources.

CI AND THE WEB

Timely, strategic, and reliable information can allow any organization to gain an edge on competitors, and the Internet is perfect for monitoring the competitive environment. It has been noted that traditional research skills have not disappeared, yet the nature of the Web has given the competitive intelligence professional the ability to gather leads and find quality and unique information more quickly and inexpensively. The key is to know where to find the information on the Web and how to manage and analyze it to gain knowledge.

Much of the information for CI cannot be found using general search engines (Weiss, 2001). But, although definitely less expensive than the traditional commercial database route, evaluating Web information takes time, and data must first be analyzed for importance and reliability before using them for CI purposes.

Global company information portals are key to assessing the current business environment. Want to get the big picture? CorporateInformation, Business.com, Hoover's Online, and CEOExpress are good places to start. Specialized resource pages that have already been compiled, such as the CI Resource Index, supply the investigator with news and tools for strategic planning and competitive intelligence. The Web site of any industry or professional association is an excellent source of information and can offer an organized jumping-off point. The Society of Competitive Intelligence Professionals (SCIP) site features discussion groups, employment opportunities, publications, and other valuable resources for the CI researcher.

The place to begin to study a specific competitor is at its very own Web site. Next, try looking for company affiliations with the reverse link lookup available in Google. Be aware that it is fairly simple for a company to track who comes to its site, and many organizations have been known to lead identified competitors to alternative Web sites (Weiss, 2001). Masking your IP address, and thus your identity, can be done with services such as the Anonymizer. The Anonymizer allows you to filter your way in safely and ensure that you are collecting the same information as other visitors.

The growing popularity of the Web has increased the quantity and accessibility of publicly available information. Accessing public company information is now easy with SEC filings available in the EDGAR database. A Canadian-based equivalent for filings can be found at SEDAR (System for Electronic Document Analysis and Retrieval).

Look at places on other sites where companies are mentioned and see what people are saying about them. Web discussion groups are an excellent source for current insider information—rumors, conflicts, and new industry developments. The popular DejaNews forum, taken over by Google, can allow you to "eavesdrop" on investors, competitors, and employees voicing opinions, complaints, and any circulating rumors. Find out what customers are saying about products and services on a consumer watch site like Epinions. Listen in on biotech and related industry discussions by employees and industry insiders at the Biotech Rumor Mill.

Conference call multimedia sites are another great way to keep up with corporate and financial news. A researcher can even listen in on live broadcasts with BestCalls.com, a searchable database of conference calls with an upcoming-calls schedule. ON24 can also allow you to get updates on corporate and financial news. Analysts answer listeners' questions on Vcall, the investor broadcast network of streaming audio financial calls and interviews.

Job postings also supply vast amounts of valuable information if you look closely enough. A newly advertised position can offer insight into how the structure of a company may be changing and any new developments on the horizon. Try the popular Monster job board or HotJobs, Yahoo!'s career site. Other employment-related sites include Vault, which covers working conditions, corporate strategy, product lines, salary ranges, and much more. Designed for both the employment seeker and the employee recruiter, WetFeet offers an insider's guide to information about hundreds of different companies in a variety of industries.

To find timely intellectual property information, you can make selective free patent searches at Delphion, the U.S. and European patent offices, and Patent Alert, a free service for anyone who registers. Patent Alert searches the U.S. Patent and Trademark Office database on the researcher's behalf and delivers the information directly to e-mail inboxes daily, weekly, biweekly, or monthly (Sherman, 2001b).

Keeping current with industry news is vital to the competitive intelligence professional's agenda. The American City Business Journals Web site, bizjournals.com, offers free searches of business articles from across the United States. Other news alerting services include NewsAlert and NewsEdge.

Much of the online information that is valuable to CI researchers is buried and cannot be found with general-purpose search tools. Knowledge of these invisible Web resource sites, tools, services, and directories is crucial to practicing CI on the Web. But finding the information does not guarantee accuracy. With any information you retrieve on the Web, remember to be critical at all times. Investigate, analyze, and never take anything you find immediately at face value. Check and double-check your sources. Without confirming your findings, without having complete confidence in what you will use to make decisions, you do not have competitive intelligence. I cannot emphasize it enough. Verify everything.

THE NEXT INSTALLMENT

The Internet has traditionally had an open environment. Web researchers are accustomed to getting much of their information free. But how long services and content are going to stay free is questionable. Due to the declining stock market, there is less venture capital available to fund Web firms, and companies are spending less on Web advertising. Companies are now charging fees in return for value-added services, precision, and guarantees of reliable content. And with all the new search technology, we still do not have any real organization on the Web.

Order, substance, cost, and emerging technologies are major issues that hover over the researcher. The trends that are transforming the Web as we know it are affecting the very way in which we think about, and interact with, online information.

THE NEW MODEL

So what will the next business model for the search industry be? We remember its beginnings with directories such as Yahoo! which charged Web developers to have their sites listed. We have also seen companies paying for placement in the unknowing searcher's results lists. And the Web's system of ad-supported, free content has been eroding for some time now. Yahoo! began charging fees for its auction services, and Britannica.com's free content lasted a mere 17 months before the walls went up again (Brethour, 2001). In just the time it took to write this chapter, several formerly free Web services—all good resources for CI—have begun charging fees.

In the beginning, the "Big Five" search engines boasted large indexes and focused their efforts on portalization, advertising, and electronic commerce, neglecting their primary function of offering precision and relevancy search functions for the Web researcher. As a result, their supremacy waned, as increasingly new, clean, robust, ad-free engines emerged, bringing with them the power to make money in different ways (Green, 2000).

There is no doubt that new challenges for Web researchers will be shaped by commercial rather than just technological forces. We know that researchers will pay for quality information. But will we soon get only the Web we pay for? If the industry pushes too hard, will Web searchers turn away? There will have to be some sort of balance. Google has been a prime example of an engine that has not compromised a good search for money earned on advertising and expensive value-added services (Sullivan, 2001a).

The search industry will have to keep improving search standards without giving up quality. Northern Light practiced this quiet equilibrium with its two content choices for a long time. But it seems everyone in the industry is trying new ways to make money. The new generation of search tools, like SurfWax, have designed their utilities to offer their best search options for a price. One thing is certain: If the search industry bombards us with fees for useful Web search services, researchers will demand advanced features, customization capabilities, networking functions, information transferring abilities, precision, relevancy, and content for their search tools.

THE ACCESSIBLE WEB

Technological developments are opening up exciting new resources to Web researchers. They are erasing the language barrier and making the Web easier to access for people with disabilities. They are also giving us new ways to find and share information.

AltaVista, using SYSTRAN software, was the first to introduce an innovative free translation service called Babel Fish. You can send an e-mail in Spanish to your business contact overseas by simply keying the English message in the translation box. You can also search the Web in other languages to get a new perspective from results originating in the source country. Although, admittedly, translation on the Web still has many limitations, one can only assume that the technology will get better.

Voice and text simulation and recognition technologies that can work with any browser or search engine are now emerging. Initially designed for persons with disabilities, some products can key text from the user's voice and read search results aloud. Current voice synthesis and screen-reading software includes Dragon NaturallySpeaking, JAWS for Windows, KeySpeak, and Screen Reader.

Research into linguistic analysis, combined with efforts in the area of artificial intelligence, will be key elements in the way in which we ask for and find information. Increase in bandwidth will see more media mounted on the Web, and image and speech technology will improve to make it just as easy to search multimedia as it is to search text (Sherman, 1999). Peer-to-peer (P2P) networking technology will no doubt fundamentally change the way that information resources are shared. It is nearly impossible to predict what will appear next or how current systems will be enhanced, but we can be optimistic that technology will shape the future of Web research.

LET'S GET SOME ORDER AROUND HERE

There were those who believed that the Web would precipitate the demise of all traditional libraries, historically the repositories of human knowledge. But most people now realize that that is not the case. The Web has no real control, no standards, and no central scheme of organization. However, major efforts to introduce a system for categorizing and organizing virtual information are under way.

Metadata, basically defined as data about data, is the use of metadata tag descriptors embedded into the source code of a Web site, which search engines scan for site analysis (Bushko, 2001). The Dublin Core Metadata Initiative (DCMI), in the tradition of libraries categorizing and organizing information, has developed elements including type, source, rights, publisher, format, and others as an alternative to search-engine spider indexing. Newly created content on the Web would not be automatically indexed by spiders and housed in an engine's database. Instead, the Metadata Initiative wants publishers of Web information to submit their content, applying to it appropriate metadata tag descriptors, which then can be traced (Zelnick, 2000).

Systematic archiving is the essence of the Open Archives Initiative. This is an attempt by the academic world to gather together free digital research collections, by way of meta-tagged information, into a searchable space (Kiernan, 1999). Although currently a scholarly venture, the Open Archives Initiative may inspire others who use the Web for communication and dissemination of information to undertake similar collaborative projects. "Binding" similar electronic collections by making them interoperable with one another may be the future of obtaining order on the Web.

THE SEARCH CONTINUES

Some interesting search tool technology has been developing. Offline search agents that can work independently of browsers may become more prevalent. Copernic Agent, a program you download to your computer, works parallel to the Web. It is a new-generation metasearch management tool that performs varying tasks in differently priced versions. These include removing dead links from results, re-running saved queries, and e-mailing search reports. Shifting the processing power from the server onto the researcher's desktop could be a significant step in offering more search options and improved analysis of results capabilities (Green, 2000).

Despite the revolutionary improvements in search engines, they still cannot "understand" what the researcher means in a query. So far, natural language searching systems like Ask Jeeves, which allows you to key a direct question, have failed to offer quality results. People, rather than spiders, are increasingly shaping the Web. We see the success of personal intervention offered by search tools like Northern Light and Vivísimo, which present content aggregation and analysis. Taking this a step further, the people at About.com have been boasting all along that they are "the Human Internet." They provide topical resource pages with annotated Web site links recommended by recognized experts.

In the future, smarter spiders may be able to judge the relevance of a document and the quality of the links it contains. There are now attempts to interpret a researcher's question and "think" about what has actually been requested. Instead of keying instructions into a query box, researchers will instead define a goal and leave the how and what up to the search technology (Green, 2000). The next generation of search engines will be designed to provide more relevant results and more direct answers to the user (Notess, 1999). And a day may come when a system has the ability to provide each person, whether a novice or an expert, with a common denominator of equal-quality results.

Search agents may soon be able to learn and adapt to researchers' preferences and establish patterns based on user characteristics and information requirements. Recent reports indicate that Google is set to offer personalized search results, taking into account the demographics of the researcher (Sullivan, 2001a). Gender, age, and even location could determine what you see in your results list. Some industry executives predict this is the next major innovation in the attempt to provide better search results (Sullivan, 2001a).

Still, the invisible Web persists in hiding valuable information from the Web researcher. Price and Sherman have identified another "opaque" Web: sites that, while technically able to be spidered, cannot be detected by general search engines (Lanza, 2001). In the future, search technology will be designed to work much harder to infiltrate these sites. The contents of the invisible Web will gradually become more accessible as an increasing number of intelligent agents and resources emerge that are specifically designed to delve beneath the surface.

CONCLUSION

The Web is indeed evolving. As it continues to grow, we can expect exciting new search tools and improved approaches to seeking information online. But the question remains: will there ever be an organized Web-based world?

The very architecture of the Internet suggests not. The next generation of search tools will continue to shift in response not only to technological influences but to social and economic ones as well. Searchers of the Web play an integral role in the development of the search industry, and it is they who will ultimately fuel the changes.

In the meantime, we must be wise and apply intuition, resourcefulness, and sound judgment at all times. Alan Kay, a Fellow at Apple who revolutionized personal computing, once said, "The best way to predict the future is to invent it" (George, 1999). With the rate of technological developments accelerating and searchers becoming increasingly savvy, one thing is certain—the future looks bright.

Differentiating Good Online Information From Bad[1]

JENNIFER RICHARD

The Internet has changed the practice of competitive intelligence. Few would argue with this statement, although many would suggest that the Internet's primary contribution has been to speed access to information and facilitate its dissemination following analysis, rather than dramatically altering how information is analyzed or its content. Ease of access to online information has afforded many researchers the opportunity to relocate without being disadvantaged in terms of business development opportunities.

Unfortunately, despite the advantages offered by the World Wide Web, many analysts continue to face the challenge of distinguishing good online information from bad. Indeed, the lack of editorial control on the Web has frequently been identified as a concern both in journal articles and on Web sites that discuss the evaluation or reliability of online information. The often-heard statement that "anyone can publish on the Web" cautions analysts to evaluate the information that they are gathering. Though the statement does have some merit, it is important to remember that all information, regardless of format or media, should be viewed with a critical eye.

To elaborate on this point, here are a few examples that illustrate the need to evaluate all sources of information. An obvious example of questionable material in print, viewed daily as you

---

[1] Jennifer Richard—Acadia University

pass through the cashier's line at your local grocery store, is the tabloid newspaper. Many of these papers carry stories of conspiracy and celebrity that are far beyond belief or reality. However, there is justification for a healthy dose of skepticism as you move to more reputable newspapers. You will know, if you've ever been quoted, or misquoted, in a paper like *The New York Times* or the *Chicago Tribune*, that information from these sources should be verified in another authoritative source. Corrections and retractions are daily occurrences in mainstream, reputable newspapers, and they are usually only printed when required.

Researchers are normally encouraged to use scholarly resources, given the tendency of many popular magazines to make liberal use of unverifiable, secondhand information. Indeed, it is not uncommon for many of the better-known magazines to use out-of-context quotes or portions of studies published in primary sources like *The Journal of the American Medical Association* or the *Harvard Business Review*. It is often this secondary coverage that is picked up by other mainstream media and then widely broadcast, leading to changes in behavior that can be detrimental to society.

One recent example of this phenomenon is the notion that autism may be caused by a vaccine. A single study, supported by anecdotal evidence, persuaded numerous families to stop immunizing their children against a number of childhood diseases including mumps, measles, and rubella. Subsequent studies have since proven that the onset of autism is often around the time of a child's last vaccine and, most important, that this is merely coincidence. An article on the Web site Quackwatch documents the development of this story and explains many of the falsehoods and incorrect assumptions surrounding it. This is but one example of the usefulness of the Web for clearing up misinformation about a poorly researched story.

Scholarly, peer-reviewed publications are not immune to these problems. For instance, the journal *Nature* retracted a piece of primary research for the first time in its 80-year history after additional studies on the same subject disproved the research findings. The November 29, 2001, issue offered an article entitled "Transgenic DNA Introgressed into Traditional Maize Landraces in Oaxaca, Mexico" (Quist & Chapela, 2001) that added to the hotly debated issue of genetically modified food. On April 4, 2002, a retraction suggested "that the evidence available is not sufficient to justify the publication of the original paper."

Credibility is often assumed for printed bound materials such as dictionaries and books; however, these resources should also be reviewed critically. The name *Webster* is a recognized reliable standard for dictionaries, but this name is now in the public domain, so anyone can publish a "Webster's Dictionary." Reference works such as directories and anthologies have varying criteria for inclusion in their publications. Some simply require a fee.

CRITERIA FOR EVALUATING INFORMATION ON THE WEB

Five major criteria are useful for evaluating online information. These are authority, accuracy, objectivity, currency and scope, and structure, or "look and feel." When usability is added as a sixth marker, Web site designers, e-commerce merchants, students, and many others find themselves with a useful set of tools for designing and evaluating online information sources.

Indeed, recent studies suggest the importance of these criteria for Web site design. One fairly large study involved more than 1,400 participants and sought to determine the makeup of a credible Web site. The researchers identified two major factors associated with credibility—trustworthiness and expertise. Data analysis led the study authors to propose seven guidelines for creating a credible Web site. The seven guidelines are: convey the "real-world" aspect of the organization in your site, make the site easy to use, include markers of expertise (authority), include markers of trustworthiness (links to outside materials and a focus on content), tailor the user experience, avoid overly commercial elements, and avoid pitfalls of amateurism (accuracy and currency) (Fogg et al., 2001).

In the following paragraphs, we explore these criteria in more detail. Further insight may be obtained online through a number of Web sites that address this important issue of information evaluation. Examples are found in Figure 4.1.

Figure 4.1 Web Evaluation Sites

An Educators' Guide to Credibility and Web Evaluation
http://lrs.ed.uiuc.edu/wp/credibility
UCLA College Library: Thinking Critically about
World Wide Web Resources
http://www.library.ucla.edu/libraries/college/help/critical/index.htm
Evaluating Web Sites
http://www.lib.umd.edu/UES/evaluate.html
Checklist to Evaluating Web Sites
http://www.lib.umd.edu/UES/webcheck.html
Ten C's For Evaluating Internet Sources
http://www.uwec.edu/library/Guides/tencs.html
Resources for Evaluating Internet Information
http://info.wlu.ca/~wwwlib/libguides/internet/eval.html
The Good, The Bad, & The Ugly or, Why It's a Good Idea to
Evaluate Web Resources
http://lib.nmsu.edu/instruction/eval.html
Evaluating Information Found on the Internet
http://www.library.jhu.edu/elp/useit/evaluate/index.html
Evaluating Quality on the Net
http://www.hopetillman.com/findqual.html
The Six Quests for The Electronic Grail:
Current Approaches to Information Quality in WWW Resources
http://www.ciolek.com/PAPERS/six-quests1996.html
Bibliography on Evaluating Web Information
http://www.lib.vt.edu/research/evaluate/evalbiblio.html
Hoax? Scholarly Research? Personal Opinion? *You Decide!*
http://www.library.ucla.edu/libraries/college/help/hoax/index.htm

---

AUTHORITY

There are a number of specific indicators that fall under the general criterion of authority. These include authorship, credentials, affiliation, and domain information.

There are numerous Web sites that provide obvious hints about their reliability through their authority. Web sites of educational institutions, governments, and nonprofit, government-sponsored organizations such as the National Institutes of Health are examples. On the other hand, a researcher might be advised to make use of sources other than the Web site of the Wine Institute to obtain medical information on the topic of fetal alcohol syndrome.

Another example is a personal Web site selling immortality through the use of the author's own patented magnetic rings. In this example the Web site's author actually does have a legitimate patent registered at the United States Patent and Trademark

Office. However, the patent application does not make the same claims as the Web site. The author provides images of famous scientists and inventors such as Albert Einstein, Thomas Edison, and Nikola Tesla in an attempt to persuade the reader to associate him or her with more legitimate scientists and inventors. This ploy is meant to increase the author's credibility in the eyes of the reader.

Finally, the domain name or URL can help to distinguish between authoritative and unreliable sites. A clever application of the hostname *Whitehouse* in the United States is a good example of how URLs can be used to mislead users. The .gov site is the official site of the U.S. White House. The .com version of this name is a pornographic site. The .net version is a satirical site and an almost exact replica of the official government site. Though the intent of the authors of the .net site may be simply to lampoon the official site, it is clear from the comments page that the average person is confused by the official appearance of this Web site. Daily topics have included "Should the color of the Whitehouse be changed to pink?" and "Spanish lessons sponsored by Taco Bell."

Questions concerning authority:
- Who is the author of the Web site?
- What is the domain type (e.g., .com, .edu, or .gov)?
- Are background information, current affiliation, experience, and credentials provided?
- Is the site maintained by a well-known or reputable organization?
- Does it have accurate contact information such as phone numbers and addresses?
- Can the contact information, affiliation, and credentials be verified in another source?

ACCURACY

The term *accuracy* as an evaluative category refers to issues such as the verifiability of the information supplied by the Web site. Typographical errors, grammatical errors, and information that contradicts generally known facts may be clues to a less than reliable source. Some encouraging news is reported in a recent study in *The Journal of the American Medical Association* regarding health information on the Internet. It concludes that although coverage of health information in both English and Spanish is poor and inconsistent, the accuracy of the information found on the Web is generally good (Berland et al., 2001).

Questions concerning accuracy:
- Is the information verifiable?
- Is the information error-free?

OBJECTIVITY

This category is also referred to as "point of view" or "bias." It is important to note that many e-commerce Web sites have a particular bias that is obvious, overt, and acceptable, as they normally offer information, such as that found in white papers, with the intent of increasing sales of specific products. In these instances, readers implicitly accept that the Web site advances a particular point of view but assume that it is accurate with regard to the information provided. In this instance, the Web becomes a useful resource for the advertising and marketing of products, provided there is no purposeful misleading of clients. On the other hand, objectivity as a criterion retains particular relevance when a searcher suspects that information is being withheld or manipulated.

There are a number of interesting tactics that can be employed to influence searchers' confidence in a Web site. The use of the label "award-winning" and links to well-known reputable organizations are two very popular ways of bolstering a not-so-credible Web site. For example, blue-ribbon awards are provided by an Internet service provider (ISP) to all of the Web sites it hosts, so any site can display an award. The spoof or joke site LiverAid (no longer on the Web), whose ostensible purpose was to arrange liver transplants for aging rock and roll stars, provided links to legitimate organizations such as the American Liver Foundation and the Canadian Liver Foundation.

Any Web site can link to reputable and credible organizations. An easy check for a concrete relationship between any two organizations is to go to the reputable site and see if there is a link to, or any information regarding, the questionable site. You may even contact someone at the reputable site and ask about any questionable links.

Questions concerning objectivity:
- Do the facts on the Web site seem reasonable based on prior knowledge?
- Is there any indication of bias? If so, is the bias clearly stated?
- Is the site sponsored by a commercial organization?
- Is it trying to sell you something?

SCOPE

The category known as scope, or alternatively as coverage or content, goes hand in hand with that of objectivity. Using this criterion, a searcher should inquire whether the topic is covered comprehensively and for whom the information is written or to whom it is targeted. One very disturbing site on the topic of the life and times of Martin Luther King, Jr., illustrates the importance of examining a site fully before recommending or relying on the information provided.

At first glance the site appears innocuous. The front page is beautifully laid out, with subheadings such as "Civil Rights Library" and "Death of a Dream." There are even PDF-formatted flyers that teachers are encouraged to distribute in their classrooms. Further, the site's .org domain implies reputability. It is not until you view the second page of this site that you discover that it really is a "wolf in sheep's clothing." All of the material found on this site is racist in nature. In fact, this is an anti-King Web site.

Questions concerning scope or coverage:
- Who is the intended audience?
- Is this site for scholarly purposes, general information, or merely entertainment?
- Are both sides of an issue or topic provided, along with balanced supporting information?
- What geographical area is covered?
- What time period is covered?
- Is this the original document or has it been edited or abridged in some way?

CURRENCY

This category is also referred to as "timeliness." Currency involves evaluating problems on a Web site such as broken links, out-of-date information, and update information indicating the last time the page was revised. A common complaint about the Web is that only recent information is available and that the information does not go back far enough to be useful for in-depth research. However, old online information can also occasionally be dangerous. An example of this problem might be dated information on a drug that does not take into account the findings of more recent studies that highlight previously unforeseen side effects.

Questions concerning currency:
- Does the Web site give information on when it was last updated?
- If so, has it been updated recently?
- Is some of the information clearly out of date?
- Are there many links that are broken and no longer connect to the resources listed?

STRUCTURE

One final criterion that may also be very important to searchers and designers is the structure and general design, or look and feel, of a Web site. This may include features such as white space and the variety of fonts. Too many fonts often make a site visually disconcerting or simply too busy. Navigational features, like scroll bars, a frame enclosing a table of contents, a site map, or a listing of basic categories, can be very helpful and can make a site more pleasant to use. Other options that make a Web site more user-friendly include the ability to turn off graphically intensive sections and to skip introductions that require downloads like the RealOne™ Player digital media software application or Macromedia® Flash™ player.

IMPORTANCE OF VERIFICATION

If there was just one piece of advice to offer analysts and researchers seeking to distinguish good online information from bad online information, what would it be? Never depend solely on information gathered from the Internet, regardless of the authenticity or authority of the information.

Most information found on the Web is relatively recent. Indeed, most electronic information only goes back as far as the early 1990s. As more money is made available for retrospective projects, the depth of coverage of information on the Net will grow. This cannot happen too soon, as is evidenced by a very serious case of a medical researcher at Johns Hopkins University limiting his background research to electronic information before performing a test on a patient. This researcher used Medline, a very authoritative source. Unfortunately, the Medline database offers information only as far back as 1966. Sadly, important information that would have helped this researcher make an accurate assessment was available in 1950s-era studies published in hard copy. The researcher missed key information, and the patient died (McLellan, 2001).

Administrators, users, and designers constantly promote the notion that everything you need is available on the Web. Unfortunately, this is not true.

RESOURCES FOR VERIFICATION

The use of more traditional resources to verify online information is crucial. Probably the best resource you can use for verification is a knowledgeable person. This individual may be a librarian, an information specialist, or a colleague who specializes in the field that is being researched. The use of e-mail and telecommunications has increased our personal access to expertise all over the world, and in general, many individuals are willing to share their knowledge.

Libraries of all types, corporate, academic, and public, are now working on joint initiatives to provide reference services 24 hours a day, 7 days a week, over the Internet, bringing together expertise from all over the world to provide service. Indeed, librarians are the perfect candidates for assisting with the retrieval of online information, as they are normally trained and experienced in searching and reference interviewing. In most instances, librarians also possess the ability to distinguish accurate from inaccurate online information, are unbiased by commercial concerns, and have the ability to use multiple sources—books and proprietary databases (Anhang & Coffman, 2002). Further, it appears that these services are needed, given recent survey findings that suggest Web searchers are in most instances not retrieving what they need by themselves (Berland et al., 2001).

A second excellent set of resources is Web-based peer-reviewed or scholarly publications. Many are freely available, often through an online U.S. government information source. Important examples include Medline for medical information, AGRICOLA for soil science and agriculture, and ERIC for educational information. Other resources are subscription-based. Access to these tools may vary from institution to institution in Canada and the United States. The number of peer-reviewed electronic journals is increasing dramatically. Indexes and abstracts that provide a gateway to this information are expanding, and in some cases, prices are becoming more reasonable due to consortia buying practices.

FACT OR FICTION

Many of the false stories and much of the misinformation floating around in cyberspace actually come directly to us through the use of electronic mail. These include pleas for help for destitute people in foreign countries who will be able to repay millions of dollars for the short-term use of our bank account, chain letters, parents requesting money on behalf of dying children, and warnings against fictitious computer viruses. A number of online resources are available for researchers seeking to determine the existence of a hoax. Examples of these may be found in Figure 4.2.

Figure 4.2 Hoax Web Sites

TITLE	URL
HoaxBusters	http://HoaxBusters.ciac.org
Urban Legends Reference Pages	http://www.snopes.com/snopes.asp
Urban Legends and Folklore	http://urbanlegends.about.com
Health Related Hoaxes and Rumors	http://www.cdc.gov/hoax_rumors.htm
The Museum of Hoaxes	http://www.museumofhoaxes.com
TruthOrFiction.com	http://www.truthorfiction.com
Urban Legends Research Centre	http://www.ulrc.com.au
Hoaxes	http://www.icsalabs.com/html/communities/antivirus/hoaxes.shtml
Virus Hoaxes and Netlore	http://www.hoaxinfo.com
Top Ten Dot Cons	http://www.ftc.gov/bcp/conline/edcams/dotcon
Internet Fraud Watch	http://www.fraud.org/internet/intset.htm
Internet ScamBusters	http://www.scambusters.com
The AFU & Urban Legends Archive	http://www.urbanlegends.com

A typical example of a hoax is as follows. The clues that should place doubt in the mind of a reader are in bold and italics.

Example of a Hoax

FW: Warning! Spider in the toilet! **Importance:** High
I'm told this isn't a joke. Take it or leave it!:
Please pass this on to everyone on your email list:

According to an article by *Dr. Beverly Clark*, in the *Journal of the United Medical Association (JUMA),* the mystery behind a recent spate of deaths has been solved. If you haven't already heard about it in the news, here is what happened. Three women in Chicago turned up at hospitals over a 5 day period, all with the same symptoms: Fever, chills, vomiting, followed by muscular collapse, paralysis, and finally, death. There were no outward signs of trauma. Autopsy results showed toxicity in the blood. These women did not know each other and seemed to have nothing in common. It was discovered, however, that they had all visited the same restaurant (*Big Chappies*, at *Blare Airport*), within days of their deaths. The health department descended on the restaurant, shutting it down. The food, water, and air conditioning were all inspected and tested, to no avail.

The big break came when a waitress at the restaurant was rushed to the hospital with similar symptoms. She told doctors that she had been on vacation, and had only gone to the restaurant to pick up her check. She did not eat or drink while she was there, but had used the restroom.

That is when *one toxicologist*, remembering an article he had read, drove out to the restaurant, went into the restroom, and lifted the toilet seat. Under the seat, out of normal view, was a small spider. The spider was captured and brought back to the lab where it was determined to be the *South American Blush Spider (arachnius gluteus),* so named because of its reddened flesh color. This spider's venom is extremely toxic, but can take several days to take effect. They *live in cold, dark, damp, climates*, and toilet rims provide just the right atmosphere.

Several days later a lawyer from Los Angeles showed up at a hospital emergency room. Before his death, he told the doctor that he had been away on business, had taken a flight from New York, changing planes in Chicago, before returning home. He did not visit Big Chappies while there. He did have what was determined to be a puncture wound on his right buttock, as did all of the other victims.

Investigators discovered that the flight he was on had originated in *South America*. The *Civilian Aeronautics Board (CAB)*
ordered an immediate inspection of the toilets of all flights from
South America and discovered the Blush spider's nests on four
different planes! It is now *believed* that these spiders can be anywhere in the country. So please, before you use a public toilet, lift
the seat to check for spiders. It can save your life! *And please pass
this on to everyone you care about*.

Red Flags and Explanations

☑ Statements like "I'm told this isn't a joke. Take it or leave it!"
  or "And please pass this on to everyone you care about"
  should be obvious red flags.

☑ Dr. Beverly Clark (Beverly Clark is actually a wedding
  apparel line) and the *Journal of the United Medical Association
  (JUMA)* are names not verifiable in Medline. *JUMA* is used to
  add credibility and to be confused with the well-known
  JAMA, The Journal of the American Medical Association.

☑ Both Big Chappies Restaurant and Blare Airport do not
  exist.

☑ Including a medical professional ("One toxicologist . . .")
  lends creditability, but because the person's name is not
  given, there is no way to verify that he exists or that the
  parts of the story pertaining to him are true.

☑ *Arachnius gluteus*, the alleged scientific name of the spider,
  gives an air of authenticity; however, there is no spider with
  this name. The direct translation is "butt spider." *Blush spider*
  is a term that refers to varicose veins.

☑ "Live in cold, dark, damp, climates" and "South America"
  are contradictory: South America is not cold.

☑ The Civilian Aeronautics Board does not exist, though this
  name could be easily confused with the Civil Aviation Board
  that disbanded in 1984.

☑ "Beleived"—misspelling. In addition, you probably noticed
  grammar and punctuation errors throughout the document.

Before concluding, there are two tips worth passing on to
readers seeking to make use of the information found in Figures
4.1 and 4.2. If a URL is no longer working, put the title of the
Web page in quotation marks and then use a search engine such
as Google. You will likely find the page. Internet service
providers, as well as universities and businesses, often change

their naming schemes for one reason or another. In many instances, however, the information remains on the Web. The second tip is that if this doesn't work, try using the Internet Archive's Wayback Machine to find cached information for the last five to six years.

CONCLUSION

The Web has opened up endless opportunities for researchers and analysts. However, it can also be viewed as an ever-changing mass of good and bad information. Researchers need to be ever-vigilant in their pursuit of the good, or information that is accurate, authoritative, current, comprehensive, and balanced. They also need to understand how to assess online information and where to look for help in doing so.

5

Protecting Your Company From Web-Based Competitive Intelligence[1]

CAROLYN M. VELLA AND JOHN J. MCGONAGLE

Businesses and other institutions are becoming increasingly reliant on the Internet to conduct their activities at all levels. Already we see a wide variety of reasons for using the Internet, and the quantity and quality of attractive features and services available online will only increase. The following are several examples of how businesses currently use the Net:

- To set up a Web site to serve as an electronic billboard that tells anyone who reads it about themselves, their capabilities, their personnel, and their experience
- To establish a Web site for the use of customers or others with whom the business connects, providing them with directories of locations, downloadable forms, online catalogs, and ways to track orders
- To develop sites to assist in the effort to recruit new employees or even to subtly advertise that the business is for sale—to the right buyer
- To launch separate Web sites for new projects or for existing subsidiaries and affiliates in an effort to show how large they are while still making themselves accessible

Whatever the reason firms use the Internet, the placement of data in cyberspace also creates a new area of vulnerability for

---

[1] Carolyn Vella and John McGonagle—The Helicon Group

businesses. That vulnerability is to the competitive intelligence efforts of their competitors.

As a new-frontier data depository, the Internet is already being studied by experts seeking to predict what kinds of data will most likely be posted (Weiss & England, 2000) and what that means in competitive terms (Vibert, 2000). That, in turn, has led to increasing efforts by CI professionals to explore and then exploit information on the Web for CI purposes (e.g., Kassel, 2001; Lang & Tudor, 2001). As with so much else in business, these actions have resulted in a reaction. That reaction is the application of defensive CI techniques to the Internet.

HOW IS CI EXPLOITING THE INTERNET TODAY?

Perhaps the easiest way to show how CI is exploiting the Internet today is by relating a series of cases, all of which are based on real work we have done.[2]

Unindexed Materials

Businesses put materials on their home page assuming they cannot be found if the firm has not indexed them or listed them on the site map. However, trained CI Web searchers use a technique borrowed from headhunters called X-raying to discover this hidden information (Silverman, 2002). X-raying involves using one of several search engines and tying the search to the company's name with commands such as *host:* or *url:* followed by the company's home page address and key search terms.

In one case, as we worked our way through a target's complex of multiple home pages, we were able to locate a hidden link to a test site the target had set up. That site was actually the final test of a new set of Web pages to be released in connection with the launch of a new service. The hidden link easily led us to this page, the existence of which we had previously identified through a search for Web sites using terms reserved by the target for what appeared to be a new marketing initiative.

---

[2]All facts have been slightly modified to protect the identities of clients and competitive targets.

Hidden Anchors and Notes

Some Web page designers use key terms to help them keep track of Web pages as they are developed and updated. These terms, while not a part of the actual text of the page, can sometimes be accessible to skilled searchers. We have found situations in which key terms were used as if they were page markers, leading us to new sites with new data.

In one case, we looked for a hidden link in a Web page. We suspected it was there because the target had reserved a number of domain names that seemed to be indicative of a new marketing initiative. We eventually found it by searching for a new Web site using the domain names themselves. One of them turned out to be a new Web site, ready for launch, complete with biographies of executives assigned to the project and its marketing materials. From that site, we could go back to the home page and thus confirmed the location of the secret link.

Inbound Links

Inbound links are those that connect independent sites to a company's site but of which it may not be aware. Inbound links can be located using advanced features in search engines such as AltaVista or HotBot®. They often disclose sites that host current or former employees' résumés and that include a link from their own page to the company's pages.

Such pages can be a gold mine to CI professionals seeking someone to interview. In addition, they can often hold otherwise unavailable details about a firm. Using this technique in one case of ours, we located a résumé for an IT specialist who had been a consultant to our target. Not only did this give us a name to pursue for a potential interview, but the résumé itself was also a real find. In describing his experiences at the target organization, the IT specialist provided a list of every firm that had been involved with the company in a major Web-based marketing project.

Job Advertisements

In another case, a chain retailer was aware that its most aggressive competitor was probably expanding. The retailer needed to know how many new stores and distribution centers were in the works, as well as how much the competitor was planning to spend on its expanded logistics needs.

Starting with the premise that these new stores would need staff, we began by searching through job clearinghouses at sites like HotJobs and Monster. There we found advertisements for the kinds of personnel that would be needed to staff these new units and functions. That alone served to confirm the expansion process. However, the advertisements, as a part of selling to potential new hires, also indicated where the expansion was to take place and included brief notes on the probable supply chain and related software and warehousing issues. This information, combined with other research including zoning applications and calls to securities analysts, helped us to model the competitor's expansion process as well as its logistics spending.

HOW DO YOU STOP THIS?

As CI develops, businesses eventually come to realize that "if we can get this on them, then they can get this on us!" To defend against Web-based CI efforts aimed at your firm, you must first understand that you can foil the CI efforts of competitors at least to some extent. You can accomplish this by making yourself virtually invisible to CI monitoring efforts. And doing so successfully is, above all, based on understanding the ways you can be tracked. Once you have that understanding, strategies and tactics to minimize or avoid detection in the future can easily be developed. Essentially, you and your firm will be practicing *defensive competitive intelligence.*

WHAT IS DEFENSIVE CI?

Initially, efforts to blunt active CI efforts were often called counterintelligence by many. While this term seems to accurately describe what is being done (that is, countering competitive intelligence), it has fallen into disfavor. As a term taken from the world of governmental and military intelligence and including within its scope so-called direct action, counterintelligence carries connotative baggage with it into the business world. Implicit within *direct action* is the notion that opposing intelligence personnel and physical assets can be removed, that is, destroyed, as a part of the counterintelligence process (McGonagle & Vella, 1998).

Given the distasteful overtones of this term, CI professionals have been striving for a new label. While *protecting against competitive intelligence* accurately describes the process, other terms such as *protecting a competitive advantage* are being used to encompass this concept in a world that likes short terms and parallelism of expression. Among them, the most accurate label is probably *defensive competitive intelligence.*

Regardless of what term or phrase is used, what should be kept in mind is that when professionals talk of defensive CI, they are not talking about something that is a mere annex to existing corporate security programs or an adjunct to staff functions that serve to enforce current legal protections of certain classes of data. They are talking about CI that supplements other information protection regimes, while not actually being part of them.

WHAT ABOUT CORPORATE SECURITY AND LEGAL PROTECTION PROGRAMS?

CI is the collection of public data by legal and ethical means and the conversion of that data into intelligence through the use of analysis. Various legal stratagems, such as trade secret protection and confidentiality and nondisclosure agreements, aim to protect critical categories of information assets by making those who violate certain patterns of behavior subject to legal, usually civil, penalties. Someone who collects competitive data by inducing a former employee of a competitor to violate a nondisclosure agreement, for example, is involved in illegal conduct because such activity violates civil law.

Similarly, if someone goes through a business's trash in a jurisdiction where that is not against the law or poses as a student to try to interview a product manager, his or her conduct is not illegal as it does not involve the actual commission of a crime. Rather, it is unethical. It is the job of your legal staff and those working with them to deal with enforcing the civil protections available for certain classes of business data. It is the role of both businesses and trade groups such as the Society of Competitive Intelligence Professionals (SCIP) to establish standards of ethical behavior when collecting data for CI.

Ways in which competitively sensitive data might be collected can, of course, involve criminal activities. The criminal activity may arise from how data are collected, such as in a burglary, or from the effort to gather protected data, such as by violating the

Economic Espionage Act of 1996. It is traditionally the role of corporate security, working with the law enforcement community, to protect a business against these efforts (McGonagle & Vella, 1999).

HOW DO YOU DEVELOP A DEFENSIVE COMPETITIVE INTELLIGENCE STRATEGY?

To develop a defensive competitive intelligence strategy, you should first try to determine what areas of your activities are of greatest interest to competitors. You can then focus your efforts on protecting those areas. However, since you cannot know with any real certainty what your competitors are focusing on, you should approach this task in a disciplined manner. We have found that there are seven key points in identifying the data you should protect:

- Protect the information that would be most difficult for your competitor to develop. Of greatest importance is to protect data that would require your tacit or active cooperation to develop or obtain. Most often, you will find that this information will relate to subjects like intentions and goals.
- Remember that competitive information has a half-life. The half-life of data is the period of time for which raw data retain at least 50 percent of their accuracy and/or relevance. This varies widely with the type of data. So, protect competitively sensitive information only for as long as is necessary.
- Protect the competitive data that are crucial to completing a profile on your firm. For example, if your firm is increasing its market share, there is no reason to tell your competitors (through press releases or attached graphs) exactly how fast you are growing.
- Protect data that are already partially protected in some other way. In particular, focus your protection efforts on the subject matter of information already being protected as trade secrets. For example, if your marketing plan is a trade secret, protect information from which someone could derive critical elements of that plan.
- Identify the information that is critical to your operation as a business. This varies from case to case. The information may be identified in terms of how intimately related it is to

the immediate success or failure of your firm. Focus first on protecting this core before moving to protect other data that are not associated with your essential activities.

- Review the CI you are already collecting on your competitors. From that, determine what pieces of raw data are critical to efforts to produce your CI analysis. Next, determine what pieces of data on competitors have been difficult or impossible for you to locate. Then look at the data about your firm that can be easily accessed. What types of information are you surprised to see out on your own Web site? Move to protect all of that data.
- Identify the data analysis techniques most likely to be used in your industry or market. Protect those key bits of information vital to completing that type of analysis.

WHAT IS INVOLVED IN IMPLEMENTING A DEFENSIVE CI PROGRAM?

Once the data, or classes of data, in need of protection are identified, those running a defensive competitive intelligence program must provide guidance on what to do next. The use of an easily understood set of rules can make that relatively simple to do.

We have developed a set of nine such precepts, using the familiar model of reporters: who, what, where, when, and why. In our model, the when is as soon as possible, and the who is everyone (see McGonagle & Vella, 1998, for additional information on these precepts). These key precepts fall into three separate categories: what to do, how to proceed, and where to act.

Implementing a Defensive Intelligence Program

I. What to Do
   Precept 1: Seek to control only critical, not all, information.
   Precept 2: Do not tell everyone everything.
   Precept 3: Continually watch for sources of CI on your firm.

II. How to Proceed
   Precept 4: Preventing disclosure is preferable to impeding it.
   Precept 5: Do not ignore simple solutions.
   Precept 6: Pay attention to details.

III. Where to Act

Precept 7: If you cannot prevent disclosure, conceal some information.

Precept 8: If you cannot conceal it, make it harder or more costly to acquire.

Precept 9: The top may be harder to control than the bottom.

A PROGRAM FOR PROTECTING YOUR COMPANY FROM INTERNET CI INITIATIVES

The best way to protect your firm from the loss of competitively valuable data is to conduct a one-time review of your vulnerabilities and then to engage in regular reviews following that. The precepts we have provided will help you determine where best to focus your review activities as well as your initial audit. However, you may find that it is easier to sell a defensive CI program after you identify the vulnerabilities that exist now.

To help you in that effort, what follows is a broad-scale program indicating where and how to review your Internet-based vulnerabilities.

Your Web Site

Start by visiting your own Web site. Go through every page. Note which pages are old. How far back do press releases and announcement files go? If Dave Smith left the company and was replaced by Sharon Brown as vice president of sales, did anyone go back and remove Dave's biography from the Web site?

Find out whether there is any formal, enforced policy on removing materials from the Web site. You may be surprised to find that while there is a policy on adding materials, there is often none on removing them.

Now look for mistakes on your Web site. Are there pages or slides that were mounted in error? In one classic case, we found that a firm had put up the draft version of a quarterly press release. It still showed the deletions and additions that were made in producing the final version. Being able to read such edits can offer very telling insights into what has really been happening at a company. In this particular case, key phrases such as "continuing growth in sales to key customers" were clearly marked to be deleted. What obviously had happened was that when the final edit was done, the page was saved still showing changes and then put up in that form. No one in the firm checked to see what it looked like on the Web.

Next, look at the pages themselves, one by one. What kinds of data do you see on them? Does the personnel page include an unnecessary table of organization? Does the technical center's flashy page include catchphrases that describe important internal initiatives? Do your e-mail and mailing lists for press releases and other materials ask recipients to identify who they are, whom they work for, and why they are asking for materials? If not, ask yourself why not.

Now, sit back and look at your pages as a Web designer might. For what purpose are they intended? Are your lists of regional offices designed to showcase how many you have or to drive customers to use them? Who is the primary audience of your Web site—customers, shareholders, or suppliers? Do you want that sort of information visible to your competitors?

Next, determine what is on your Web site but is not indexed. You may well be surprised to see that it supports "temporary" lists of people attending upcoming meetings, test pages not ready for release, draft materials, versions of pages never used, previous versions of current pages, and materials removed from the index but not from the site. Never assume that these materials cannot be found and read. They can—and they will be.

All major Internet browsers allow their users to read certain things about your pages, variously called code and source data. These are usually just bits of information on when the page was mounted and by whom, when it was last changed, and what software was used. Most of the time the contents are innocuous and of no competitive value, but sometimes designers put additional notes to themselves in them or add searchable terms to the headers to be activated later. Take them out.

The Invisible Web

Now, move to the way the Web relates to your home page. Start by checking into the pages of related organizations, your subsidiaries, and your affiliates. What do they say? To what sections of your home page are they linked?

Sometimes, links on outside pages can accidentally allow people unplanned, or even unauthorized, access to pages on your site. In one case we worked on, we were trying to find an open-source article on a change in certain rules. One search engine gave us what was evidently the home page of a practitioner in that area. We did not have a complete copy of the final draft of the revised rule and noted that this home page had a link to the proposed changes. We clicked on the link and voilà! We found that we had been transported into the members-only archives of a professional association that had this text. That was not evident at first but was soon obvious, when we simply went from that page to "Home." What this practitioner had obviously done was copy the address of the page that contained these changes while online in the members-only section. In so doing, he actually added his own password and thus provided a back door into the organization's pages. Do any of your affiliates do that?

Also, check the Web sites of your affiliates and subsidiaries for specific details. Are they providing sketches from your facilities to show their expertise? Are these sketches too revealing?

Move now to the companies that do business with you: your suppliers, your consultants, your distributors, etc. You can go to their Web sites, if they are few in number, and search for your firm's name. What are they saying?

In addition, for suppliers or consultants who have worked on particularly important projects, such as building plants with new capabilities, look for an anonymous case study on their pages that is used to demonstrate their expertise. Is that case study you? What does it tell your competitors that you prefer they not know? You will sometimes see descriptions, plans, and even photographs about how they redesigned your plant and what it can do now.

External Sites You Use

Now, move to the external sites your company uses, such as job listings and association directories. What are you, or they, saying about your firm? Does a review of past job listings show a pattern that is helpful to a competitor? For example, do you always advertise on Monster when you are opening a new office?

Alter links that create these listings of unnecessary content. Rather than noting how many new facilities you are opening and when, why not say you are "aggressively expanding"? If you need to provide specific data to entice the best applicants for your job openings, consider reserving some of the data for those who actually apply and providing it after (rather than before) you speak to them. That way you can warn the applicants first about keeping confidential what you are about to tell them.

Also check external sites to see what you do *not* have to protect. For example, if your senior managers always serve on association committees and the association always posts a current biography of these key members, why should you worry about keeping these same biographies off your own home page?

Links Back Home

Next, check into inbound links, those that link back to your home page. What do they show? Don't forget to check inbound links to your subsidiaries and affiliates. The most common link of importance you will find is to résumés of former (and sometimes even present) employees and consultants. How much detail are they disclosing about what they did and, most important, about what you are still doing? If it is too much, contact them and ask them to make changes.

Follow up links that start from colleges and universities. Increasingly, colleges and universities are using their Web sites to promote the activities of their faculty. Do they also discuss the consulting contract you gave one of their professors?

Many of these schools use the Web to provide information about courses and research projects being undertaken by the faculty. You may be surprised to find that one of your mid-level managers, going part-time for an advanced degree, has just had his or her paper published on the Web. Is that a problem? Let us give you one example of such a case.

In searching for information on the marketing strategy of a target, we found a recent paper done by a student in a fairly arcane area of mathematical modeling. It was clear that the subject of the study was the target. The paper involved efforts to determine how to allocate costs across several markets as well as across different groups of customers.

When we presented our findings to the client, it saw the same thing we did. The client's CI manager then located someone in the company who was familiar with this area. She took one look at the outline of the paper and observed that it was a way of calculating costs across state lines for large customers. The discovery was an intelligence breakthrough for our client, who had suspected that the target was moving in that direction. The paper was the first hard evidence that the target was doing the computer modeling necessary to calculate costs in this way. Harmless? No. Harmful.

REGULAR REVIEWS

Obviously, you cannot track down every link to your Web site and every link to those links. If you did, you would be searching the Web forever. Approach regular defensive Internet reviews as a competitor would. Do not waste your time checking everything. Rather, focus your efforts on the subject matter and areas that are currently most sensitive. Search under your firm's name as well as under its nicknames and under new, even unused, domain names. Take several of the following approaches to help ensure the security of your data, and train others to do the same (McGonagle & Vella, 1998).

- Never use the same search engines again and again. If you use Google this time, switch to the HotBot® or Ask Jeeves search engine next time, and so on. No engine or crawler covers even half the Web.
- Educate those who maintain your Web page, as well as those who provide content, to review what they post before they post it and then to look at it once it is on the Web, preferably not on their own computers. Also remind these workers to remove materials in a timely manner.
- Find out how long different items are kept on your Web site. For example, some public firms keep analyst briefings, including audiocasts and overheads, mounted for years. Others remove them after three months or less. While many firms have a complete press release library, others, perhaps with an eye towards defensive issues, keep only the most recent press releases online.
- Review descriptions of your firm at commercial sites that provide industry- or company-specific data for a fee. Do not limit your review to Dun & Bradstreet. Look for broad-ranging sites such as 1Jump as well. Most of the data there, and at similar sites, are captured from public, often published, sources. So, if they are listing all your officers and shareholders, for example, and you are a private firm, you can elect either (1) not to give such data to these companies in the future or (2) to keep the data off your own site.
- Make sure that outsiders designing or redesigning Web sites do not use internal terms of art or catchphrases they have heard from your employees. In doing so, they have given your competitors more to start with than they deserve.

- For new Web-based initiatives, make sure that they are not mounted on, or even linked to or from, your home page until they are ready to become operational.
- Look for Web page designs that are helpful to consumers, not competitors. For example, if you want to make available to customers a list of all 75 of your sales offices, wouldn't they find it easier to use if they could be given the address of the one closest to their ZIP Code? Not only is that more customer-friendly, it is competitor-hostile, for it makes a competitor seeking that list ask for locations possibly hundreds of times.
- Consider design options that make it more difficult for a competitor to save an entire page. Some frames, JavaScript elements, and other options have this often unintended consequence.
- Feel free to ask why things are put up. Speeches and presentations by your executives may be interesting, but are they too revealing of overall strategy? To what articles or interviews are you providing your own links? Not every interview with every employee deserves to be given its own link. In fact, there are some interviews, usually with your very top officers, that you are better off not drawing attention to. They can provide a great deal of assistance in profiling (Vella & McGonagle, 2000).
- Caution your contractors and consultants that they can, inadvertently, become a window into matters that are competitively sensitive. Ask them to hold off publicizing what they are doing in any detail for several months.
- Save time and money while protecting your company by linking to sources of data on your firm. More and more public firms in the United States are directing those wanting to review documents filed with the U.S. Securities and Exchange Commission (SEC) to the SEC's own Web site, rather than posting documents on the company Web site. Then competitors are at the mercy of the limitations of EDGAR when trying to review such filings. You may want to do the same with articles on your firm.
- Consider subscribing to or using software that monitors changes in targeted home pages. Then use it on your own.
- Regularly check what new domain names your own firm has filed for. Do not assume that your emerging Internet strategy is hidden. Skilled CI professionals can turn to services that allow them to see what domain names you have

reserved and when. Looking at these lists can help them determine where your strategy is going. Should your firm be filing for other domain names to mask the intent of the new names? The reservation of multiple names makes it that much harder for your competitors to keep you in their sights.

- Should your new domain names be reserved by a subsidiary that does not carry the parent name? Some firms use such relatively anonymous entities to hold all of their patents, trademarks, and other intellectual property assets.

In your efforts to protect your firm, always remember that you cannot possibly protect everything. If you try to protect all your information, you may impair or destroy your firm's ability to communicate with important stakeholders and run the risk that the business may not survive in a competitive environment. Instead, shield your intelligence—develop and implement a defensive CI program.

Linking Management Thought With the Online World

6

Analysis: Why It Is Important[1]

CRAIG FLEISHER

This is a time of new and varied business challenges and opportunities for competitive business analysts and competitive intelligence in general. Analysts must help their companies contend with a host of traditional competitive threats, including hostile and potentially hostile competitors, empowered consumers, and simmering market conflicts. At the same time, they are grappling with a new set of intelligence questions that have emerged in the new information and communication technology (ICT) era and online world that this book encompasses. Intelligence questions posed by decision makers to today's competitive analysts have become more complex and require faster processing.

Today, the threats to companies almost invariably involve more than one company, geographic boundary, marketplace, and product/service issue. In this environment, as never before, analysts are challenged to develop answers to difficult questions and support their judgments with unique and useful information. They must do so against a backdrop of shrinking budgets, chaotic and ephemeral markets, demanding executives who have precious little time for planning, evolving ICT, more global and sophisticated intelligence targets, multi-point international competition, and a frequent overload of data that often illuminates matters but also makes it harder to distinguish fact from fiction.

At the same time, the opportunity for intelligence to contribute to and enhance a company's well-being is as good as it has ever been. New technologies, including sophisticated analytic

---

[1] Craig Fleisher—University of Windsor

applications, have helped make analysis work faster, more sophisticated, more efficient, and more comprehensive in using information (Fleisher, 2001). Improved and more convenient delivery of just-in-time learning, primarily through digital means, has helped the professional workforce show steady improvement in its CI-related knowledge, skills, training, and abilities (Vibert, 2001).

Nevertheless, many questions remain about the importance of analysis and the value it can bring to competitive organizations. In this short chapter, I will try to respond to such questions by identifying what analysis is, how it is performed, the critical needs it serves, and the shifting organizational priorities for analysts and analysis.

WHAT IS ANALYSIS AND HOW IS IT PERFORMED?

Intelligence analysis processes involve three steps: (1) collection, (2) analysis, and (3) synthesis. Collection takes place using open or closed data sources. Analysis involves a variety of scientific and nonscientific techniques to make conclusions or inferences from the data. Synthesis normally produces an analysis product, such as a chart, graph, table, summary, visual, or other communicative aid, to deliver to the client. A formula for placing CI analysis into this broader CI context is as follows:

> Understanding Business Situation and Client's Needs (known in business as Key Intelligence Topics or KITs—Herring, 1999)—determines → Type of Analysis—determines → Type of Data Needed—determines → Type of Data Collection

Analysis usually takes place at multiple levels within an organization. Strategic analysis is arguably the most vital form of intelligence because it provides a framework within which other forms of intelligence collection and analysis take place, offers an overall assessment from the top down rather than from the bottom up, and helps to provide a basis for policy formulation, resource allocation, and strategy development. Strategic intelligence analysis helps to discern and make sense of important trends, to identify and extract patterns that would otherwise not be visible, and to provide an overall picture of the evolving opportunity and threat environment, as well as the level of organizational impact that might be experienced under certain specified contingencies.

Its focus on macro-level issues rather than the more detailed levels of analysis and its day-to-day irrelevance for many intelligence consumers are weaknesses of strategic analysis.

Strategic intelligence analysis provides guidance for relevant tactical and operational assessments, and work done at the tactical and operational levels in turn helps to shape the strategic intelligence focus. Strategic assessments should be useful for intelligence analysis consumers, providing forecasting estimates that will help to reduce uncertainties in ways that feed into policy development processes, as well as providing a basis for more informed decision making and more effective resource allocation. As strategic analytic methodologies mature, they will also offer the basis for predictive or anticipatory assessments that can serve to provide warnings of potential high-impact activities. Although there exist extensive treatments on the kinds of specific techniques and tools that the business analyst might use (Fleisher & Bensoussan, 2002), analytical initiatives that would fall under the rubric of strategic intelligence analysis include the following:

- **Overall opportunity and threat (O&T) assessments.** These analyses are used to assess the levels of dependence and vulnerabilities of critical customers, markets, products, and processes all along the value chain, the nature of competitive activity that could affect these areas, the kinds of competitive changes that could have a significant impact, and the likelihood of such activities taking place.
- **Sector or competitor assessments.** Such analyses focus on opportunities, risks, threats, and vulnerabilities in particular areas, such as company infrastructure, specific geographic locations, certain customer types, or particular sectors of the product/service market, such as frozen foods or aircraft rental. These assessments can also highlight emerging or threatening competitors that are likely to impact the competitive marketplace or market space terrain.
- **Trend analyses.** These are used to illuminate changing opportunities, risks, threats, and vulnerabilities. Trend analyses might include baseline assessments, performed so as to better recognize departures from the current status, or they might focus on the future in an effort to determine in what ways the matter is developing and what can be done to anticipate and address impending issues. Trend analysis is most effective when it is linked with careful attention to fundamental drivers in the social, political, economic, cultural,

technological, aesthetic, customer, legal, environmental, and sectoral areas (Cartwright, 2001) that will shape the future industry and macro-environment.

- **Anomaly detection.** Strategic analysts search for anomalies that provide indicators of emerging challenges. In this context, anomalies can be understood as developments that do not fit typical or known patterns. The detection of anomalies or novel patterns can be a major anticipatory element. This process requires data on tactical and operational efforts, and it also reinforces those efforts. Anomaly detection requires systematic environmental scanning, as well as the integration of tactical and operational intelligence reports that identify and highlight specific aberrations from the norm. This task is often done with sophisticated new analytic application software that can quickly ferret out anomalies across a wider range of data inputs than ever before. With the array of Web tracking software available to today's analysts, analytic applications will only get more valuable over time as the Internet takes a more prominent place in organizations' market planning.

- **Analysis of future environments.** The business environment is constantly changing, most notably the online business environment. Strategic intelligence analysis must take that into account. It must attempt to provide assessments of potential future environments in the marketplace and the likely impact of competitive activity within those environments. Considerations of social as well as political and economic impacts will have to be factored into intelligence assessments.

- **Potential impact assessments.** Because of the macro-level view taken by strategic analysis, it also offers a good approach for assessing probable cascade effects of impending competitive action and activity. The potential for widespread effects can be recognized most readily as a result of in-depth strategic analysis—which in turn offers opportunities to develop both protective and amelioration strategies. The capacity for effective and rapid reconstitution of operations following a crisis or disaster might depend on such analysis.

Tactical analysis is a necessary and important complement to work done at the strategic level. It is the natural link between macro-level analysis and the micro-level focus on individual cases.

In physical space, geography helps to differentiate tactical from strategic, but on the Internet, this component is lacking, which makes the distinction between strategic and tactical somewhat more tenuous. At the same time, however, the strategic and tactical levels are mutually reinforcing. Strategic intelligence analysis provides the framework for tactical assessments, and these assessments in turn help to feed strategic analysis. With a highly dynamic interrelationship among the various levels of analysis, each level is strengthened by and strengthens the others.

The kinds of prominent studies that come under the umbrella of tactical analysis include the following:

- **Cluster and pattern analysis.** Cluster and pattern analysis is designed to discern temporal patterns, the use of particular marketplace attack methods, commonalities of targets, and attempts to build profiles of competitors, including executives and key line and staff personnel.
- **Stimulus-response analysis.** Stimulus-response analysis is designed to identify potential actions that could be taken by competitors in response to specific known or predicted events. This analysis could be used both proactively in developing warnings and reactively in lending significance to seemingly innocuous activities.
- **Value constellation analysis.** Companies involve a dizzying array of stakeholders in the conduct of their business operations. This analysis is designed to identify the important partners, allies, venture partners, outsourcing partners, and agents a company utilizes.

Operational intelligence analysis overlaps with investigation and is often oriented to individual cases. It involves technological assessments of the methods used for marketplace battles, specific investigations of competitive threats, and the like. An important component of operational analysis is identifying the particular vulnerability or vulnerabilities that have been exploited and providing guidance on how it or they can be minimized or eliminated.

Another component of operational analysis is the potential ability to provide attribution during or shortly after an intrusion. The data collected during an incident, combined with the profiling efforts provided at the tactical level, could lead to attribution. While there are significant policy and legal questions associated with such a capability, its importance to the overall analytical process cannot be overstated.

In physical space, physical geography often helps to separate operational and tactical from strategic, but ICTs and competition in the market space on the World Wide Web make these distinctions more tenuous. At the same time, all three levels are mutually reinforcing of one another. With a highly dynamic interrelationship among the various levels of analysis, each level is strengthened by and strengthens the others.

CRITICAL NEEDS SERVED BY ANALYSTS

Although it can be difficult to scope out and measure the unique value added by analysts and the analysis process within the larger organizational CI effort, Langley (1995) notes that the analysis process serves intermediate decision-making purposes such as reducing the number of input variables; providing more time for decision making as opposed to facts absorption; providing connections among seemingly unrelated data and information; providing a context by relating information to organizational mission, objectives, and strategy; and creating a working hypothesis by making a story out of disparate business environment information.

Godson (1987) states that analytic outputs serve four organizational purposes:

- They predict future developments and explain the implications to decision makers.
- They make data more meaningful and provide guidance to decision makers who are considering goals and alternative means of achieving them.
- They provide warnings of major developments, events, trends, and assessments based on empirical evidence, helping policy makers avoid unpleasant surprises.
- They offer pieces of current information on specialized topics of concern to decision makers.

A major question with respect to the importance of analysts in satisfying organizational needs is whether organizations can perform as well in the marketplace in the absence of analysts. Certainly, some organizations perform well in the marketplace without having an analysis unit or individuals formally designated as analysts. In reality, however, this question has not been empirically studied in a corporate setting. Studies performed in governmental intelligence settings suggest that analysis plays an important role in organizational success and that its absence results in less successful outcomes (Commission on the Roles and Capabilities of the United States Intelligence Community, 1996). It seems reasonable that similar studies in a corporate setting would produce similar results.

SHIFTING ORGANIZATIONAL PRIORITIES FOR ANALYSTS AND ANALYSIS

All of these changes add up to a fundamental shift in organizational priorities for analysts. Though change is uneven among different industries and sectors, it is possible to decipher the outlines of a transformation toward improved organizational analytical capabilities through the following principles.

Adding Value to Intelligence

A priority for intelligence analysis is to deliver a product that adds context and meaning to the raw data and information collected. In today's information-overloaded and news-rich physical and digital environments, intelligence must compete for the decision maker's attention as never before. As John Gannon (1996), former deputy director of the Central Intelligence Agency, commented, "It is our challenging but rewarding job to keep telling these smart but overworked folks what's happening in a complicated world."

Keeping ahead of the competition, and keeping the attention of intelligence consumers/users, cannot be taken for granted. In light of some authorities calling the insufficient and poor training of analysts a primary reason for the low effectiveness of CI programs (Werther, 2001), what will ensure that the analyst stays relevant?

One way to stay relevant is to build and maintain subject matter expertise, continuity, and depth within the organization's analytical ranks. Information alone will not be useful to the consumer if it is not interpreted correctly and presented in a credible way by a recognized expert. This issue has been addressed in some organizations through the creation of a senior-level council that is responsible for workforce strategic planning and addresses the areas of CI recruitment, assignments, core skills and standards, and training. Other organizations have relied upon the continuous delivery of learning opportunities, through apprenticeships, traditional classrooms, and virtual instruction, by which analysts can upgrade their capabilities. Finally, some organizations have carefully selected certain realms of analytical focus to be outsourced to specialist companies that can provide the needed services more efficiently and effectively than internal resources. The variety of ways that best-practice CI organizations have attempted to address this need is ably cataloged in several recent studies (American Productivity and Quality Council, 2000; Lackman, Saban, & Lanasa, 2000; Prescott, Herring, & Panefly, 1998).

Answering Questions in Real Time

One of the consequences of an analyst getting closer to internal clients is that the type of key intelligence topics (KITs) and questions the analyst faces will change. Analysts have traditionally met intelligence needs through the publication of regular briefings and overviews that are tailored to the client's agenda and special intelligence requirements. These documents can also be supplemented just in time with several personalized electronic or paper memos that respond to questions raised by prior briefings.

The same question-and-answer process is played out at other levels of today's organizations, where analysts may provide daily or, when a crisis erupts, minute-by-minute or hourly intelligence support. In today's rapidly changing business environment, the vast majority of an organization's analysis will be done in response to specific questions from analytical clients. Over the course of a typical year, an analyst or analytical team may provide hundreds of briefings on virtually every substantive issue covered by the organization.

Concentrating Resources

In today's information-overloaded environment, successful analysts must be vigilant about prioritization. Few business organizations maintain a level of in-house analytical resources sufficient to provide them with a continuing competitive advantage. Because of this fact, successful analysts are now required to utilize the latest in information technology. They must use all available sources, including in-house, open, and closed sources; stay abreast of the latest and smartest analytical techniques; and continually press for clarification of their clients' critical intelligence needs.

Organizations must also find new and innovative ways to build flexibility into their collection and analysis efforts so that these priorities can be addressed on an as-needed, critical basis. This flexibility is seldom considered among the priorities of organizing CI but has become increasingly important in CI resource-constrained contexts.

Forging Partnerships

The final priority concerns how the organization, its data collectors, and its analysts relate with other parts of the broader community. Partnership is a concept that has taken hold throughout the private and public sectors as organizations seek to take advantage of others' specialized expertise and resources. One recent step in this direction has been broadening and deepening cooperative efforts between CI and other elements of the organization through the building of formal and informal networks, including such stakeholders as corporate information specialists, information systems and applications development personnel, university talent, information acquirers in associations, planners, and customer support experts throughout the organization.

Nearly all analysis will, in all likelihood, move toward stronger partnerships and collaboration in the years ahead. Rarely does all the expertise on any particular issue reside in one part of an organization or business unit. Tapping into analytic expertise across the entire value chain of the organization and coordinating on collection activity will be important to overcome those all too commonly experienced budget and personnel constraints.

Looking Over the Horizon

The focus on custom tailored support helps make analysis more relevant and useful to the client. It also ensures that intelligence resources are going where there are demonstrated needs. However, providing this type of support makes an enormous claim on an organization's resources, particularly its people, data collection facilities, and time. At worst, analysts risk becoming prisoners of their inboxes and being unable to put daily events in a broader context, which is essential if they are to provide timely warnings of emerging opportunities or threats.

Although this is not a new problem, most organizations are trying to balance the need for current analytical support against the need to look ahead. The challenge is to step back and consider opportunities and threats that the organization might face tomorrow, next week, or next year. Analysts have to look beyond the immediate and obvious threats and consider those forces and trends that might be moving slowly but inexorably toward their organizations. This is the only way the analyst can highlight for policymakers the sort of low-probability, high-impact events that could seriously affect the organization's competitiveness. Analysts must continuously subject conventional wisdom to strenuous tests. Giving policymakers a sense of the possible, rather that just a sense of what is most likely, must remain a key priority for intelligence. It is one of the aspects of analysts' work that sets them apart from others.

Providing On-Call Direct Support

Analysis is most relevant and useful when it is provided directly to the intelligence consumer. Analysts can be extremely beneficial when they are deployed on-site and are in regular contact with the organization's policy developers, negotiating teams, and frontline decision makers. These on-site representatives provide "one-stop shopping" for those internal clients who need their expertise. On-site representation also ensures that the analysts remain close to their clients and agendas, gain useful feedback from consumers, and better help target collection to meet specific intelligence needs. Such direct support has recently become more important, since today's busy decision makers often do not have time to wait for critical information. Consequently, analysts must do whatever they can to help their clients get the answers they need in a timely way.

SUMMARY

Leading CI authorities such as Ben Gilad (1998) and Liam Fahey (1999) have recently suggested that excellent analysis is the key to a successful CI practice. Intelligence is often a company's first line of defense and offense. Maintaining this capability into the future will require that analysts and CI practitioners exploit every opportunity to provide analysis that is persuasive, relevant, timely, and prescient. Analysts must help ensure that senior decision makers have the essential insight they need to preserve their organizations' competitiveness; to protect existing and future customers, products, and services; to give negotiators the information and insights required to produce agreements and arrangements that advance the company's interests and well-being; and to give their sales and frontline customer contact personnel the advantage of early warning and dominant marketplace awareness.

There are other challenges for analysis apart from the changes in the world around organizations. The demands, expectations, and responsibilities of analysts are ever-changing as intelligence consumers contend with their particular difficulties. Contemporary analysts are expected to offer more direct and immediate support than in the past, resolve different types of queries, work more closely with their counterparts responsible for information collection, package their analysis in a variety of new forms, and deliver it through whatever means are best suited to the recipient.

In fulfilling this mission for the future, CI organizations and members of the analytical community face many fresh challenges and priorities. Success will be determined, at least in part, by how well they manage their scarce resources, balance often conflicting demands for current intelligence against the need for longer-term analysis, continue to develop both broad and deep analytic expertise, and forge new relationships with others both inside and outside their organizations.

7

Management Thought: The Connection With CI

CONOR VIBERT

How pervasive are the skills required to practice CI? If we think of CI as primarily a process of research and analysis that supports decision making, we can see the requisite skills being developed by many of our children. According to Principal Everett MacPherson, teachers at New Minas Elementary School in the Annapolis Valley of Nova Scotia are noticing that projects such as "How to save the polar bears" or "Why is our country a good place to live?" are frequently researched online. How are these youngsters making a case for keeping the bears content and numerous in the Far North? With a little parental help, children as young as eight, nine, and ten are offering insights gleaned from digital encyclopedias such as the MSN® Encarta® online encyclopedia, search directories that include Yahoo!, map providers such as Maps.com, and Environment Canada's WeatherOffice (Vibert, 2001).

Few elementary or high school instructors set out to teach competitive intelligence to their students. However, they are interested in learning how to more effectively incorporate the Internet into their curricula. What is important for the field of CI is that, from an early age, children are learning how to undertake targeted online research. Slowly, these same skills are being enhanced through incorporation into university curricula around the world, with the consequence being a growing pool of candidates capable of practicing CI (albeit, not at the level of the seasoned professional) upon entry into the workforce.

One important message of this book is that while the practice of online research and analysis is still in its infancy in the commercial and government sectors, colleges and universities can play a leading role in shaping how CI evolves in the next decade. Consider a scenario where classrooms serve as living labs and safe practice fields for young online analysts:

Nineteen- and 20-year-olds use the Web to identify new and emerging technologies in key regional industries, conduct social responsibility audits of publicly traded corporations, identify key internal stakeholders of acquisition targets, and track the communication patterns of key industry competitors. In these same classrooms, virtual teams of geographically distributed students view presentations via Webcasts, communicate using ICQ chat software, undertake multimedia presentations prepared in the Microsoft® PowerPoint® presentation graphics program, and critique their colleagues in real time with the help of information obtained from online regulatory and commercial databases.

In some postsecondary institutions, this scenario is real. For others, it is not very far off. Aside from helping students become proficient in Internet technologies and gain an understanding of online information sources, efforts to develop competent CI practitioners need to address the issue of personal insight. The assumption of this author is that analytical insight can be developed through training and practice. Some of this experience cannot be gained in the classroom and will only be developed in the field. However, the time needed to become a competent CI practitioner can be dramatically shortened through solid application and understanding of tried-and-true theory.

Unfortunately, the idea that academic training and insight can contribute in a meaningful manner to the development of CI as a field and of competent practitioners is not shared by all. Indeed, some CI professionals question the relevance of academic thought and training when it comes to preparing CI practitioners for the harsh realities of the business world. One set of writers even argues that "in competitive intelligence, industry knowledge counts far more than educational or professional background" (Gilad & Herring, 2001). This argument is flawed for a number of reasons:

> First, the definition of the term "competitive intelligence" is itself debatable with writers and practitioners struggling to come to agreement on a common understanding (Fleisher, 2003). Second, practices falling under the guise of CI are numerous and more often than not overlap with those found in other professions. Finally, the statement has not

been tested. Aside from anecdotal evidence, there is no solid empirical support for this argument. (Vibert, 2003, p. 133)

This section of the text argues that academic theory can guide practice and aid CI professionals in their quest to understand and predict competitor behavior, customer reactions, and market conditions. Why is this so? The answer is to think of CI as simply a highly useful way of researching and understanding organizations and their actions. Organization theory is a body of knowledge that explains how organizations do things, how they are structured, and why some organizations do things better than others. CI is the process or practice of research. The ideas housed under the heading of organization theory can improve the process or practice of research and thus of CI.

The objective of this chapter is to link CI with contemporary management thinking. Building on the ideas of Craig Fleisher in Chapter 6, it offers reasons, along with a number of examples, as to why CI trainers and practitioners should care about the concepts that form the core of organization theory and much of strategic management thought. Explicitly, this chapter responds to the question, Can academic insight inform the practice of CI? Then, to help readers make sense of the broad conceptual toolkit available to them, the text distinguishes concepts with economic origins from those with a noneconomic slant.

The remaining chapters in this section build on these ideas. Chapter 8 links them to the online, day-to-day information gathering, analysis, and dissemination activities of researchers. While Chapter 7 relates academic thought to CI, Chapter 8 connects academic thought to Web-based CI. The ideas presented will help readers improve their research efforts through an increased understanding of how organizations function, as well as an appreciation of new ways to compete.

Chapter 9 applies organization theory to Web-based CI. It introduces the idea of online research missions, analytical frameworks that can help practitioners and researchers undertake Web-based CI and offer their organizations a competitive advantage. Chapter 10 extends these ideas by presenting a number of case examples of research missions that tie together organizational concepts, online information sources, and analytical frameworks. Finally, Chapter 11 places Web-based CI in a larger spectrum, that of knowledge management.

ABOUT ORGANIZATION THEORY

So what are these concepts that we refer to? Business schools, their star professors, and consultancies such as McKinsey & Company, The Boston Consulting Group, and Bain & Company have played a role in developing ideas that help explain why organizations look and act as they do and why some succeed and others fail. Their ideas also help analysts and observers understand "what is feasible for organizations themselves and for the wider social system," as well as "some inherent contradictions which limit the impact that individual actors can have" (Hall, 1996, p. 25). These ideas are captured under the heading of organization theory, which encompasses perspectives originating in diverse fields of inquiry, including economics, sociology, political science, anthropology, biology, and psychology.

To simplify matters, consider that these concepts can be divided into two groups: concepts with economic origins and concepts without economic origins. Those with economic origins are normally referred to as "economic theories of the firm" or "models of business organization conduct." As with most disciplines, no definition exists to unite those seeking to understand why companies act and organize as they do (Grant, 1996, p. 109). A few ideas are, however, accepted by most management thinkers.

First, a theory of the firm is normally an "abstraction of a real world business enterprise designed to address a particular set of its characteristics and behaviors" (Machlup, 1980). Second, most theories of the firm seek to predict the behavior of firms in their competitive environments (Grant, 1996, p. 109). Third, these concepts are implicitly managerial in their orientation (Gioia & Pitre, 1990, p. 590). That is, they are rarely critical of management activity and seek to offer insight that supports managers.

In addition, most economic theories of the firm reject the idea that executive decisions are made under conditions of perfect knowledge. For the most part, these theories also do not agree that the sole objective of the firm is to maximize profits.

A second group of concepts is noneconomic in origin. Researchers and writers in this tradition are interested in the analysis of organizations, not just business enterprises. Performance or effectiveness from this perspective is not limited to the corporate bottom line or externally imposed market measures. Desired outcomes may take many forms, including survival and legitimacy.

There is also recognition that corporations may not be autonomous actors or behave in a manner consistent with the decisions of managers. Most companies employ many individuals, all of whom have distinct opinions and viewpoints. Finally, thinkers in this tradition do not shy away from looking closely at the relationships between performance or effectiveness and internal structures and cultures (Grant, 1996).

HOW CI CAN BENEFIT FROM THE CONCEPTS OF ORGANIZATION THEORY

Before proceeding to our next chapter, it is important to return to the concern expressed by Gilad and Herring, noted on page 98: can academic insight inform the practice of CI? The answer is yes. Why might a CI practitioner have an interest in understanding management concepts developed at institutions such as Harvard, Stanford, or the Massachusetts Institute of Technology? Aside from the simple response of "they can improve analysis," a number of reasons can be offered.

To begin with, "if organizations are understood then individuals [in this instance, CI practitioners] have a tool by which they can deal with the reality that they face" (Hall, 1996, p. 25). That reality is an uncertain competitive landscape that is more often than not in flux. Although labeled as theories, most of the concepts presented in this chapter and the next are based on real-life corporate experiences. Whether they explain the behavior of small businesses, large corporations, not-for-profit entities, or government institutions, these ideas are the result of observation, data collection, and data analysis. They exist and are referenced in this book because evidence exists to support them. They are also noteworthy because the evidence and core ideas have passed the critical review of academic peers and have developed a following among scholars.

Another justification for connecting the practice of CI with the ideas or concepts of organization theory is that it helps to distinguish CI analysts from one another on the basis of their work. At a personal level, effective incorporation of these ideas into analytical tasks can lead to a career-related competitive advantage over one's peers. Borrowing a page from one of the concepts described in the following chapter, the resource-based theory of the firm (Barney, 1991), let's assume that analysts possess a competitive streak. In their quest for recognition and reward, analysts will strive to consistently produce work that either saves or makes money for the company, that is difficult to imitate, and that cannot be matched in terms of availability and quality. The breadth of concepts described in the following chapters offers CI professionals an enhanced knowledge base to use in differentiating their analytical services.

John Prescott, coeditor of the *Journal of Competitive Intelligence and Management*, offers a different perspective. Many disciplines have multiple origins and multiple fields of practice. Competitive intelligence is no different. Its practice is not specific to any one industry. Indeed, it is difficult to identify an industry that might not benefit from CI. Be it the field of law, computer science, patent analysis, pharmacy, marketing, accounting, medicine, or geography (Prescott, 1999), no one profession can claim ownership of the practice of CI. The same argument applies to ideas or concepts that influence its path of development. Just as military intelligence and the information sciences have played a role in CI's evolution, so too can the ideas grouped under the heading of organization theory.

Another reason is philosophical in nature. Consider how the CI process was described by David Campbell earlier in this book. In its most basic form, CI involves the collection, analysis, and dissemination of competitor and market information. Although they are often couched in the language of corporations, these steps are performed by individuals, acting alone or collectively, with or without the aid of technology. The process is quintessentially human in nature. It is also commonly accepted by many CI professionals and forms a part of what may be considered a paradigm (Kuhn, 1962) or school of thought regarding what analysts and researchers should be doing when they practice CI. This paradigm has been socially constructed.

This viewpoint suggests that when we think of CI, much of what we know is the result of our previous interactions with other CI professionals or entities. Our discussions, how we have communicated our ideas to decision makers or negotiated with clients, the rhetoric that we have been exposed to, etc. (Gergen, 1985), have all played a role in forming our understanding of CI. As a result, how we view an action as straightforward as a price increase in a competitor's product may be the result not so much of our own analytical abilities but rather of how they have been modified through discussion, interaction, and presentation to other decision makers and colleagues.

Yet, just as we are influenced, so too can our ideas be influential. The management concepts discussed in this book can help CI professionals improve decision making by enhancing the credibility of their arguments and create or socially construct an environment accepting of their analysis.

The origin of the next point is the philosophical position termed relativism. One strand of relativism holds that no form of knowledge is more valid than another. From this perspective, knowledge of any particular event or activity is not objective or universally accepted, nor does it have definite foundations. Relativism counters "the view that what is true, good, beautiful, or what exists, can hold for all times and places" (Smith, 1998, p. 35). It is also subjective and tied to specific contexts.

The implication for CI and the management concepts outlined in this book is obvious. These concepts explain corporate behavior. Many explain why some firms obtain a competitive advantage while others do not. Others focus on why some companies survive while others disappear off the map in a matter of a few months or years. Still other perspectives explain organizational growth or decline. The common feature in most cases is that these approaches explain why companies act as they do, why they look as they do, and why they might succeed or fail. Picture one company or its actions analyzed through dozens of different lenses.

These concepts can also help overcome a researcher bias toward the use of online information sources. A 2000 study by the American Productivity & Quality Center (Prescott & the Society of Competitive Intelligence Professionals, 2000) argues that most North American business professionals consider the Internet to be the most effective tool for obtaining information about suppliers, customers, and competitors. Unfortunately, this also suggests that many professionals may rely too heavily on online information sources for intelligence needs (Windle, 2003). Exposure to new management concepts offers researchers and CI analysts a portfolio of mental frameworks within which to position different information strands.

Use of these concepts can also improve organizational decision making. Among the purposes for which analysis is used within corporations are the formation of connections among seemingly unrelated data and information and the creation of a context for relating information to the company mission and strategic objectives (Langley, 1995). The insight of analysts forms these connections and creates these contexts. New styles of thinking such as those presented in the following pages inform insight.

Another reason that CI professionals should pay attention to contemporary management thought is the potential for these ideas to resolve a number of concerns related to analysis. In arguing why analysis is often done so poorly, Fleisher and Bensoussan (2003, p. 114) suggest four points. First, "individuals frequently do analysis on the basis of the data they have as opposed to the data they should have." Second, many corporate researchers and CI professionals suffer from "tool rut," or the overuse of the same analytical tools. Third, most analysis is based on historical data and financial ratios. Finally, many analysts are business school graduates whose insight stems primarily from instruction by accountants and finance professors. The multidisciplinary roots of organization theory offer an alternative set of frameworks to overcome these shortcomings.

Finally, broadening the toolkit of analysts and researchers to include managerial concepts can also help establish the credibility of CI as a distinct profession. What are the prerequisites for a profession? One model suggests "commitment to serve others, adherence to a published code of ethics, a mastery of specialized knowledge, standards for measuring knowledge, and active participation in a professional society" (Fleisher, 2003, p. 86). Most important for this argument is a sixth characteristic: specialized knowledge of other related fields. Organizational theory can be thought of as a related field.

These are but a few of the reasons to justify the use of organization theory by CI professionals. Together they suggest that analysis and the practice of CI can only be improved by exposure to new ideas such as these.

8

Management Thought: Ideas That Can Improve CI

CONOR VIBERT

How can the concepts of organization theory improve the practice of Web-based CI? In the previous chapter, we justified the connection of these ideas with competitive intelligence. In this chapter, our focus will be on demonstrating connections with the online world.

Earlier, we made the case that effective incorporation of ideas from organization theory would help analysts distinguish their work from that of others. Over time, this in turn would lead to a personal advantage that would be sustainable if their work proved valuable, difficult to imitate, and unmatchable in terms of timing and quality. Our argument is that CI professionals and researchers can develop a reputation for uniqueness and effectiveness by incorporating the concepts of organization theory into their analytical efforts.

But how might this occur? One approach is to use an existing research process, such as collecting the data, analyzing them, and then disseminating them, and to justify the results using one of the concepts discussed in this chapter. A second approach is to use the concepts to improve the CI process itself. In the following paragraphs, we examine the concepts and suggest how online researchers may use them to improve their own analytical abilities.

Whether intended or not by the authors, in the eyes of a reader, almost all organization theories or concepts may be interpreted as offering a rationale for action or behavior. To frame the discussion, let's assume that these concepts can be grouped under five headings, which are illustrated in Figure 8.1: those that suggest how companies might organize themselves, those that offer insight into how corporations might be led, those that explain how companies compete, those that suggest how workers and society in general can be protected, and those that recommend ways in which deficiencies or deviant behavior might be corrected.

Figure 8.1 An Organizing Framework for Organization Theories

	THEORIES OF ORGANIZATION	ECONOMIC THEORIES OF THE FIRM
Organizing	• Bureaucracy theory • Contingency theory • Configuration theory • Postmodern theory • Chaos theory	• Evolutionary theory • Property rights
Leading	• Strategic choice theory • Symbolic interactionism • Dramaturgy • Metaphorical perspective	• Stakeholder theory • Knowledge perspective
Competing	• Resource dependence theory • Population ecology theory	• Game theory • Resource-based theory • Chicago School theory
Protecting	• Institutional theory • Sensemaking perspective • Rules-based theory • Poststructural feminism	• Agency theory • Transaction cost economics • Knowledge perspective
Correcting	• Critical theory • Marxist perspective	• Behavioral theory • Bain-Mason perspective

In the following pages, brief overviews of a selection of the theories are grouped under each of these headings. In many cases, each description represents but the tip of the iceberg of an extensive collection of insight. For the purpose of this endeavor and for simplicity, each theory is categorized under one theme. These groupings are by no means all-inclusive and serve simply to provide the reader with an idea of the underlying themes. In each overview, suggestions are offered as to how researchers might make use of these ideas, as well as how online information sources might be employed to improve their analysis. As noted earlier, the next chapter offers examples of specific Web-based applications or analytical frameworks.

ORGANIZING

If asked where to begin when explaining how a competitor, customer, or supplier organizes itself, many professional analysts would start with the idea of a bureaucracy.

A CI practitioner might find this idea useful when scanning a competitor's online regulatory filings for changes to its management or operational structure. For the purpose of this discussion, it is important to understand that the bureaucracy is a historically universal form of organization (Pettigrew & Fenton, 2000). Until the early 1960s, bureaucracy theory was the preeminent means of describing organizations, originating with Max Weber's (1947) thoughts in the early twentieth century on the ideal machine-like organizational form. As the following description illustrates, despite the dramatic technological achievements of the twentieth and early twenty-first centuries, Weber's characterization of organizations as bureaucratic retains its sense of timelessness.

> A bureaucratic firm, according to Weber, has certain rational features. Bureaucracies are organized in a clearly defined hierarchy of offices, each level having a clearly defined, explicit authority and responsibility. Each level is responsible not only for its own actions, but also for the actions of the department below it. This creates a chain of command. Employees are appointed, not elected, to positions on the basis of their technical competence. Each position is filled by a free contractual relationship. While they are completely free to do as they wish in their private lives, employees of a bureaucracy are subject to strict controls at work, and must adhere to the rules and policies of the organization. The firm should also be the primary employer of each individual. (Tawney, 1958)

Bureaucracy theory matters for another reason. One might almost ask if the approaches noted in the following pages can be thought of as a response to these ideas. The contingency perspective is one example. Theorists of this tradition consider there to be no one best way of organizing a business. Instead, an extended program of research was guided by an assumption that the most appropriate organizational form is one that furthers the objectives of the firm (Pettigrew & Fenton, 2000). This approach can be summarized as follows:

The relationship between an organization's environment and its structure is deterministic. That is, aspects of an organization's context (environment, technology, task, size of firm, etc.) determine its structure. Structures that more closely mirror the requirements of an organization's context are more likely to be effective than those that do not. There is no single best way to structure an organization, though every individual situation has a best solution. If there is a simple rule of thumb that can be drawn from Structural Contingency theory, that rule might be that there can be only one best structural solution in a specific contextual situation. Within a given situation, there are no alternatives, only one best choice. (Schreyogg, 1980, p. 304)

How might these ideas be used in concert with the Web to improve analysis? Consider the case of a private company that is quite effective at limiting information disclosure about itself. An online analyst seeking to build a mental portrait of this entity might consider identifying publicly traded competitors that are similar in size, use similar technologies and work processes, and operate in the same industry. Commercial Web sites such as Hoover's Online and Yahoo! Finance can help with this process. Once competitors have been chosen, annual reports to government regulators, competitor Web sites, and online news articles can help the analyst build his or her portrait.

A related style of thinking is the configuration perspective (Miles & Snow, 1978; Miller & Friesen, 1978; Mintzberg, 1979; Miller, 1986). It seeks to identify ideal organizational types that blend strategy with structural features. The common theme that binds configuration theorists is that organizations can be reduced to a few types that are internally coherent (Mintzberg, 1979; Miller, 1986; Pettigrew & Fenton, 2000).

Different researchers have formulated and provided evidence to support the existence of different types of organizations. One set of theorists (Hinings & Greenwood, 1988) uses the term *archetype* to describe different organizational configurations. Organizations are groupings of structures and systems that are held together by a specific set of values and beliefs. Structures and systems refer to the set of roles and responsibilities of employees, the decision-making mechanisms that allow policies to be made and resources to be allocated, and the organization's recruitment, appraisal, and compensation procedures and policies. Values and beliefs refer to ideas about the organization shared by most employees. Most employees can be expected to share a number of similar values (Hinings & Greenwood, 1988). The entity's overall purpose and its basic organizing principles are generally well accepted, as are the criteria by which outsiders judge the organization's performance (share price, ability to meet performance expectations, and ability to deliver services without controversy).

These design patterns are maintained or destabilized by a number of dynamics. These include the organization's operating context, deep-seated employee values, the conflicting interests of various groups within the organization, the power these groups have to implement ideas, and their capacity to transform ideas into concrete action (Hinings & Greenwood, 1988).

Knowledge of the configuration approach can aid the online research efforts of a CI practitioner in the following manner. Indicators of an organizational change can often be difficult to spot from a distance. This approach specifies some indicators that are useful for identifying a transformation in the offing. Press releases from company Web sites may signal the existence of conflict by documenting new hiring activity among senior managers. Employee values can be gauged by comparing those stated on corporate Web sites with those expressed in commercial chat groups. A changing operating context can be inferred by examining corporate financial performance as demonstrated in regulatory documents alongside industry trends found on industry association Web sites and in online trade journals.

In terms of noneconomic approaches to organizing, two other perspectives are important. The postmodern approach (Clegg, 1990; Cooper & Burrell, 1988; Gergen, 1991; Parker, 1992) rejects the notion of rational thought and bureaucracy as a legitimate style of organizing. Postmodernists believe that humans are essentially observers who construct interpretations of the world around them. From this perspective, no interpretations are universal and multiple realities exist simultaneously (Montagna, 1992). Clegg defines this form of organization by contrasting it to what it is not.

> Where modernist organization was rigid, postmodern organization is flexible. Where modernist organization was focused on the strategic business unit and specific end products, postmodern organization is centered on the management of the work force core competencies. Where modernist consumption was premised on mass forms of

consumption, post modernist consumption is premised on niches. Where modernist organization was premised on technological determinism, postmodernist organization is premised on technological choices made possible through de-dedicated micro-electronic equipment. Where modernist organization and jobs were highly differentiated, demarcated and de-skilled, postmodernist organization and jobs will be highly de-differentiated, de-demarcated and multi-skilled. Employment relations assume more complex and fragmentary relational form, such as subcontracting and networking. . . . Within the core enterprises and countries of postmodern organizational forms, control will become less authoritarian in the workplace as new forms of market discipline substitute for the external surveillance of supervision, and changes are fostered by extensive deregulation. Internal markets within large organizations will increasingly be created as cost centers and profit centers, and surveillance will be lessened as more flexible manufacturing systems are adopted within which workers become their own supervisors. (Clegg, 1992, p. 35)

Postmodern insight suggests that online analysts should explore *outlier organizations* to gain meaningful intelligence. Outliers are companies that are either extremely successful or extremely poor in their operations. A keyword search of the Web sites of major newspapers will identify outliers. For the positively exceptional companies, articles about them written by external sources will often be found on their Web sites. For those performing poorly, one might examine quarterly regulatory filings or simply recent news stories. This body of knowledge also suggests a visit to the home pages of futurist organizations or government agencies, such as the Bureau of Labor Statistics, that highlight work-related trends.

Chaos theorists (Thietart & Forgues, 1995; Levy, 1994) suggest a second distinctive noneconomic perspective on organizing. They have borrowed ideas originating with physicists, mathematicians, biologists, and astronomers that attempt to explain the behavior of complex systems. Chaos theory may be defined as the study of complex, nonlinear dynamic systems (Lorenz, 1963). This school of research and theorizing holds that simple systems give rise to complex behavior, while complex systems give rise to simple behavior. Organizing from this perspective can be described as follows:

Chaotic organizations are driven by the counteracting forces of change and stability. These forces contain the seeds of order and chaos. On the one hand the forces of change are stabilizing because of their tendency to push the system out of its orbit. Experimentation, incoherence, diverse and diverging activities from the organization thrust are all sources of instability. They create demands that are not necessarily consistent with planned objectives. On the other hand, forces of order and stability are used to close a system which is considered too complex by most people. Search for order is an attempt to build islands of certainty where purposeful action can be undertaken. Furthermore, order is a means to create the illusion of management. This illusion is forged by individuals who are confronted with the impossible challenge of achieving a mission without having the capacity to succeed. Order can also create resistance to change and leave an organization in a state of limbo. (Thietart & Forgues, 1995, p. 28)

Why might a Web-based CI practitioner care about chaos theory? Its most apparent use is for gaining insight into the long-term stability of a complex organization such as a multi-firm joint venture or alliance. Analysts might use chaos theory to consider questions such as, Is the relationship going to hold together? The Internet holds clues to the answer. Examples of previous collaboration or conflict between partners can be identified through scans of archives of major newspapers. Strategic overlaps or complementary aspects of the partner organizations may be found in SEC regulatory filings or on the company home page of each partner. Backgrounds of managers can be determined through search engines. Key issues that might help or hinder the relationship can be found on industry association Web sites or in the business press.

If economic theories are to be considered, at least one perspective stands out as offering insight into how companies or other operating entities might organize. An evolutionary perspective (Nelson & Winter, 1982) distinguishes itself from many other economic approaches by attempting to shed light on the internal workings, or black box, of the organization.

LEADING

Organizational theorists have long had an interest in understanding how leaders impact the management of large corporations. CI practitioners can benefit from these insights by using them to predict behavior. One important perspective is termed "strategic choice." Strategic choice theory (Chandler, 1962; Child, 1972) implicitly recognizes the role of managers and leaders in creating the competitive environment and structuring the organization.

> The boundaries between an organization and its environment are similarly defined in a large degree by the kinds of relationships which its decision makers choose to enter upon with their equivalents in other organizations, or by constraints which more dominant counterparts impose upon them. In view of these essentially strategic and political factors, environmental conditions cannot be regarded as a direct source of variation in organizational structure. The critical link lies in the decision maker's evaluation of the organization's position in the environmental areas they regard as important, and the action they may consequently take about its internal structure. (Child, 1972, p. 10)

What is the connection of the Internet and its vast library of information to this perspective? One signal that these ideas may send to the reader is that competitive environments are in one sense a construct of executive leaders. If one can understand how one's competitor perceives the competitive environment, then one can often predict its moves.

One means to predict behavior is to examine the past. The past performance of senior executives can often be determined from online resources. Sources of information include corporate financial regulatory filings, the competitor Web site, and a simple search on a search engine such as Google. Identification of previous employers can open the door to archived annual reports, press releases, news stories, and other sources of information.

Another approach that addresses corporate leadership is termed "symbolic interactionism." This theory refers to the human capacity to create and use symbols to communicate. In this regard, meaning is derived from social acts, gestures, and the creation of significant symbols. Strong organizational leaders manage symbols very carefully. Consider for a moment the symbolism associated with the cutting of a ribbon at a hospital opening by a corporate CEO, the goodwill generated by an executive's public apology for a product defect, or the sponsorship of a community event by a multinational. Further, think of the symbolism connected with the practice of linking company leaders in press releases to good corporate financial performance.

One means by which this concept can support the practice of more effective online analysis is as a tool for assessing changes in competitor public relations activity. Competitors' press releases and executive speeches found on their Web sites can be monitored over time to identify those executives who are being publicly associated with successes and those who are not. Who is seen by the media, and who is hidden from sight? How have things changed over time? Answers to these questions can often serve as indicators of careers in ascendance or descent or divisions experiencing problems.

The stakeholder approach (T. M. Jones, 1995; Freeman, 1984) implicitly suggests that a key characteristic of good leaders is an ability to deal fairly with stakeholders and effectively prioritize the myriad of issues that face them on an ongoing basis. Consider that point in the context of Microsoft. Its important stakeholders, aside from individual customers or software programmers, range in the hundreds or even thousands. Implicit in this argument is the idea that the issues of stakeholders are as important as those of shareholders and must be given equal consideration.

A number of different versions of stakeholder theory exist. One version is summarized as follows:

> The firm can thus be seen as a nexus of contracts between itself and its stakeholders.
>
> Top corporate managers, because they contract with all other stakeholders either directly or indirectly through their agents and have strategic positions regarding key decisions of the firm, can be considered the contracting agents for the firm. The firm is thus recast as a nexus of contracts between its top managers and its stakeholders . . . Firms exist in markets in which competitive pressures do influence behavior but do not necessarily penalize moderately inefficient behavior . . . Given that the contracting process gives rise to commitment problems, efficient contracting will be profoundly affected by the costs of solving these commitment problems. Because these commitment problems abound, firms that solve commitment problems will have a competitive advantage over those that do not. Further,

because ethical solutions to commitment problems are more efficient than mechanisms designed to curb opportunism, it follows that firms that contract through their managers with their stakeholders on the basis of mutual trust and cooperation will have a competitive advantage over firms that do not. (T. M. Jones, 1995, p. 420)

Online researchers can use these ideas to identify the key issues facing a competing CEO. Stakeholders can be identified by monitoring ongoing media stories about the company using any of a number of different sources. The competitor Web site, industry associations, government regulators, activist groups, and online annual reports will provide useful information about most of the important stakeholders. Many of the key issues will be identified in the competitor online annual report and press releases, as well as on the industry association Web site.

Finally, the connection of the knowledge perspective to leadership is somewhat less obvious but just as important. It suggests that, in the long run, human capital is the only asset that might offer a corporation a sustainable competitive advantage over its rivals. Thus, by definition, the most important role of any senior manager or leader is to develop and protect the corporate knowledge base or human resource assets. From this viewpoint:

> Firms are institutions for the production of goods and services (Grant, 1996). If this idea is taken as a starting point, then a knowledge-based theory of the firm suggests the basis of any existing or potentially sustained competitive advantage is the knowledge possessed by its employees. Knowledge takes on many different meanings. It may refer to information, processes, designs, ideas, or the abilities that reside in employees, etc. It may be tacit or explicit (Kogut & Zander, 1992). What ever its manifestation, knowledge ultimately sustains the firm financially (Grant, 1996). Successful organizations recognize knowledge as an asset and will strive to acquire, develop and protect it. This theory of the firm describes how organizations manage knowledge and suggests that for protection, successful entities will use the tools of the legal system as well as proactively develop specific internal mechanisms and structures. (Spender & Grant, 1996)

A knowledge perspective suggests a role for an intellectual property audit. What is a competitor trying to protect? How do these efforts fare when compared to those of other players? The

Web sites of government patent and trademark offices allow online researchers to determine specific patent and trademark assets. Online annual reports often identify key copyright material, and commercial (but free) online sources such as FindLaw can often provide the employment contracts of key executives.

COMPETING

Among the most important areas of insight found in the body of knowledge known as organization theory is that of how companies compete. Population ecologists (Hannan & Freeman, 1976) view the corporate world in terms of populations of organizational forms that compete over time for scarce resources. They seek to explain why some forms survive or do not survive over time. Commonly researched forms include restaurants, independent gas stations, and community newspapers. To get a sense of the importance of competition, consider the number of dining establishments that opened and closed in your neighborhood over the last few years.

A population refers to all companies within a particular boundary that have a common form. Each population occupies a specific niche or a distinct combination of resources and other constraints that are sufficient to support an organization form (G. R. Jones, 1995). Organizational forms follow a particular life cycle that includes three stages: variation, selection, and retention (Hannan & Freeman, 1976).

Variation refers to the creation of new structures and the replacement of old forms. It occurs primarily at the time the companies are formed. Organizational forms are then selected according to how well they fit their environment. In general, most organizations cannot freely change themselves. Inertial pressures keep them the same (Hannan & Freeman, 1984). Indeed, selection processes tend to favor organizations with structures that are difficult to change. Such structures reliably produce collective action and are accountable.

Reliability and accountability are indicated by the extent to which a form is reproduced. For instance, consider the case of large professional accounting firms. Walk into the offices of Deloitte & Touche, PricewaterhouseCoopers, or KPMG. Look around and glance at their brochures. Also take a peek at their Web sites. You will note the similarities. This is an organizational form that has survived and prospered.

Those forms that will survive are then retained. Mechanisms used to retain specific organizational forms include the development of standard operating procedures, the use of socialization processes created for new employees, and the acceptance of common bureaucratic principles such as a clearly defined hierarchy of offices with each level having its own particular authority and set of responsibilities.

For researchers, using the Web to locate key resources can suggest which organizations will survive and which will not. IPO activity, which can be tracked through commercial Web sites, can also be used to identify industry segments that are supportive of new organizations. Further, for firms that have survived, business plans available through the U.S. Securities and Exchange Commission Web site can help to identify the features of these organizations that promote accountability and reproducibility.

Resource dependence theorists (Pfeffer & Salancik, 1978) argue that organizations will be competitively successful if they can reduce uncertainty in their operating environments. Because they cannot supply all their needs internally, organizations require resources from their operating environment. This interdependence most often leads to a complex set of relationships in which one organization attempts to influence its resources while in return its resources attempt to influence the organization. As such, organizations must attend to the demands of those environmental factors that provide resources necessary for their continued survival (Pfeffer, 1982). Therefore, to a certain extent, organizations are dependent upon their resources for stability (Pfeffer & Salancik, 1978).

This perspective leads CI practitioners to ask questions about control. For instance, which entities really control specific industries? How independent are boards of directors in any industry? How influential are bankers or lawyers or engineers in the auto industry? The movie industry? How about the aerospace industry? Online government regulatory documents can help answer questions like these by identifying executives and board members and aspects of their personal backgrounds such as current and former employers.

Resource-based theorists (Barney, 1996) address competition from a different perspective. They focus their attention on answering questions such as, Why do the successes of firms such as Wal-Mart or Toyota appear so enduring? This perspective may be summarized as follows:

The firm must be concerned not only with profitability in the present and growth in the medium term but also with its future position and source of competitive advantage. Firms must think about how they will compete when their current strategies are copied or made obsolete.

Competitive advantage can be sustained only if capabilities creating the advantage are supported by resources that are not easily duplicated by competitors.

Resources must be valuable (rent producing) and non-substitutable. In other words they must contribute to a firm capability that has competitive significance and is not easily accomplished through alternative means.

Strategically important resources must be rare and/or specific to the firm. They must not be widely distributed within an industry and/or must be closely identified with a given organization. Although physical and financial resources may produce a temporary advantage for a firm, they often can be readily acquired by competitors. On the other hand, a unique path through history may enable a firm to obtain unusual and valuable resources that cannot be easily acquired by competitors. (Hart, 1995, p. 998)

Which firms will have a sustainable competitive advantage over time? This is an interesting question for a CI professional. Commercial online information sources such as Hoover's Online, which classify companies according to industry and, in some cases, markets served, can quickly help to narrow down the possibilities. Online government regulatory documents can offer the financial information needed to assess whether a firm's competency is valuable. Trade press stories about the company, accessible through sites such as Competia.com, should allow the researcher to determine whether substitutes exist and whether imitation is difficult or not.

Theorists of the Chicago School (Stigler, 1957, 1961) suggest that the key to profitable growth is competition based on price and market dynamics. Each company has a different set of inputs that it uses to produce a different set of outputs. Competitive forces make the acquisition and transformation of these inputs a complex process.

From this vantage point, firms exist to enhance efficiency in products and distribution (Conner, 1991). These efficiencies determine the size and scope of the firms. If a firm can make efficiency gains, it will grow; if not, it will shrink as competitors erode its source of competitive advantage (Conner, 1991).

The role of new entrants to an industry is to impose the need for efficiency on established firms. New entrants possess specific information that allows them to accomplish tasks that those without it are not able to do. Among the most important forms of information that an organization can possess is the knowledge of how to become more efficient. Unfortunately, this knowledge is often difficult to acquire (Stigler, 1961). New entrants typically possess such knowledge and it is they, through their drives for efficiency, that force others to improve their efficiencies.

As a result, industry participants that do not become efficient with their means of production and distribution will earn lower long-run profits than those that do. One need simply ponder the impact of innovations such as the personal computer, the Microsoft® Windows® operating system, and Napster to understand the relevance of this last point.

Integral to this process is the natural movement of firms towards equilibrium. Although a new entrant might have an initial advantage in terms of efficiency, many of its competitors will imitate it over time. They will become just as efficient and the playing field will return to normal (Conner, 1991). Soon, none of the firms in the industry will enjoy above-average profits until a new entrant again sets a new benchmark for efficiency.

The importance of the Chicago School theory to practitioners of Web-based CI is that it forces them to think about the threat of new entrants to an industry and the potential changes that may result from the introduction of new products or services. Adherents to this way of thinking might consider undertaking a patent analysis using the United States Patent and Trademark Office to identify key technologies that are being used in other fields. CI practitioners may also want to examine the Web sites of venture capital firms to see what new products are being funded. Further, serious researchers may look for breakthrough ideas in the documents supporting IPOs associated with an industry of interest. These are available through commercial Web sites such as Hoover's Online or the SEC Web site.

PROTECTING

Events such as the Exxon Valdez oil spill, the Challenger disaster, and the chemical spill at Bhopal bring to mind some of the problems associated with large-scale organized behavior. Academics have responded by seeking to develop explanations that might decrease the likelihood of similar future incidents or behaviors. Underlying their efforts is an assumption that the workplace and society can be made safer and more welcoming. The theme of protection from deviance should be of interest to CI professionals as it may help to indicate weaknesses of competitor operations.

Why do so few airlines allow smoking on airplanes? Why is drinking on the job no longer tolerated in many companies? Why are the auditing procedures of most major accounting firms so similar? Institutional theory answers these questions and others. It holds that organizations are to a considerable extent shaped in their structures by the need to fit with the demands and expectations of the wider institutional environment. These demands and expectations stem from cultural norms, standards set by professional bodies, requirements established by funding agencies, etc. (Donaldson, 1995; Powell & Dimaggio, 1991). For example, as practices that promote safety or improve the workplace for women are adopted as the norm across society, so too are they adopted in most organizations. Institutional theory may be summarized as follows:

> Firms operate within a social framework of norms, values and taken-for-granted assumptions about what constitutes appropriate organization level behavior. Economic choices are constrained not only by . . . technological, informational and income limits . . . but by socially constructed limits that are distinctly human in origin like norms, habits and customs. Firms' tendencies toward conformity with predominant norms, tradition, and social influences in their internal and external environments lead to homogeneity among firms in their structure and activities, and . . . successful firms are those that gain support and legitimacy by conforming to social pressures. (Oliver, 1997, p. 699)

What is a Web-based application of institutional theory that might be of use to an online researcher? Well, this perspective suggests that competitors will copy successful others. Thus, in the event that an analyst's efforts to build a portrait of an organization fall short, he or she should examine the peculiarities of similar competitors. For instance, if a challenge was to identify the key risks faced by a particular private competitor, a curious online researcher might want to peruse in detail the online annual reports of other key competitors or business plans of newer start-ups, all available online through a number of different avenues.

A second theory that offers insight into how organizations might protect themselves from undesirable outcomes is the rules-based approach (Mills & Murgatroyd, 1991). In a nutshell, if an analyst wishes to understand the functioning of a company, he or she should learn its rules and identify who makes the rules, who enforces them, and who resists them (Helms Mills & Mills, 2000).

An analogy can be made to the game of North American football. It is extremely difficult to understand if one does not know the difference between pass interference and the play of a highly skilled defensive back or the importance of having linemen remain stationary before the snap of the ball. These are subtle rules. The referees enforce the rules, an often unenviable task when one considers the difficulty of distinguishing, in many instances, a holding call from a legitimate block when two 300-pound linemen are involved. Coaches often try to resist enforcement of the rules by badgering the referees. Finally, league officials make the rules. If changes are desired, then the solution is to lobby the officials.

The Internet offers unique opportunities for CI practitioners to make use of the concepts of a rules-based perspective. One example is to use these ideas to build a portrait of an industry playing field. New entrants to an industry seeking to protect themselves by learning how things are done may find this exercise of interest. Information useful for this purpose can be found on the Web sites of professional or industry associations, government regulators, competitors, suppliers, and customers, as well as in industry trade journals.

Agency theorists (Jensen & Meckling, 1976; Eisenhardt, 1989) address a different concern. Senior managers or executives cannot be trusted to act in the best interests of shareholders. Given the threat of moral hazard and the consequences of adverse selection, shareholders or principals can protect themselves from the uncertain behavior of managers or agents by putting in place safeguards to their interests.

> Using the metaphor of the contract, agency theory addresses the agency issue in which one party (the principal) delegates work to another (the agent), who performs that work. Agency theory is concerned with resolving two problems that can occur in agency relationships. The first is the agency problem that arises when the desires or goals of the principal and agent conflict and when it is difficult or expensive for the principal to verify what the agent is

actually doing. The second is the problem of risk sharing that arises when the principal and the agent may prefer different actions because of the different risk preferences. In the corporate world, an agency relationship exists between a firm's outside stockholders and its managers to the extent that stockholders delegate the day-to-day management of their investment to those managers. (Jensen & Meckling, 1976, p. 306)

One branch of this perspective, principal-agent theory, offers specific insight on how to protect against deviant behavior. According to this theory, the solution is to construct optimal managerial contract(s) given different levels of outcome uncertainty, risk aversion, and information. The best contract will be a behavior-oriented contract that stresses protective measures such as hierarchical governance, an outcome-oriented contract that emphasizes mechanisms such as market governance or the transfer of property rights (Eisenhardt, 1989), or a hybrid of the two.

An online analyst may use these ideas to assess whether a competitor's CEO and executive team will act in their own best interests or those of their shareholders. A CEO acting in his or her own best interests may focus on short-term share price gain at the expense of the longer term. This may create opportunities for patient competitors. Information useful for making such an assessment, such as employment contracts, share price history, company risk factors, personal backgrounds of executives, and competitor financial statements, is often readily available on the Internet.

CORRECTING

Organizations are not normally created to ensure the occurrence of accidents and systemic discrimination. However, in some instances, individual or organizational behavior does occur that might be labeled "deviant." Often deviance is simply in the eye of the beholder. Understanding such concerns in a competitor organization can provide a CI professional's client or employer with a competitive advantage. Academic insight offers remedies or explanations for these matters from the points of view of workers, employees, shareholders or principals, organizations and, to some extent, greater society.

Among the most obvious of perspectives promoting correction is Marxism. Marxists (Pfeffer, 1982) suggest a need for revolutionary change in order for workers to overcome the oppression of capitalist owners. The lens in this instance is that of workers. The villains are, of course, capitalists who seek to de-skill their employees. Pfeffer (1982) summarizes the main points of this worldview as follows:

> Employers seek an inexpensive, relatively powerless labor force that can be controlled to work in concert with their interests. The means of production (technologies) are selected that have the effect of de-skilling the labor force, thus ensuring social control over the labor force. Employment relationships are structured so that the power and control are largely hidden, yet largely achieved. Attempts to de-skill and control the labor force have within them forces that produce resistance on the part of the labor force. These forces include lack of motivation and effort, absenteeism, turnover, and collective action taken through labor unions. A cycle of conflict and change is engendered by the struggle between capital and labor. (Pfeffer, 1982, p. 163)

What is the online application of these ideas? An analyst may have an interest in determining factors that may cause a competitor's facility to shut down or its labor costs to increase. Such factors can often be identified by finding out which unions operate within a competitor organization and then perusing their Web sites. Issues pertinent to workers employed by a competitor will often be found on these sites.

When faced with such worries, behavioralists (Cyert & March, 1963) suggest a different response. If pressing, the issue can be dealt with quickly using insight from the past. Any course of action may not necessarily be the best, but it will be good enough, and it will be chosen from a few but not all feasible alternatives.

> Most organizations, most of the time exist and thrive with considerable conflict of goals. Except at the level of non-operational objectives, there is no internal consensus. Conflict is resolved by constructing acceptable-level decision rules, sequential attention to goals and by having individual subunits deal with a limited set of problems and a limited set of goals. . . . Organizations avoid uncertainty . . . by solving pressing problems rather than develop long run strategies and . . . they negotiate the environment. They

impose plans, standard operating procedures, industry tradition and uncertainty absorbing contracts on the environment. . . . Search is stimulated by a problem and is directed toward finding a solution to that problem. . . . Organizations adapt over time . . . When an organization discovers a solution to a problem by searching in a particular way, it will be more likely to search in that way in future problems of the same type. When an organization fails to find a solution by searching in a particular way, it will be less likely to search in that way in future problems of the same type. (Cyert & March, 1963, pp. 116–124).

A CI practitioner can use the ideas of this approach to assess a competitor's response to an operational concern. For instance, one means to identify a problem that a competitor might have is to scan the market for solutions. What wares are management consultants selling? What IT systems are hot? What financial instruments are being marketed towards firms in the industry? Knowledge of these products and services available on the Web sites of vendors combined with insight regarding the activities of a competitor can often point to a capability not possessed by that organization.

Finally, responses by scholars to the ideas of the Bain-Mason perspective (Bain, 1968; Mason, 1939) suggest that deviant organized behavior can be overcome by competing on price and quality. In this instance, deviance refers to ideas of the Bain-Mason perspective that were dominant through much of the mid-twentieth century and that others felt needed to be corrected. What was so troublesome to many was the implicit prescription that industry participants direct their behavior towards blocking competition rather than actually going toe-to-toe with innovative new entrants.

This thinking characterized many North American industries of the 1960s and 1970s, including the auto industry, and can still be seen today in industries such as softwood lumber. The Bain-Mason paradigm suggested that firms seeking to obtain high returns should focus on creating and/or modifying the structural characteristics of their industry. The implication was that they would be rewarded for their participation in the right industry (Teece, 1985). The logic behind this was that if industry profits were high, all would benefit. Therefore, any attempts to alter industry structure should be blocked. Blocking adversaries or protecting high industry profits meant creating difficult barriers to entry, reducing the number of firms in the industry, increasing product differentiation, or reducing demand elasticity. Thus, the aim of organized behavior from this perspective was to shield the firm, to the maximum extent legally possible, from competitive forces (Porter, 1980).

Unfortunately, the ideas of the Bain-Mason paradigm still linger to this day. Indeed, the Internet is well suited to helping online researchers spot efforts by competitors to alter an industry's structure. For instance, many regulators post letters from industry or competitor lobbyists on their Web sites. Industry associations normally list their position clearly on their Web sites. Further, merger activity is easy to track, allowing industry concentration to be assessed over time.

Organizing, leading, competing, protecting, and *correcting* are terms we use to categorize organization theories. We might have used five different categories instead. The result would still have been the same—a body of concepts that can improve the online analytic capabilities of CI professionals. We now move on to specific Web-based applications of these ideas.

Web-Based Research Missions: Incorporating the Internet Into Analysis

CONOR VIBERT

"In competitive intelligence, industry knowledge counts far more than educational or professional background" (Gilad & Herring, 2001). Some CI professionals question the relevance of academic thought and training for preparing CI practitioners for the harsh reality of the business world. Despite such pessimism, the growing complexity and uncertainty of today's competitive landscape suggests a role for established analytical frameworks and approaches. As Michael Porter (2001) noted in *Harvard Business Review*, despite the dramatic impact of technological innovation and the Internet on daily commercial activity, most of the goals and objectives of our major business institutions remain unchanged.

This chapter reinforces this important notion. While change appears pervasive, much remains the same, and a great deal of contemporary organized behavior can be comprehended. The online information resources of the Internet are an important aid for developing quick and coherent explanations. They also present a significant opportunity to ground the practice of competitive intelligence in current management thought. In this chapter we suggest a series of online research missions to help observers make sense of the behavior of our major institutions. Individually, each couples insight with real-time information in a manner that improves analysis. Building on the work of Dodge (1999), these missions share a number of common features.

First, an opening remark, termed a *mission overview*, sets the context for the online activity. Second, a *mission statement* is presented that defines the mission to be undertaken. Third, a series of *mission guides*, or context-specific questions, direct the online analyst toward queries that fit the parameters of the underlying ideas being applied. Fourth, *mission sources*, or Web sites hosting information useful for responding to the mission statement, are suggested. Fifth, a *mission source rationale* outlines how the online information might be retrieved and used in the context of the mission and theory under examination. Finally, a *mission display* proposes how the researcher might present the results of the mission to readers, in a matrix or graphical form or as text.

The remainder of this chapter presents a series of selected research missions that complement many of the ideas presented earlier in this book. Specifically, with respect to theories of organization, examples are offered that will help you identify corporate power holders, clarify historical paths of corporate growth, assess which companies truly control specific industries, estimate which companies might survive over time, undertake a social responsibility audit of a corporation, expand your mental horizons, and understand corporate behavior from the point of view of a modern Marxist. In terms of economic theories of the firms, research missions are suggested that will help you to identify new disruptive technologies, assess whether a CEO and his or her team are working in the best interests of their shareholders, prioritize the stakeholder-related issues facing a corporation, develop a portfolio of intellectual property belonging to a company, and understand how leaders might make key CI-related decisions.

These missions are intended as examples of how the Internet can be used to improve analysis, with a number of assumptions in mind. Their domain is public corporations with shares traded on U.S. stock exchanges. The online information sources highlighted are not exhaustive but are simply representative examples. The information sources cited are for the most part free and publicly available. Although some online resources, such as a number of those found at the information portal Hoover's Online, are available for a fee, this chapter focuses on free information. It also adopts the sage advice suggested in Chapter 3 by focusing on helping analysts acquire a toolbelt of Web information resources to gain access to a number of invisible sites (Novack, 2001; Price, 2002). Finally, as we proceed, remember that the content of many of these Web sites may change, and what is provided free one day is often a pay-for-use offering the next.

Before we move on to the first research mission, it might be useful to know that instructional guides for systemic research processes are freely available on the Web for those striving to improve their analytical skills from the comfort of their office or home. Indeed, a veritable cottage industry of easy-to-follow analytical processes now exists, and it is starting to cover a large number of important areas of interest. Where might one look?

- A longstanding favorite is Polson Enterprises, formerly known as the Virtual Pet Web site. Clearly laid out here is a series of steps with associated links.
- If you are interested in legal research, check out the Web site of Ballard Spahr Andrews & Ingersoll, LLP, The Virtual Chase.
- For a union perspective, you may want to consider the Corporate Research page at the Web site of the American Federation of State, County and Municipal Employees.
- Some of the better research process offerings available through a business school Web site are those of the University of Southern California's (USC) Marshall School of Business. Among the Research Guides at its library is "Emerging, niche, obscure, illegitimate, and other difficult to research industries."
- If you would like to approach analysis from the point of view of a social or environmental activist, then you should take a peek at the Resources page of the CorpWatch Web site. One of the guides offered is entitled "Hands-On Corporate Research Guide."

We now begin our illustration of online research missions, starting with those fitting under the heading of organization theories. The first study complements the contingency perspective.

RESEARCH MISSION: IDENTIFYING CORPORATE POWER HOLDERS

Mission Overview. Even in the largest organizations, a limited number of individuals or departments make the important decisions. In times of dramatic change, these are the individuals or departments that will be retained or counted on to add value. One means of identifying them is to seek out those individuals who hold power. This is the domain of strategic contingencies theory (Hickson, Hinings, Lee, Schneck, & Pennings, 1971; Vibert, 2000a).

Mission Statement: Which departments or individuals are powerful within an organization?

Mission Guides: Which people occupy senior positions of authority in the company? How might one identify those employees or officers who own significant shares in the company? Which individuals act publicly for the organization? Which create dependencies? Which people acquire resources, and which reduce uncertainty?

Mission Sources: Online information sources that might prove useful for this exercise include 10K Wizard, FreeEDGAR, Google, the U.S. Securities and Exchange Commission (SEC) Web site, BusinessWeek Online, CNN/Money, Competia.com, and Yahoo! Finance.

Mission Source Rationale: Two obvious sources useful for identifying individuals in positions of authority are the corporate Web site and its regulatory filings. Most firms will identify their top management team and offer brief profiles of each member. The company's 10-K Annual Report form filings and its most recent DEF 14A form filings will also name key officers. These are financial documents filed by publicly traded organizations with the SEC. They may be accessed through numerous Web sites including those of the firm, 10K Wizard, and Yahoo! Finance. Online information sources useful for understanding share ownership levels of insiders include FreeEDGAR and Yahoo! Finance.

Corporations are cautious regarding whom they profile or mention. Thus, some corporate representatives will be far more visible than others. To identify these individuals, consider a search of the press releases and articles found on the company's Web site. A simple number count of references may signal the relative importance of the individual in the eyes of the employer. A second means of assessing visibility is to use a search engine like Google with keywords such as the name of the individual and the name of the company. If one excludes hits originating from the company Web site, a search of this nature can offer a hint of visibility in the eyes of external stakeholders.

Dependence can be assessed by numerous means. One interesting approach is to examine the profiles of the executive team and others available on the company Web site or in its SEC filings. Look for similarities in background such as common previous employers, education, alma mater, employment starting dates, and length of tenure with the corporation. Through this approach one can often identify coalitions within the executive team itself.

Individuals who reduce uncertainty or acquire resources are often noticed and rewarded. Scan the press releases on the company Web site and look for mention of heroic activities. Who is credited with a major sale or acquisition? Who is commended for a turnaround strategy or legal maneuver? Search the major business press, such as BusinessWeek Online or CNN/Money, with the company name as a keyword. Use a tool such as Express, found on the Web site of Competia.com, to identify industry magazines that might focus on companies and industries not covered by the national press. Again, in these cases, look for stories that mention the company and specific individuals.

Mission Display: One means to present such data is to construct a matrix with six columns, labeled "Authority," "Share Ownership," "Visibility," "Dependence," "Resource Acquisition," and "Uncertainty Reduction." Each row should correspond to either an employee of the company or a department or group within the organization. Each box should contain a ranking or score for the individual or department with respect to the column topic.

For the purposes of this study, assume that ten employees of the company have been listed in the rows. For "Share Ownership," assign a score of 10 to the individual with the largest number of shares. To the individual among the ten with the smallest number of shares owned, assign a score of 1. For each characteristic demonstrating visibility, follow the same logic. At the end of the exercise, total the scores for each individual. With the exception of the CEO, the person with the highest score is likely to be the most influential in the corporation among the group of individuals rated.

RESEARCH MISSION: STRATEGIC GROWTH—
WHAT WE CAN LEARN FROM HISTORY

Mission Overview. Arthur Chandler (1962) suggests that when it comes to organizational growth, structure follows strategy, and the most complex type of structure is the result of the combination of several basic strategies. Expansion of volume led to the creation of an administrative office to handle one function in one local area. Growth through geographical dispersion brought the need for a departmental structure and headquarters to administer several local field units. The decision to expand into new types of functions, vertical integration, called for the building of a central office and a multi-departmental structure, while the developing of new lines of products, diversification, resulted in the formation of the multidivisional structure, with a general office to administer the different divisions. These ideas fall under the heading of strategic choice theory (Chandler, 1962; Child, 1972).

Mission Statement: Identify a company's current strategy and structure according to Chandler's (1962) framework.

Mission Guides: Using online information sources, identify and provide evidence of the points in time when the company underwent an initial period of expansion in volume, geographic dispersion, vertical integration, and diversification. Is the organization that you are studying currently following one of these four strategies? If so, which one?

Chandler (1962) suggests that most organizations follow the structural path of an administrative office leading to departmental structure, which in turn leads to a central office with a multi-departmental structure, followed by a general office with a multidivisional structure. Find online evidence of your company's current location in Chandler's continuum of structures.

Mission Sources: Online information sources that might prove useful for this exercise include Vault.com, Hoover's Online, WetFeet, Google, CorporateInformation.com, 10K Wizard, and the SEC Web site.

Mission Source Rationale: Increasingly, corporate histories are available and can be easily accessed by digital analysts. Online sources where you may find or link to such information include the Snapshot feature of Vault.com, the Fact Sheet feature of Hoover's Online, WetFeet, and the organization's own Web site. There are many means to identify a company Web site. Aside from an online quest guided by a search engine such as Google, you might want to consider linking to it through CorporateInformation.com.

If no formal history is available, consider examining press releases. In many instances, these may span a number of years, offering insight into current and past stages of the company's evolution. If the company's shares starting trading publicly for the first time in 1996 or beyond, its S-1 form is an ideal place to look for initial public offering (IPO) information. Its S-1 form should be available from the SEC Web site, 10K Wizard, or Hoover's Online, as well as from many other sources. A history of the company will be contained in this document.

When researching the structural features of a publicly traded corporation, you may find two specific sources of use. Hoover's Online offers listings of subsidiaries and their locations, the locations of manufacturing facilities, and companies fitting under the umbrella of the corporate hierarchy. Another important source of information is the company's 10-K form Annual Report filings with the SEC. Facilities, subsidiaries, and the corporate hierarchy are usually laid out in this document.

Mission Display: The company's strategy may be presented in an organized manner. A suggestion is to construct a matrix with columns labeled "Expansion in Volume," "Geographic Dispersion," "Vertical Integration," and "Diversification." Rows should be labeled by year. In each box, provide online evidence of the occurrence, along with the URL of the information source.

RESEARCH MISSION: INDUSTRY CONTROL— WHICH CORPORATIONS REALLY MATTER

Mission Overview: Organizations are externally constrained. Organizations attempt to manage their external dependencies, both in order to survive and in order to gain autonomy. In turn, these entities strive to make others dependent upon them to maintain power and stability. These ideas fall under the heading of resource dependency theory (Pfeffer & Salancik, 1978; Pfeffer, 1982).

Mission Statement: Identify those organizations upon which a firm is dependent.

Mission Guides: Are any particular industries overcompensated for on the boards of firms participating in this industry? In many firms it is not uncommon for members of the top management team to have spent significant portions of their careers with other firms. In the case of your organization, is there any pattern to the origins of the top management team? Are their any implications for the organization?

Mission Sources: Online information sources that might prove useful for this exercise include 10K Wizard, the SEC Web site, Hoover's Online, Companies Online, CorporateInformation.com, and Yahoo! Finance.

Mission Source Rationale: Dependence can be assessed through many means. One approach is to identify the home industries of members of the boards of directors of the major players in each industry. Such an assessment should help identify some of the key resources needed by organizations seeking to prosper in a particular industry. For example, if the boards of directors of firms competing in Industry X include large numbers of bankers, executives from construction companies, and equipment manufacturers, then these industries will probably receive a lot of attention from the company under examination.

A second approach would be to investigate the backgrounds of executives employed by each major competitor. Are they predominantly marketers, accountants, engineers, or lawyers? In which industries did these individuals previously work? Are there common past employers? Are there common prior training grounds for key executives such as specific university research institutes, government labs, or professional associations?

Information on board makeup and executives may be found using company Web sites and insights from recent filings of SEC forms DEF 14A (Proxy Statement) and 10-K (Annual Report). The search feature of a company's Web site is often quite useful for discovering more detailed material on different individuals. If an industry magazine can be identified, you may also want to consider a search using that individual's name. Finally, another useful angle is to search by name and corporate affiliation with a search engine such as Google. Corporate profiles found through Yahoo! Finance may also be of help. Each identifies the major institutional owners of firms.

Mission Display: If you are assessing the members of boards of directors, one means to present your data is to construct a matrix. Each column should correspond to one of four or more firms competing in the industry. Each row should correspond to the home industry of each director on each corporate board. Each box might list the specific firms that employ the board member, the individual's name, and the URL of the information source.

Data on top management team members can be presented in a similar manner. Each column of the matrix should correspond to one of four or more firms competing in the industry. Each row should correspond to an industry in which each member of the senior management team was previously employed. Each box may list the specific firms that previously employed the executive and the individual's name, as well as the URL of the information source. Similar matrices can be drawn if it appears that other factors are important, such as professional training, hometown, and universities.

RESEARCH MISSION: SURVIVAL—
THE ONLY THING MORE IMPORTANT THAN PROFIT

Mission Overview: Population ecology seeks to explain why certain organizational forms survive over time (Hannan & Freeman, 1976). Its basic premise is that forms vary, are selected, and then are retained. Selection processes tend to favor organizations with structures that are difficult to change. Difficult-to-change structures are those that reliably produce collective action and are accountable. Reliability and accountability are indicated by the extent that a form is reproduced. Numerous forms of organization exist.

Mission Statement: Is an industry attractive to new organizational forms?

Mission Guides: What new organizational forms are being created in a particular industry? Does the industry provide adequate resources that might favor the survival of a new organizational form? This latter question can be answered by considering the six sub-questions listed below.

1. Are there journals or magazines that target their content toward readers employed in this industry?
2. Are there professional or industry associations in existence to meet the needs of firms or employees in this industry?
3. What is the relative industry growth rate?
4. Which regulators focus a significant amount of attention on firms operating in this industry?
5. Which types of professional service firms, practice areas, or supporting industries have arisen to meet the resource requirements of companies in this industry?
6. Is there a significant body of venture capital available to new start-ups in your industry?

Mission Sources: Online information sources that might prove useful for this exercise include the SEC Web site, 10K Wizard, Hoover's Online, Business.com, Competia.com, vFinance.com, Wall Street Net, the American Society of Association Executives (ASAE) Web site, Hoover's Online IPO Central, and IPO Express.

Mission Source Rationale: Recognizing the birth of a new organizational form is not always easy. On some occasions, in no uncertain terms, the popular press will spell out the unique character of an operating entity. Recent case studies include Napster, Amazon.com, and eBay. In other instances, a researcher may have to determine an organization's distinctiveness. One means of doing so is to identify the business models of new publicly traded entities operating in a particular industry. These are often described in the SEC Form S-1 Registration Statement (or business plan) filings of new industry entrants. Again, the relevant firms in each industry can be identified using 10K Wizard, and a keyword search of each document can be undertaken by going to the original filings in the SEC EDGAR database, available at the SEC Web site.

Initial public offerings can provide additional data on the viability of new organization forms. Insights from population ecology can aid CI professionals in their efforts to assess whether organizations born through the IPO process will survive over time. More specifically, among the most important of indicators of future survivability is birth into the right value chain segment. In this instance, *right* refers to a value chain segment that is resource-plentiful.

One indicator that a segment is resource-plentiful is the level of IPO activity. Segments with large numbers of new entrants are normally resource-rich. Investors are voting with their checkbooks. IPOs can be quickly and easily counted by first accurately defining the value chain segment and then counting the number of S-1 forms filed by firms entering that segment in the past year, using 10K Wizard or IPO Express. To obtain insight into industry-specific IPO activity, search by either "Done Deals" or "Deals in Registration" using the databases at Wall Street Net.

Another means to assess whether the resources of a firm's niche are sufficient to ensure the survival of a significant number of similarly structured companies is to examine whether structures are in place to support it. These structures or support mechanisms include industry-specific journals or magazines identifiable through Web sites such as Competia.com, Business.com, and Hoover's Online; professional and industry associations and regulators that can be linked to through sites such as the ASAE Web site, Competia.com, Yahoo! Finance, and Business.com; and professional service firms offering customized service. A helpful Web site for identifying the competencies of law firms is FindLaw. Wall Street Net is useful for identifying underwriters or investment banks specializing in a specific industry.

Another important indicator is the existence of a healthy pool of firms offering venture capital to promising organizations in this industry. These may be identified using online sources such as vFinance.com and the National Venture Capital

Association Web site. Those segments with large numbers of interested venture capital firms should have higher levels of available resources than those without.

Finally, among the simplest of indicators is the industry growth rate. Is it promising, or has it been in the doldrums for years? Industry reports available through CorporateInformation.com or assessments obtainable through Quicken.com are interesting sources for this information.

Mission Display: Is an industry attractive to new organizational forms? A means to present evidence in response to this question posed by the Mission Statement is to construct a matrix. Label each row as a year and each column as a specific subindustry or value chain activity. In each box, list the number of IPOs per year in each activity.

For the first question in the Mission Guides, regarding the identification of new organizational forms in an industry, it may prove helpful to put your data in tabular form. Each row should correspond to a separate business model. Columns should be labeled "Description," "Industry," and "Company."

For the second question in the Mission Guides, which relates to the adequacy of resources that might favor the survival of a new organizational form, again construct a matrix. Each row should be labeled as a specific industry, such as those found on Hoover's Online. Columns might be labeled "Industry Journal," "Industry Association," "Industry Growth Rate," "Industry Regulator," "Professional Service Firm Capabilities," and "Availability of Venture Capital." Each box should offer a brief textual response to the question and provide a URL to link to the information.

RESEARCH MISSION:
IMAGINING WHY FIRMS ACT AS THEY DO

Mission Overview: When we think of large organizations and attempt to understand their behavior, many of us think in terms of metaphors (Morgan, 1980), as do many management writers.

Mission Statement: Describe in detail two metaphors that characterize your organization.

Mission Guides: One metaphor should describe the organization from the point of view of the corporation itself. A second metaphor should capture the company from a different perspective—that of employees or outside analysts. You should offer evidence to support your choice of metaphors.

Mission Sources: Online information sources that might prove useful for this exercise include CorporateInformation.com, Google, WetFeet, Northern Light, The Motley Fool, Global Unions, the Corporate Watch Web site, the Web site of the U.S. Occupational Safety & Health Administration (OSHA), FindLaw, the SEC Web site, and the Web site of the Arthur J. Morris Law Library of the University of Virginia School of Law.

Mission Source Rationale: Where might you get ideas for a metaphor or two and the evidence to support them? Sources may include online chat groups, corporate Web sites, press releases, news reports, regulatory documents, records of court cases, corporate profiles, student projects, boycott reports, and so on.

For the corporation's perspective on itself, search its Web site. Look for examples of speeches by executives, press releases that describe the company, and statements that depict its culture. These may often be found in job ads posted on the site or in the human resource section. You may also want to visit WetFeet, a human resource site that often lists corporation-friendly profiles. Consider employing the Northern Light search engine—now a fee-based service. Use terms such as the company name and *case analysis* or *corporate culture.* You may be surprised by what you discover.

You might find it helpful to see if your firm has a corporate profile listed at Vault.com. Such profiles often describe a corporate culture from the point of view of employees. Chat groups, which can be quickly accessed through sources such as Fool.com or Google Groups, are often a forum for disgruntled employees. Their views normally differ from those of the corporation and may on occasion offer a more balanced portrait of its culture.

Does your firm have a union? If so, it might have a Web site. You will probably find a link to the union at a site such as Global Unions. Or the company may be the subject of a boycott. The Corporate Watch Web site offers links to sources that might supply evidence of this. Has your company been the target of a regulatory body administrative action? The Web site of the Arthur J. Morris Law Library of the University of Virginia School of Law offers direct links to such sources at a page entitled "Federal Administrative Decisions & Other Actions."

Has the corporation been an object of concern to OSHA? A keyword search on the OSHA Web site may supply useful information. If the company has undertaken illegal activity or is being sued, you might be able to find evidence of this using the Find-Law search engine of legal news and case commentary. Read the corporate 10-K Annual Report or its 10-Q quarterly reports. Firms must be truthful when filing documents with the SEC. If there is bad news, it will be evident here, as they are obliged to comment on court challenges that may have a material impact on their bottom line.

Mission Display: The mission display for this perspective is simply a description of the metaphor.

RESEARCH MISSION: THE RELEVANCE OF MARX'S IDEAS 150 YEARS LATER

Mission Overview: An underlying premise of Marxist theory is the state of perpetual conflict between labor and capitalists (Marx, 1859). A Marxist view of organization would suggest the following:

> Employers seek an inexpensive, relatively powerless labor force that can be controlled to work in concert with their interests. The means of production (technologies) are selected that have the effect of de-skilling the labor force, thus ensuring social control over the labor force. (Pfeffer, 1982, p. 163)

Of interest is whether Marx's ideas are still relevant almost 150 years after he wrote, with Friedrich Engels, his famous work *The Communist Manifesto*.

Mission Statement: In terms of your organization, is there evidence to suggest Marx may have a point?

Mission Guides: Using SEC Form 10-K filings for the last three to five years for your company, complete the following tasks:

1. Track the ratio of number of employees to total revenues of the firm. Is there evidence that this ratio is increasing, decreasing, or remaining the same?
2. Track the ratio of salary and administrative expenses to the total revenues of the firm.
3. Identify any incidences of layoffs or facility closings.
4. Identify any incidences of outsourcing.
5. Determine whether employees of this organization are unionized and, if so, to which union they belong.

Mission Sources: Online information sources that might prove useful for this exercise include CorporateInformation.com, Google, Quicken.com, Global Unions, the Corporate Watch Web site, 10K Wizard, the Web site of the SEC, and the Negotech Web site.

Mission Source Rationale: Read the management discussion section of the company's 10-K filings for this year and three or five years ago. Hoover's Online and the company Web site may also provide a description of the company's history. Company profiles available through Yahoo! Finance offer a list of significant events that should include any layoffs and plant closings. Financial information is available from numerous sources, including Quicken.com, CorporateInformation.com, and Hoover's Online.

Information as to whether employees are unionized can be accessed by numerous means, including a keyword search using a popular search engine such as Google; a keyword search of the company's regulatory documents, including its 10-K and S-1 filings; and a search of union directories using an online portal such as Global Unions. For firms operating in Canada, Negotech, a vehicle of Human Resources Development Canada, allows keyword searches by company name as a means to identify the existence of unionized labor in an operating entity. Issues common to workers in the Canadian arm of a large corporation are often shared by their American counterparts.

Mission Display: For each company, construct a matrix. Label each row as a particular year. Label columns as "Ratio of Employees to Total Revenues," "Ratio of Salary and Administrative Expenses to Total Revenues," "Incidents of Layoffs or Facility Closures," "Incidents of Outsourcing," and "Existence of a Union." Within each box, offer the needed particulars, along with URLs of the information sources.

RESEARCH MISSION: AN EXERCISE IN CORPORATE SOCIAL RESPONSIBILITY

Mission Overview: How should corporations work? Some writers suggest organizations should be organized and should behave in a humane manner. *Humane* can mean different things to different people. One definition of a humane organization is an entity that is socially responsible in its actions. Writers of this tradition are often categorized under the critical theory perspective.

Mission Statement: Has the recent behavior of your firm been socially responsible?

Mission Guides: You may find that the organization's view of its level of socially responsive behavior differs somewhat from that of external observers. The following questions should be responded to from both points of view:

1. Is the firm financially stable?
2. Is there any evidence to suggest that the organization does not respect its physical environment?
3. Are the products and services of the organization manufactured, developed, and delivered to consumers and clients using the highest available standards?
4. Are there any reasons to accuse the firm of not treating its human stakeholders with dignity and compassion?
5. Is the corporation supportive of local community needs?

Mission Source: Online information sources that might prove useful for this exercise include Quicken.com, CorporateInformation.com, Google, the OSHA Web site, FindLaw, the SEC Web site, the U.S. Environmental Protection Agency (EPA) Web site, the Web site of the U.S. Consumer Product Safety Commission, the Right-to-Know Network (RTK NET), Competia.com, NewsLink, Epinions, PlanetFeedback, the Web site of the Arthur J. Morris Law Library of the University of Virginia School of Law, Environment Canada's National Pollutant Release Inventory, and the Search Systems Public Record Locator.

Mission Source Rationale (Vibert, 2000b): Is your company on shaky financial ground? Is it apt to take risky actions to stay afloat? Read the Research Reports available at CorporateInformation.com, or contrast your firm's performance to that of its major competitors using Quicken.com. For the most up-to-date financial information, examine the financial statements found in your company's most recent SEC 10-Q Quarterly Report filing.

Perhaps your company has faced a regulatory body administrative action. You will find links to pertinent sources at the "Federal Administrative Decisions & Other Actions" page at the Web site of the Arthur J. Morris Law Library of the University of Virginia School of Law. This is one avenue to assess the company's performance with regard to the quality of its products and services as well as its respect for the environment. If the firm is having problems with the quality of its consumer products, the Consumer Product Safety Commission Web site may offer evidence in terms of recent product recalls or warning letters. You may also want to visit Epinions for comments providing insights on specific products and PlanetFeedback for customers' perspectives on how the firm is operating.

Is the company a major polluter of the environment? The environmental databases of the EPA, available through RTK NET, will offer evidence one way or the other. For companies operating in Canada, a similar source is the National Pollutant Release Inventory sponsored by Environment Canada. At the level of individual states, a useful link is the Search Systems Public Record Locator. Many states provide online access to court documents and information on the registration of corporations conducting business in the state. The U.S. federal courts maintain records of bankruptcy proceedings against companies.

You may also want to consider identifying and then reading the online versions of magazines targeted at specific industry segments. Competia.com's Express is a useful tool for this purpose.

Is your company treating its employees with respect? If so, it should be clear of lawsuits. To check if this is the case, scan its most recent 10-K and 10-Q filings using the keyword *litigation*. Also try using the search engine at FindLaw. An examination of cases falling under the jurisdiction of the state and U.S. district courts should give some evidence as to whether the company has been the object of potentially damaging legal actions. Has it been the target of investigations by OSHA? Try a keyword search on the OSHA Web site.

When seeking to determine how proactive your organization is in terms of supporting the community, consider undertaking a keyword search of its Web site. Firms are often quick to highlight their good deeds and will probably not hide their successes in this regard. You might also consider doing a keyword search of the online newspapers that serve the communities within which your firm's facilities are located. A good Web site for finding local newspapers is NewsLink.

Mission Display: In order to present your ideas in a coherent manner, you may want to consider developing a matrix with seven columns, entitled "Social Responsibility Category," "Company Perspective," "Evidence That Counters the Company Perspective," "Description," "Information Source," "URL," and "Rating." Ratings could be offered in absolute terms, such as on a scale of 1–10, or relative to the performance of other companies on the criteria listed in the rows. The rows should be entitled "Financial Position," "Respect for Environment," "Respect for Customers,"

"Respect for Human Stakeholders," and "Respect for the Community."

RESEARCH MISSION: WHO'S MINDING THE FORT?

Mission Overview: How do principals (shareholders) protect their interests from agents (managers)? Agency theory (Jensen & Meckling, 1976) suggests that when shareholders have complete information about the business context, behavioral contracts should be used. When information is incomplete, shareholders should protect their interests by choosing between variants of a behavioral or an outcome-based contract. Behavioral contracts are enacted through the use of hierarchy, boards of directors, MIS systems, and budgets (Eisenhardt, 1989). Outcome-based contracts are enacted through market governance or the adoption of a mentality of "just come back to us with the final product."

Mission Statement: For the organization under study, are the top management team and its CEO acting in the best interests of shareholders?

Mission Guides: For each member of an organization's executive team, indicate whether the compensation package or formula is primarily outcome-based or behaviorally oriented. Offer evidence to support your assertion. Relative to its most recent annual share price performance and that of its three major competitors, was the most recent compensation of the firm's CEO in the best interests of shareholders?

Mission Sources: Online information sources that might prove useful for this exercise include CorporateInformation.com, Business.com, Quicken.com, BigCharts, FindLaw, 10K Wizard, Hoover's Online, and the SEC Web site.

Mission Source Rationale (Vibert, 2001): Agency theory helps analysts understand not only how and whether shareholder interests are being protected but also whether compensation packages are warranted given the financial performance of the organization. You will find the firm's 10-K and DEF 14A SEC filings particularly useful for responding to these questions. Aside from offering up-to-date financial results, they will also provide insight into how well executives are compensated.

Alternative sources for financial results include the Hoover's Online and the CorporateInformation Web sites. Both list major competitors, in the Fact Sheets of the former and the Research

Reports of the latter. In most cases, the DEF 14A form details executive compensation packages for the previous few years, including bonuses and stock options. In some instances, it provides the employment contracts of key executives. Employment contracts and compensation formulas are sometimes found in 10-K and S-1 forms. Executive employment contracts may also be listed on the FindLaw Web site. BigCharts is an excellent source of share price graphs, charts, and diagrams, as is Quicken.com. You may also want to consider doing a journal search of compensation or human resource magazines and journals.

Mission Display: When seeking to understand whether the executive team (agents) of a particular organization have acted in the best interests of their shareholders (principals), you might want to present relevant analytical data in text form or construct a matrix. If the latter, each column should correspond to one of the executives. Rows should offer financial performance and compensation information for the corporation and its executives, perhaps as follows:

Row 1: Base salary
Row 2: Stock options granted
Row 3: Any bonus payments
Row 4: Compensation figures as a result of exercising stock options
Row 5: Average share price growth over the last year
Row 6: Average revenue growth over the past year
Row 7: Average profit growth over the last year
Row 8: Total change in compensation for the executive over the past year

A similar matrix might be constructed to compare the performance of one CEO to that of another, with each column corresponding to a different competitor.

RESEARCH MISSION:
STAKEHOLDER ISSUES—SETTING PRIORITIES

Mission Overview: A stakeholder is any group or individual who can affect or is affected by the achievement of an organization's purpose. Stakeholders are defined by their legitimate interests in the corporation (Donaldson & Preston, 1995). Top management teams need to address stakeholder needs if they are to succeed.

But which issues matter? Which issues should attract the attention of top management teams?

Mission Statement: Which stakeholder issues should matter to
your organization and why?

Mission Guides: Who are the major stakeholders of your firm?

What are the major issues facing your firm and others operating in this industry?

Imagine you are a member of the corporation's top management team. From this perspective, rank the issues according to
their perceived legitimacy, the urgency with which each needs to
be addressed, and the potential impact of each on the corporation (Suchman, 1995).

Mission Sources: Online information sources that might prove
useful for this exercise include CorporateInformation.com, Com-
petia.com, Business.com, FindLaw, BusinessWeek Online, For-
tune.com, Yahoo! Finance, the ASAE Web site, CNN/Money, the
SEC Web site, and the USC Marshall School of Business Web site.

Mission Source Rationale: Among the most important online
sources for identifying stakeholders and issues of importance to
them are the industry associations that represent the company
and its competitors. They are often tasked with lobbying regulators and government organizations on matters of consequence
for all players. Two useful listings of industry associations appear
at the ASAE Web site and in the Express feature of
Competia.com. Major institutional shareholders may be found by
glancing at corporate profiles at Yahoo! Finance. The industry
association Web sites normally discuss issues of importance to
their members and government regulators that are being targeted for lobbying. The regulator Web sites, which may also be
located through the Competia site, usually describe significant
industry or market issues from their point of view.

Also worthy of examination is the Web site of the company in
question. What topics are mentioned in its press releases? Are
there any executive speeches posted on the site? Does it appear
that they are responding to any important concerns?

Another angle is to peruse the most recent 10-K Annual
Report or 10-Q Quarterly Report filed by the company with the
SEC. Who are its customers, suppliers, creditors, competitors,
etc.? These documents also reference issues of importance,
including operating losses, litigation, regulatory changes, and
new product offerings of competitors.

Keyword searches can be conducted using 10K Wizard.
Another approach is to use the CorporateInformation Web site.

Take a peek at the Research Reports for the company being examined. They often mention many key external stakeholders by name. Along the same lines, Yahoo! Finance identifies competitors of publicly traded corporations.

Finally, look at what the popular press is saying about the organization. Is it controversial? If so, the issue(s) in the news are most likely being addressed by senior management. In many instances, especially with young organizations, news stories may be few and far between. Good sources for such information can be found by looking at stories associated with the various online profiles of the firm, such as those found at Hoover's Online or CorporateInformation.com. You may also want to consider business news sources such as Yahoo! Finance, CNN/Money, Fortune.com, BusinessWeek Online, or the like. These sites are general sources of business news and offer internal search engines that can be queried by company name.

In many instances, even more targeted sources of information are needed. In this case, we refer to industry-specific online magazines. One approach for identifying these sources is to use the Express feature of the Competia Web site. A second is to access the USC Marshall School of Business Web site. Its library offers a link to industry-specific Research Guides that list a variety of publications, including journals, magazines, and trade publications.

Mission Display: Construct a matrix with each row corresponding to an issue. Three columns should be labeled "Legitimacy," "Urgency," and "Impact," respectively. A fourth column should be labeled "Total Score." Develop a ranking scheme for each characteristic and sum the totals for each issue. The highest-ranked issues are those that should command the attention of the top management team.

RESEARCH MISSION:
BRAIN MATTER—APPARENTLY, IT IS IMPORTANT

Mission Overview: Over time, human capital is the only true source of long-term success. From human capital flows knowledge. The challenge for managers of modern corporations is to capture and retain this knowledge. Successful organizations recognize knowledge as an asset and will strive to acquire, develop, and protect it (Liebeskind, 1996). This is a central argument underlying the knowledge perspective.

Mission Statement: Identify the intellectual property that your organization is trying to protect.

Mission Guides: How does your firm protect its intellectual property? Does it make use of patents, trademarks, or copyrights? Or does it rely on trade secrets?

For your firm and three of its competitors, count the number of patents registered per year for the last four years. Who is winning the patent race? For your firm and three of its competitors, count the number of trademarks registered per year for the last four years. How might you interpret these data? In its regulatory filings, press releases, or Web site, does the company identify its most important patents, trademarks, or copyrights? If so, what are they? What knowledge might this organization consider to be a trade secret?

Mission Sources: Online information sources that might prove useful for this exercise include CorporateInformation.com, the SEC Web site, and the U.S. Patent and Trademark Office Web site.

Mission Source Rationale: For many companies, these concerns can be addressed in an absolute and relative sense by taking a yearly inventory of patents, trademarks, and copyrights and then doing the same thing for competitors. Two approaches to obtaining information regarding patents and trademarks are fairly straightforward.

A first, non-exhaustive approach is to search by assignee name and year using the search features found on the U.S. Patent and Trademark Office Web site. Separate databases exist for patents and trademarks. When using these two databases, be aware that patents and trademarks are filed under the original assignee names. Thus, if a company has merged, has been acquired, or has changed its name, historical research needs to take into account original corporate names. This will afford a very high-level view of patent and trademark activity among competitors.

A second approach is to examine the recent 10-K Annual Reports and 10-Q Quarterly Reports found on the SEC Web site. A keyword search within each document using terms such as *copyright, trademark,* and *patent* should indicate the existence of activity in this regard. Competitors can be identified through the firm's 10-K form filings or in the online Research Reports of CorporateInformation.com.

Mission Display: Present the results of your research in a simple tabular display. For each of these three protective tools (copyrights, trademarks, and patents), construct a table with the years forming columns and the companies forming rows. Placed side by side, a year-by-year count of patents, trademarks, or significant copyrighted material will quickly demonstrate which firms are proactive in knowledge protection. In some instances, you will also be able to view the genesis of a patent race.

RESEARCH MISSION: SPOTTING DISRUPTIVE TECHNOLOGIES

Mission Overview: The online information sources of the Internet can help us to identify potentially disruptive technologies before they are established and recognize industry breakpoints as they approach (Strebel, 1992). *Divergence* refers to efforts by competitors to enhance the value of a particularly innovative product offering to the point where imitation takes over. A *breakpoint* is associated with sharply increasing variety in competitive offerings, resulting in more value for the customer. *Convergence* leads to a shakeout of the less efficient and a survival-of-the-fittest atmosphere. A breakpoint is associated with sharp improvements in the systems and processes used to deliver the offerings, resulting in lower delivered cost. These ideas find a home with the perspective known as the Chicago School theory of the firm.

Mission Statement: Is the industry within which your firm operates ripe for a convergent or divergent breakpoint? Identify if possible any new disruptive technologies in the offing.

Mission Guides: Strebel (1992) suggests the following questions may be useful for identifying signals of an approaching convergent breakpoint: Relative to previous years, is the level of IPO activity in the industry above or below average? Do companies target a similar set of customers, or are they really all the same? Is the role of distributors in this industry increasing or decreasing in importance? Are the products and services offered by suppliers becoming increasingly commoditized, or do these suppliers still add significant value to the end product or service of these firms?

Signals of an approaching divergent breakpoint may be found in the answers to the following questions: Has the growth rate of the industry declined over time, or is it slowing at the moment? Is there any evidence that traditional customers are looking for alternative solutions or solution providers for their needs? Is there any evidence that any of the firms are entering new markets or industries or are developing new product or service lines that are not necessarily related to their existing offerings? Are new technologies or previously unavailable resources impacting or changing the delivery of the products or services of these firms to customers? Is there any evidence of supply bottlenecks or quality problems with suppliers to these firms? Are there any new disruptive technologies looming on the horizon?

Mission Sources: Online information sources that might prove useful for this exercise include CorporateInformation.com, Google, WetFeet, Northern Light, Polson Enterprises, the USC Marshall School of Business Web site, FindLaw, Competia.com, Red Herring, vFinance.com, Hoover's Online IPO Central, IPO Express, the SEC Web site, the U.S. Federal Communications Commission (FCC) Web site, 10K Wizard, the Thomas Register, the Arthur J. Morris Law Library of the University of Virginia School of Law Web site, Multex Investor, and Quicken.com.

Mission Source Rationale: How might an analyst spot a convergent breakpoint? With great difficulty! However, signals are occasionally apparent and take the form of responses to the questions noted above. In terms of industry IPO activity, once again, take a look at 10K Wizard. Sort by "Industry," "SEC Form Type," and "Year." This will give you a quick count of yearly IPOs. When seeking to understand whether a company's products are being commoditized, examine its Web site and those of its competitors. Are they saying the same things? Do the products look alike? Try the Web site of the Thomas Register. Signup is free. The Thomas Register allows researchers to identify manufacturers through a search by product type. In many instances, specifications are listed for each product.

You may also want to make use of shopping comparison Web sites. Do the companies target the same customers, and how important is the role of distributors? To answer these questions, take a peek at the information on the company available through the Research Reports option of the CorporateInformation Web site. It usually includes major customers. In addition, you may want to examine the company's 10-K Annual Reports for current and recent years. Customers and distributors are discussed and often clearly identified. If your organization has recently made its IPO, a glance at its S-1 form should also be useful in this regard.

How might an analyst spot a divergent breakpoint? Once again, it is not an easy task, but getting answers to the queries listed above may help. Evidence of customers or competitors entering new markets can be found by scanning the press releases available on the companies' Web sites. Industry growth rates and comparisons are available through online sources such as Quicken.com or Multex Investor.

Are traditional customers seeking new partners? Hints regarding the likelihood of this can often be found by again examining the Web site of the firm. In this instance, look for announcements of new strategic partners. Finally, for further clues on these issues and others related to a potential divergent breakpoint, read the magazines or online journals that industry insiders read. These can be identified and are available through the Express feature of the Competia Web site.

Of even greater difficulty is the challenge of spotting a disruptive technology before its time has come. Where could you look to get a few ideas about what might be in the pipes? Consider the following tips:

- Make use of search engines such as Google or Northern Light, using keywords such as the industry name and *disruptive technology* or *bleeding edge technologies.*
- Try professional or industry association Web sites such as the American Medical Association Web site, available through Competia. Many offer position papers on technologies that may soon be influential.
- Examine regulatory Web sites such as those of the FCC or SEC, which offer guidance to industries on soon-to-be influential technologies.
- Read the bible of the venture capital world, *Red Herring.* Its online version allows in-depth searches by industry, technology, company, issue, product, and service.
- Identify companies being funded by venture capital firms. Some can be spotted using the DealMonitor search tool at vFinance.com.
- Find information on IPOs in registration, available through Hoover's Online IPO Central or IPO Express. This can be an excellent angle to identify an emerging idea. Registration is the last stage before a company goes public. Netscape Navigator is a good study of a previously successful IPO. From this point, consult the business plan of these firms or their S-1 forms. An even better way is to use 10K Wizard and search by industry and S-1 form for the time frame of interest.

- Scan Web sites and online magazines associated with management consulting firms such as Bain & Company or McKinsey & Company to garner a wealth of hints. Online articles often discuss hot trends, although not all address the same industries.
- Read industry-specific trade magazines, available through NewsLink or Competia.com. These publications frequently highlight new or coming technology advances in a particular sector or industry.
- Search at the USC Marshall School of Business or Polson Enterprises Web sites.
- Examine industry profiles that discuss trends, such as those found on WetFeet.

Mission Display: Responses to the questions regarding the onset of divergent or convergent breakpoints are best suited for display in tabular form. Rows should correspond to each question. Columns should correspond to the firm under study, as well as a number of its competitors. Boxes should offer textual responses to the questions, along with the information source URL.

RESEARCH MISSION: HOW DECISIONS ARE MADE

Mission Overview: How might organizational decisions be made when corporate goals are not clear, competitive environments and organizational participants change quickly, and the technologies of the organization are either poorly understood or rapidly changing? Behavioral theorists would be comfortable answering a question of this nature. Indeed, one set of researchers termed their ideas "the garbage can model" (Cohen, March, & Olsen, 1972).

Mission Statement: Identify a solution and a decision maker for a corporation facing problems.

Mission Guides: What problems is your company experiencing? What solutions are available on the market to resolve your company's problems? What individuals within your organization can address its problems?

Mission Sources: Online information sources that might prove useful for this exercise include Google, Office.com, The Motley Fool, FindLaw, the SEC Web site, and NewsLink. Copernic Agent Basic, which can be downloaded from the Copernic Web site, could also be helpful.

Mission Source Rationale: Use a search tool such as Copernic Agent Basic, or an industry list of corporate participants such as those provided by Hoover's Online or Business.com, to identify management consulting firms or software development companies capable of providing solutions. Choose one of these companies and select a number of solutions that it offers. They should be listed on its Web site. With this group of solutions in mind, identify a series of suitable problems from your company's recent 10-K, 10-Q, or 8K SEC filings, news articles, or chat groups such as those at Fool.com or Google Groups. Aggregated news articles are often available through a number of sites, including NewsLink, Office.com, and Hoover's Online.

Next, match these solutions and problems to the individual in the company who is most likely to be a relevant decision maker. Information of this nature can often be found using profiles or news releases on the company Web site, any DEF 14A forms that it has filed recently with the SEC, and general news articles about the organization.

Mission Display: For each company, construct a matrix. Label the rows with the corporate problems and the columns with the external solution providers. The individual boxes should contain textual descriptions of solutions offered by each service provider and should name an appropriate decision maker.

RESEARCH MISSION: ALL ABOUT INDUSTRIES (AND THINGS YOU DON'T WANT TO KNOW)

Mission Overview: The attributes of the industry structure within which a firm operates define the range of options and constraints facing it (Bain, 1956). Success accrues to those companies operating in the right industry. In the past, profits and revenues could be grown by blocking new firms or by lobbying government to keep out new adversaries (Teece, 1985). Ideas of this nature are commonly associated with an industrial economic perspective known as the Bain-Mason paradigm.

Mission Statement: Identify how incumbent industry players are striving to reduce or block competition within the industry.

Mission Guides: How are firms in your industry attempting to alter its structure through their lobbying efforts? Is there any evidence of a monopoly that unreasonably excludes firms from this market or significantly impairs a competitor's ability to compete? Is there any evidence of recent or expected merger activity that will leave the market substantially concentrated after the merger or make it difficult for newcomers to enter? Is there any evidence of illegal business practices?

Mission Sources: Online information sources that might prove useful for this exercise include CorporateInformation.com, Competia.com, the U.S. Federal Trade Commission (FTC) Web site, 10K Wizard, and the ASAE Web site.

Mission Source Rationale: Are organizations in a particular industry lobbying a government regulator to change the rules of industry competition? This question and others related to it can be answered in a systematic manner. To begin, identify the regulators and industry associations that deal with the industry. This can be done using the Express feature of the Competia Web site. Next, scan the industry association Web sites that speak on behalf of the companies in question. Look for areas such as "Government Affairs" or "Issues." These often list and document the concerns of member organizations and regulators, as well as the steps being taken by the industry association to address the concerns.

Then, go to the Web sites of the key regulators. If the sites have search engines, use them to find discussions of these issues or those related to the industry association. Many regulators, from time to time, invite external input in the form of written submissions as they strive to develop effective policy. In many instances these documents are available in their original form on the Web site. These submissions will often offer evidence of the lobbying activity of various industry associations, corporations, or other interested parties.

In terms of individual organizations, scan corporate Web sites for executive speeches, press releases, or statements of the corporation's position on specific matters related to the industry. Further, read the chairperson's report of the annual report for shareholders that is often found on company Web sites.

Is the firm in question undertaking illegal business practices? To find out, search its most recent 10-K or 10-Q SEC filing by the keyword *litigation*, undertake a keyword search by company name at FindLaw, use a news aggregator such as Hoover's Online to explore recent stories about the company, and scan the FTC Web site for the firm's name.

When one public company plans a merger with another, it is required by law to file with the SEC and make details of the planned merger public. Information related to tender offers and acquisitions is provided to the SEC through a number of the following forms: SC 13D, SC 13E3, SC 13E4, SC 13G, SC 14D1, and

SC 14D9. A search by industry, year, and form type using 10K Wizard will identify companies involved in this type of activity.

Mission Display: Construct a matrix. Label the rows with the various lobbying activities. The columns should have the headings "Regulator Perspective," "Industry Association Perspective," and "Company Perspective." In each box, offer evidence of how each of these three entities (regulators, industry associations, and companies) is dealing with specific efforts to alter the rules of industry competition.

This concludes our illustration of research missions.

10

Analysis: Web-Enhanced Case Studies in Real Time[1]

CONOR VIBERT

Although many CI professionals do not have access to the same level of resources found in large corporations, the playing field for solid analysis may actually be quite level when a talented researcher has at his or her fingertips the online resources of the Internet. Consultant Susan Hollett (*http://www.hollettandsons.ca*), who works in Shoal Harbour, Newfoundland, offers an example of how independent analysts may effectively practice CI despite being located away from major urban centers and employers:

> A recent project involved a multi-media company that was looking to enter the educational CD Rom market in the North Eastern United States. They wanted to identify competitors, understand their behavior and track their activities. Using the Internet and the Canadian Commercial Trade Commissioners' research, we were able to come up with a preliminary list. Armed with this, we "dug in" and searched the online business, local, and sector press; the industry and professional association Web sites; and the conference and trade show circuit for relevant information. We offered the client a multi-dimensional picture of the competition on the other side of the continent. In addition, we provided research tools and co-developed strategies that would enable them to stay abreast of changes. These strategies included the use of alert services, automatic notification of changes to "product" Web pages, and identification of the business and

[1]Some of the case material of this chapter was originally developed for an in-class study at Acadia University by undergraduate students Heather Ongo and Erin Burke. I owe them a debt of gratitude.

sector press most likely to track pertinent market niches in specific geographic areas. (C. Vibert, personal communication with S. Hollett, March 3, 2001)

Along with understanding online information sources, professionals such as Hollett also realize the importance of tried-and-true analytical frameworks for grasping the significance of business activity. In the following pages, a number of abbreviated case examples illustrate how theory can be effectively integrated with online information to inform the practice of CI. The first example explores the case of online music distributor MP3.com (Vibert, 2001), while the latter three cases address the media industry.

CASE EXAMPLE 1: MP3 AND THE CEO'S PAYCHECK (A CASE IN AGENCY THEORY)

Mission Overview. This abbreviated case study explores the means by which shareholders protect their interests from corporate managers, using the online music distributor MP3.com as an example.

Mission Statement. Did MP3.com's CEO act in the best interests of shareholders during 1999?

Mission Guides. In 1999, was the compensation package or formula of MP3.com's CEO primarily outcome-based or behaviorally oriented? Based on its share value during 1999 and relative to that of its three major competitors, was this individual's compensation in the best interests of shareholders?

Mission Sources. The mission sources for this endeavor are primarily regulatory documents filed with the SEC but sourced through 10K Wizard, company profiles made available through Hoover's Online, and an employment contract listed on the Find-Law Web site.

Mission Source Rationale. Integral to this discussion is the identification of the CEO and any important issues that might be worrisome to shareholders. One source for this information is MP3.com's 2000 DEF 14A Proxy Statement filed with the SEC. It identifies Michael Robertson as the CEO and offers the following background details:

> Michael L. Robertson founded MP3.com and has served as
> our Chief Executive Officer and Chairman of the Board
> since March 1998. From September 1995 to March 1998,

Mr. Robertson operated several Web sites that focused on merging search technologies with commerce. From September 1995 to September 1996, Mr. Robertson was President and Chief Executive Officer of Mounds, Inc., a developer of digital picture software. From January 1994 to August 1995, Mr. Robertson was President and Chief Executive Officer of Much Software, a developer of networking and security tools. Mr. Robertson received his Bachelor of Arts from the University of North Carolina. (MP3.com Form DEF 14A, 2000).

Noteworthy is that in 2000 Michael Robertson also owned 37 percent of the outstanding common stock of MP3.com (*Company Capsule for MP3.com*, n.d.).

During 1999 and 2000, MP3.com was a somewhat controversial entity. The following excerpt from a May 1999 regulatory filing suggests why shareholders were probably paying close attention to the performance of the company and its CEO:

> Our model for conducting business and generating revenues is new and unproven. Our business model depends upon our ability to generate revenue streams from multiple sources through our Web site, including:
>
> – Web site advertising fees from third parties;
> – online sales of CDs and music-related merchandise;
> – promotional activity fees; and
> – leveraging our aggregated artist and consumer information. (MP3.com Form S-1/A, 1999)

This was followed up two months later with another statement by MP3.com to regulators:

> It is uncertain whether a music-based Web site that relies on attracting people to learn about, listen to and download music, mostly from lesser-known artists, can generate sufficient revenues to survive. We cannot assure you that this business model will succeed or will be sustainable as our business grows. . . . We provide many of our products and services without charge, and we may not be able to generate sufficient revenue to pay for these products and services. Accordingly, we are not certain that our business model will be successful or that we can sustain revenue growth or be profitable. (MP3.com Form 424B4, 1999)

The inherent risk of MP3.com's 1999 business model suggested a role for the ideas that underlie agency theory. Does *outcome* or *behavioral* best describe the contract that linked Michael Robertson to MP3.com in 1999? An employment contract found at FindLaw.com suggests an *outcome* descriptor:

> 1.3 Executive shall do and perform all services, acts or things necessary or advisable to manage and conduct the business of the Company and which are normally associated with the position of Chief Executive Officer, consistent with the Bylaws of the Company and as required by the Company's Board of Directors. . . .
>
> 3.1 The Company shall pay Executive a base salary of $150,000 per year (the "Base Salary"), payable in semi-monthly payments in accordance with Company policy. Such salary shall be prorated for any partial year of employment on the basis of a 365-day fiscal year.
>
> 3.2 Executive's compensation may be changed from time to time by mutual agreement of Executive and the Company.
>
> 3.3 Executive shall be eligible for an annual performance bonus of up to $50,000 payable at the sole discretion of the Company's Board of Directors. . . .
>
> 9. . . . This Agreement does not supersede or alter in any way the terms and conditions of the Founder Stock Agreement dated March 18, 1998. (*Employment agreement*, 1999)

How well was MP3.com's CEO paid in 1999? Very fairly, if its regulatory filings are any indication (MP3.com Form DEF 14A, 2000). A search using the keywords *executive compensation* on 10K Wizard indicated that, in 1999, Robertson received $158,626 in salary, $148,500 in bonus payments, and $4,850 towards a car lease. This was an increase from a salary of $70,833. How did his compensation fare with that of other CEOs? Using the CEOs of two main competitors, ARTISTdirect, Inc., and Launch Media, Inc. (now LAUNCH, the music destination on Yahoo!), for comparison (*Company Capsule for MP3.com*, n.d.), this salary appears reasonable. The better-compensated of these latter two received $162,500 in base salary as well as stock options during 1999.

How did MP3.com perform? In an absolute sense, not well. On 1999 revenues of $22 million, it lost $42.5 million. Relative to competitors, however, it fared adequately. ARTISTdirect, Inc., and Launch Media, Inc., lost $57.8 million and $37.5 million on sales of $10.3 million and $16.6 million, respectively (*Company*

Capsule for ARTISTdirect, Inc., n.d.; *Company Capsule for Launch Media, Inc.*, n.d.). In terms of share price performance (*Stock chart*, n.d.) the results were also not outstanding. From an initial IPO priced above $60 per share, stockholders ended 1999 with shares worth half that amount. This was in line with the performance of MP3.com's major competitor, whose initial price of $35 per share melted away to $20 per share at year-end.

Mission Display: In this instance, a textual display offers as much insight as findings portrayed in matrix form. How might these results be interpreted in light of agency theory?

MP3.com shareholders chose to use an outcome-based contract to retain the services of Michael Robertson, who owned 37 percent of the company's shares. Performance in the first year as a publicly traded company was not outstanding. Indeed, shareholders saw their equity decrease significantly. However, the salary and benefits of the CEO were not excessive in light of this performance; in fact, relative to those of other chief executive officers, they were quite low. Although share price did decrease, Michael Robertson certainly did not benefit from this bad news and indeed shared the pain. Thus, at least in terms of salary and benefits paid to their CEO, the interests of shareholders were protected fairly effectively.

CASE EXAMPLE 2: WHO CONTROLS THE MEDIA INDUSTRY? (A CASE IN RESOURCE DEPENDENCE THEORY)

Mission Overview: This abbreviated case study explores important relationships of dependence in the context of the media industry. It compares the profiles of The Walt Disney Company's board of directors and executive management team with those of two of its top competitors, Time Warner and Viacom Inc.

Mission Statement: Identify those companies upon which your firm is dependent.

Mission Guides: Are any particular industries overcompensated for on the boards of firms participating in this industry? In the case of the company under study, is there any pattern to the origins of the top management team?

Mission Sources: The mission sources for this endeavor are primarily regulatory documents filed with the SEC and executive profiles made available through Hoover's Online.

Mission Source Rationale. Regulatory filings were reviewed for The Walt Disney Company (The Walt Disney Company Form DEF 14A, 2001) AOL Time Warner (now Time Warner—AOL Time Warner Form DEF 14A, 2001), and Viacom Inc. (Viacom Inc. Form DEF 14A, 2001) to identify the industry affiliations for each director. The results are presented in Figure 10.1.

Company affiliations for each board member were identified via officer profiles found using Hoover's Online. By searching with the Industry Keyword option selected, we identified the industry sector for each affiliated company.

As expected, it was found that directors from the media, finance, telecommunications, and legal industries were well represented on corporate boards in the media sector. The results also suggest heavy participation in charity and political organizations by board members. One explanation for this is the presence in the industry of the FCC as a regulator. Effective lobbying necessitates the involvement of well-connected individuals who are also normally well placed in charity circles.

In all three cases, a large number of directors either are lawyers or have a background in financial services. The concentration in financial services is mostly linked to venture capital firms and investment companies. We expected a higher concentration in banking; however, given the influence that new technologies have on the media industry, it stands to reason that the firms would have a heavy interest in venture capital. All three companies view the Internet as being an important part of their future. Each has board members affiliated with the telecommunications sector. Each board also has at least one director linked to the real estate industry.

Directors with links to the political arena present an interesting cross section of talent. For instance, it appears that The Walt Disney Company is strategically placed in Washington by having George Mitchell, a former U.S. Senator and majority leader, on its board. Mr. Mitchell also chaired the Ethics Committee of the U.S. Olympic Committee. Time Warner has a former U.S. trade representative (Carla Hills), while Viacom has George Abrams, former general counsel and staff director of the Senate Judiciary Subcommittee on Refugees; William H. Gray, a former U.S. Representative; Ken Miller, a member of the Board of Directors of the United Nations Association of the United States of America; and William Schwartz, who chaired the Boston Mayor's Special Commission on Police Procedures.

Figure 10.1 Director Affiliations in the Media Industry

INDUSTRY SECTOR	THE WALT DISNEY COMPANY	TIME WARNER	VIACOM INC.	TOTAL
Media	4	1	13	18
Charities	6	0	11	17
Education	6	0	7	13
Finance	2	3	8	13
Lawyers	1	3	7	11
Real Estate	4	5	1	10
Telecommunications	3	3	4	10
Investments	2	7	0	9
Political	3	1	4	8
Computer	2	22	2	6
Leisure	1	3	2	6
Transportation	3	2	1	6
Consumer Products	0	3	1	4
Drugs	0	1	3	4
Health Services	2	1	1	4
Retail	1	1	2	4
Diversified Services	1	1	1	3
Food/Tobacco	0	1	2	3
Insurance	1	1	1	3
Construction	1	0	1	2
Specialty Retail	0	0	2	2
Technology	0	0	2	2
Defense/Aero	1	0	0	1
Manufacturing	0	0	1	1
Metals and Mining	0	0	1	1
Utilities	1	0	0	1

The influence of interlocking ownership structures is also evident when executive roles and backgrounds are examined. In the case of Time Warner, the chief operating officer position has been split into cochairs, one being the president of AOL, the other the president of Time Warner. All the top corporate executives have expertise in the media industry. For example, Viacom President and Chief Operating Officer Mel Karmazin (Viacom Inc. Form DEF 14A, 2001) was the president and CEO of CBS before the merger. Robert Iger was president and chair of ABC prior to the merger with Disney. Michael Eisner, Chair & CEO of The Walt Disney Company, has a strong media background, which has taken him from ABC to Paramount Pictures (The Walt Disney Company Form DEF 14A, 2001). Richard J. Bressler, senior executive vice president and chief financial officer of Viacom Inc., came from Time Warner.

Dependence is a term that aptly fits this industry. Executives appear to be chosen not only for their industry background but also for their influence in a tightly knit industry.

CASE EXAMPLE 3: AN ECOLOGICAL TAKE ON INDUSTRY ATTRACTIVENESS (A CASE IN POPULATION ECOLOGY)

Mission Overview: This abbreviated case study explores the role of ecology in assessing the attractiveness of an industry for new entrants. It addresses issues related to the birth and death of companies in the context of the media industry.

Mission Statement: Is the media industry attractive to new organizational forms?

Mission Guides: Is this industry attractive to new companies? What new entities are being born into a particular industry? Does the industry provide adequate resources that might favor the survival of a new organizational form?

Mission Sources: The mission sources for this endeavor are primarily regulatory documents filed with the SEC and sourced through 10K Wizard, industry profiles obtained from Hoover's Online, and professional association Web sites linked to from Business.com.

Mission Source Rationale: In order to assess the attractiveness of the media industry for new organizational forms, we identified the relevant industry and conducted a count of recent IPOs in the category.

According to Hoover's Online, The Walt Disney Company participates in the "Media" industry (*Company Capsule for The Walt Disney Company,* 2002). A search for IPO offerings in this industry category from 1994 to 2002 using 10K Wizard discovered only one occurrence. 10K Wizard's categories differ slightly in terms of titles. "Media—Major Diversified" is the heading used by its search tool. Further examination suggests that a Fox Family Network S-1 filed in the 1998–1999 time range dealt with a sale of common stock in an attempt to restructure and reorganize News Corporation (Fox Family Network Form S-1, 1998). This was confirmed by a search using the Hoover's Online IPO Central portal. These findings indicate that there have been no new organizational forms born in the media category since at least 1994.

However, when related categories are examined, the picture becomes somewhat different. Not surprisingly, the year 2000 saw the greatest number of new public offerings, with 12 companies achieving this form of success. Analyzing the various media segments listed on the 10K Wizard Web site (as illustrated in Figure 10.2), we determined that the only subcategory that experienced IPO growth in the media industry in 2001 was "Internet & Online Providers."

Figure 10.2 IPO Activity in the Media Industry, 1996–2002

Year	Major Diversified	Motion Pictures	Theatres	TV & Music	Radio	TV Production & Programming	TV Broadcasting	Internet & Online Providers
2002	0	0	0	0	0	0	0	0
2001	0	0	0	0	0	0	0	2
2000	0	2	0	2	2	3	1	2
1999	0	0	0	0	1	2	1	0
1998	1	1	1	2	0	0	0	0
1997	0	1	0	1	1	0	0	0
1996	0	1	0	3	0	0	0	0

This suggests that players in the media category are well established. Even with the surge of investment dollars available during the period surrounding the new millennium, new organizational forms attempting to enter this category may not have been able to compete effectively with the larger established conglomerates. Therefore, they entered the industry in a support capacity.

The companies that made their IPOs in 2001 in the Internet & Online Providers segment are developing new technologies to support established players such as The Walt Disney Company and Time Warner. For example, InfoSpace, Inc., provides commerce, information, and communication infrastructure services for wireless devices (InfoSpace, Inc., Form S-1, 2001). Many pundits suggest that the future direction of media delivery will likely be towards wireless handheld devices. Indeed, InfoSpace, Inc., is developing technology that will allow organizations such as The Walt Disney Company to broadcast their programming.

Are resources available to support new entities seeking to enter the media industry? To answer this question, a search was conducted using Competia.com's Express feature. Unfortunately, "media" is not one of the major industry groups covered by this service provider. It did note a number of organizations, publications, and associations dedicated to the "Multimedia" industry. Business.com's online resources were then explored. These offer a "Media & Entertainment" industry category, where links to the following associations that support the subindustry of "Broadcasting" were found:

- The National Academy of Television Arts and Sciences
- Writers' Guild of America
- Motion Picture Association of America
- The U.S. National Association of Broadcasters (NAB), a full-service trade association that promotes and protects the interests of radio and television broadcasters in Washington and around the world (*Multimedia*, n.d.)

Connected to the issue of resource availability is the state of the industry itself. Is it growing, contracting, stagnating, or remaining the same? According to a Hoover's Online Industry Snapshot obtained in 2002, the industry categorized as "Media" had already matured. The result was that the birthrate for new organizational forms had tapered off. A "survival of the fittest" struggle appeared to be ongoing as the major players acquired smaller companies that would give them a competitive advantage (*Company Capsule: "Media,"* 2002).

Aside from resources and industry-competitive dynamics, another issue to be addressed is the role of government. Does government encourage new entrants? The breadth of the industry or sector labeled "Media" suggests that any answer will at best be incomplete. Filmmaking and broadcasting are just two of many important areas. Unfortunately, regulators that govern one area may not have jurisdiction over another. In broad terms, the FCC regulates the media industry in the United States. It controls the number of major players in the industry through the management of broadcasting licenses to prevent monopolies from forming. Currently the media industry is "working toward a government-imposed 2006 deadline to provide High Definition Television (HDTV) for viewers" (*Company Capsule: "Media,"* 2002).

Even when a firm is successful in entering an industry such as this, competitors may play a role in reducing its chances of survival. One example is EchoStar's efforts to remove Disney's ABC Family channel from its satellite service. EchoStar later settled a lawsuit with Disney and continues to carry all Disney services

(Echostar, 2002). Although The Walt Disney Company can hardly be described as a new entrant or representing a new organizational form, the case illustrates what can happen when one corporation attempts to take resources (viewers) away from another entity. The case and the FCC's role in developing an HDTV alternative suggest that while entry into and exit from some subindustries is possible, entry into others is quite difficult.

Attractive industries draw new companies. Aside from a significant body of S-1 filings, another indicator is worth noting. Given the importance of IPOs as exit strategies for venture capitalists, attractive industries should also be awash in venture capital at all stages. Unfortunately, during this time period, as noted above, there were no IPOs in the media category. Investors apparently knew what most others realized—the industry was mature and barriers to entry were high. Thus they directed their money elsewhere.

CASE EXAMPLE 4: PROTECTING BRAIN MATTER IN THE MEDIA INDUSTRY (A CASE IN KNOWLEDGE PERSPECTIVE)

Mission Overview: This abbreviated case study explores the role and importance of knowledge in the context of the media industry.

Mission Statement: How is intellectual property protected in the media industry?

Mission Guides: How are patents, trademarks, or copyrights used by firms in this industry to protect their intellectual property? What role is played by the use of trade secrets? For one company and three of its competitors, count the number of patents registered per year for the last four years. Is a patent race under way? If so, who is in the lead? For the same company and its competitors, count the number of trademarks registered per year for the last four years. What does this mean? In its regulatory filings or press releases or through its Web site, does the company identify its most important patents, trademarks, or copyrights? If so, what are they? What would this company consider to be a trade secret?

Mission Sources: The mission sources for this endeavor are primarily regulatory documents filed with the U.S. Patent and Trademark Office, as well as the Web site of The Walt Disney Company.

Mission Source Rationale. A patent search using the United States Patent and Trademark Office Web site, as illustrated in Figure 10.3, suggests that Yahoo! and Time Warner are the most prolific patent filers in recent years in this industry. Indeed, in its annual report for 2000, Yahoo! stresses the importance of patents: "We rely upon trademark, patent and copyright law, trade secret protection and confidentiality of licence agreements to protect our proprietary rights" (Yahoo! Form 10-K, 2000). Time Warner and Yahoo! are currently competing for top spot in the Internet and broadband communications industry. Both companies are securing their competitive advantage by protecting their innovations using the patent system.

Figure 10.3 Patent Activity in the Media Industry

COMPANY	2001	2000	1999	1998
Time Warner	12	12	13	27
Viacom Inc.	0	1	1	0
The Walt Disney Company	0	1	2	5
Yahoo!	23	20	23	14

On the other hand, using the same database, Viacom Inc. is leading the trademark race, as illustrated in Figure 10.4. Viacom is currently ranked third in the media industry and therefore needs to compete more aggressively in order to sustain its market share and obtain the level of competitive advantage that The Walt Disney Company enjoys.

Figure 10.4 Trademark Activity in the Media Industry

COMPANY	2001	2000	1999	1998	TOTAL FILED
Time Warner	132	166	358	223	1889
Viacom Inc.	257	381	349	213	2523
The Walt Disney Company	112	62	109	120	890
Yahoo!	14	19	21	8	107

Disney and Time Warner's intellectual property was at risk during the late 1990s, when the copyright on some of their most valuable assets was set to expire. It was one of those rare occasions when Disney and Time Warner combined forces to lobby Congress to extend copyright protections. The companies were successful in persuading Congress to pass HR 2589. The resulting law gives the media industry 20 more years of copyright protection.

Why would a major media conglomerate like Disney be concerned with protecting its copyrights? Mickey Mouse has huge symbolic value and still has a lot of commercial value. The Disney characters and brands have considerable earning potential, and they can be licensed and merchandised in so many ways. Mickey Mouse and friends are billion-dollar brands. Disney has said that Winnie the Pooh and the Hundred Acre Wood characters generate a third of its licensing revenue. Indeed, in the late 1990s, Pooh generated $2 billion a year for Disney and its licensees (Weinstein, 2002).

Firms such as The Walt Disney Company do not promote their trade secrets for obvious reasons, and they are serious about protecting them. For instance, in an ongoing court case that pits Disney against the Slesinger family regarding their royalty rights to Winnie the Pooh, the issue of information disclosure has arisen. "The next hearing in the case is expected to be about whether documents Disney has managed so far to keep sealed should remain so. [Daniel] Petrocelli [Disney's lawyer] has argued that the documents contain trade secrets and other proprietary information that could harm Disney's business if disclosed" (Wagner, 2002).

CONCLUSION

For CI analysts, the online resources of the Internet can be a confusing morass of data and information or a liberating respite from the challenges of problem solving. When informed by theory, they can resemble the latter.

The Knowledge Management Cycle[1]

DANIEL L. SILVER

This book has focused on the acquisition and analysis of information and knowledge. As noted in earlier chapters, the practice of competitive intelligence is broader in scope. It also addresses other issues, including the sharing or dissemination of insight on a timely basis. An interest in knowledge sharing is not unique to CI professionals. In recent years, it has also received an enormous amount of attention from consultants, academics, executives, information technology specialists, and others. Termed "knowledge management," it is an area of endeavor that complements the objectives of most CI efforts.

Despite the excitement surrounding knowledge management, there is significant debate and confusion as to what it is or should be. Related buzzwords such as *business intelligence* and *knowledge creation* further confound the issue. Critics argue that most implementations of knowledge management have been based on an outdated business model and a related information processing view (Malhotra, 2000). In several cases, such as data warehousing, it is difficult to justify why specific information technology solutions fall in the realm of knowledge management rather than within the scope of traditional information management.

This ambiguity about what knowledge management is and how it contributes to organizational performance has recently led some industry analysts to remark that knowledge management is a fad, just like one-minute management and total quality management (Schrage, 2000)—one that has little to do with

---

[1]Daniel Silver—Acadia University

information technology (Sveiby, 2000). However, we do not consider knowledge management a fad. Rather, it is an important new area of research and application that is necessarily passing through a period of settling and definition. Our intention in writing this chapter is to work toward a clearer understanding of knowledge management in the context of competitive intelligence, organization theory, and information technology.

We begin with a discussion of the problems surrounding knowledge management and develop a definition. The knowledge management cycle is then described within the contexts of an individual, a small organization, and a large organization. The remainder of the chapter explores the differences between how an individual and an organization can manage knowledge, current areas of research and application, and major challenges for research in the coming years.

MOTIVATION FOR KNOWLEDGE MANAGEMENT

E-commerce and the Internet have generated competitors who may be on the other side of the world physically but who are only a mouse-click away. Employees are moving from organization to organization at alarming rates, taking with them important knowledge of company operations that must be reacquired by new employees. The pace of technology, particularly information technology (IT), continues to force managers to consider organizational change associated with the implementation of electronic commerce storefronts, automated inventory procurement, and enterprise resource planning (ERP) systems. Changes in government legislation and regulatory practices provide a steady flow of new threats and opportunities. Customers are demanding new products and services that are bundled to their preference. Consequently, companies are being forced to move faster and at new levels of personalized interaction.

Dealing with these internal and external pressures and filtering through the barrage of information for relevant data requires ways of managing organizational knowledge that are rarely found in today's companies and institutions (see Figure 11.1).

Figure 11.1 Internal and External Pressures on an Organization

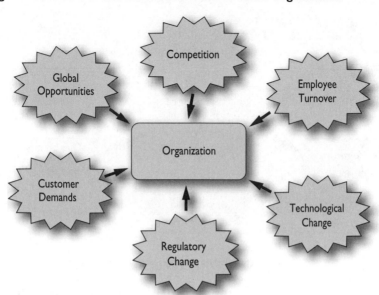

Organizations must develop management methods that accept information as a valued resource, convert that information into organizational knowledge, and then generate value-added information from that knowledge in order to address these challenges.

Figure 11.2 shows the major entities that act as sources of information for organizations. Leading companies are able to filter information in from these entities, build on their organizational knowledge, and synthesize valuable information. Fundamental to the success of their methods is the realization that information technology does not, on its own, equal knowledge management.

Since the late 1990s, books such as *The Information Paradox* by John Thorp (1998) have asked serious questions about the role of information systems within organizations, how they are managed, and the methods used to measure their benefit. Managing knowledge within an organization involves both people and information technology. We see the ultimate goal for an organization as communicating information and managing knowledge with the same efficiency and effectiveness as an individual. A later section of this chapter compares an organization's ability to manage knowledge to that of an individual and discusses significant differences.

Figure 11.2 Organizational Knowledge Environment

WHAT IS KNOWLEDGE?

Before going further, it is important to define *knowledge* and to explain how it differs from information and data. Figure 11.3 depicts a pyramid of progression from data to wisdom. *Data* can be identified as values without context, such as "the height of a column of mercury in a glass tube." *Information* can be defined as data within context, or values derived from raw data, such as "air temperature in degrees Celsius." Information, like data, can be encoded and therefore stored, processed, and communicated via paper or IT.

Figure 11.3 A Progression from Data to Wisdom

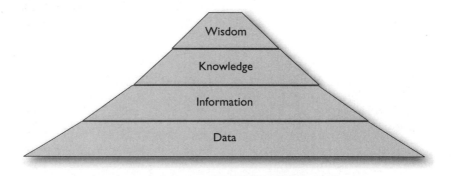

Knowledge, on the other hand, as Allen Newell (1982) points out, is a combination of information and processes whereby the processes relate a vast array of information so as to promote rational behavior and achieve desired goals. Under this definition, knowledge is uniquely linked to action, such as "it is −2 degrees Celsius and water freezes at 0 degrees Celsius, so I will bring the hose in for the winter." Similarly, Karl Sveiby (2001) defines knowledge as "the capacity-to-act" and suggests that it is the intangible asset that all organizations strive to create.

These definitions subscribe to the autopoietic epistemology of Maturana and Varela (1980) that considers that data are passed between knowledgeable entities, but knowledge is not. Autopoietic systems are open to data but closed to knowledge. After the receipt of data, knowledge must be created or interpreted inside the system in a manner that is unique to each system depending upon its other experiences.

This particular definition of knowledge supports the organizational theorist's perspective, suggesting that the majority of knowledge resides in human minds and that aspects of knowledge are lost when converted to information that can be handled by IT. Many authors, such as Hubert Saint-Onge (1996), have made the distinction between *explicit* knowledge that can be recorded within a computer (e.g., spoken words, diagrams, writing, raw data) and *tacit* knowledge that defies transformation into an information form (e.g., intuition, personal perspectives, beliefs, values, complex conceptual relationships).

We feel these are terms that complicate the discussion of knowledge management and therefore refrain from their use in favor of the earlier terms, *information* and *knowledge*. The final layer of the pyramid is *wisdom,* which we humorously define as knowledge plus benevolence, and which plays no further role in our discussion.

TWO PERSPECTIVES ON KNOWLEDGE MANAGEMENT

As stated earlier, knowledge management currently has no clear definition. One reason for this has been disagreement over the very definition of knowledge itself. A second, and more recent, reason is confusion over the role of IT in knowledge management. However, two major perspectives on knowledge management have emerged over the last five years: the technology-centered perspective and the people-centered perspective (Sveiby, 2001).

The Technology-Centered Approach

The technology-centered perspective suggests that knowledge consists of objects that can be encoded, stored, transmitted, and processed by IT devices. Proponents of this perspective see IT solutions as the answer to knowledge management problems. Consequently, many IT companies have adopted the language of knowledge management for the purposes of promoting what have popularly become known as business intelligence products and services.

Although surrounded in hype, the technology-centered perspective is important. Data mining and data warehousing technology can have a very positive effect on the collection, analysis, and dissemination of organizational information. In fact, much of the recent interest in knowledge management has been due to successful use of these technologies. Similarly, customer relationship management software can benefit both the company and the customer by influencing purchase behavior. Decision support tools can provide answers to complex questions in areas such as manufacturing and inventory control. E-commerce technologies allow Internet contact with customers so as to provide new levels of product selection, delivery, and service. Other IT developments such as intranets, portals, groupware, workflow messaging, and content management can provide systems for efficient and effective information flow and collaboration.

There is no question that IT provides powerful tools that can play an important role in a knowledge management strategy. However, many knowledge management applications continue to fail because "too many managers still believe that once the right technology is in place appropriate information sharing will follow" (Davenport & Prusak, 2000). Such a strategy must consider that it is ultimately people that turn information into knowledge and action.

The People-Centered Approach

The people-centered perspective, on the other hand, suggests that knowledge consists of process and that the most valued knowledge defies encoding, machine storage, and analysis. Human intellect and management skills are paramount. Indeed, Accenture's knowledge management practice cited the following five key success factors:

- Know the organizational community and its needs.
- Create the appropriate context that fosters learning, knowledge creation, and information sharing and trust.
- Oversee the content of information flow and fill in knowledge gaps to create value.
- Support and show by example how sharing and leveraging knowledge can benefit the organization.
- Enhance the knowledge management process by making it simple, effective, and efficient. (Manasco, 2001)

Karl Sveiby (2000) describes three major components generally involved in knowledge management: external structure (relationships with customers and suppliers), internal structure (patents, models, and computer systems, as well as internal human culture and networks), and individual competence (of professional/technical staff and of support/management staff). To Sveiby, the objective of knowledge management is to leverage the transfer of knowledge among these three components so as to create value. He makes the significant point that, when used, tangible resources tend to depreciate in value; however, knowledge, as an intangible asset, tends to grow with use. It is when knowledge is not used that its value depreciates.

The people-centered perspective views IT solutions as only a small part of an approach to knowledge management within organizations. For this reason, proponents have a tendency to shy away from IT-based knowledge management solutions, sometimes to their own detriment.

BRINGING THE PERSPECTIVES TOGETHER

The division between the technology-centered and people-centered perspectives may be driven by differences in educational background, as well as personal and professional motivations. It needs to be eliminated, for there is an important relationship between the perspectives. Knowledge management is a people-centered philosophy that necessarily involves the use of information technologies. Knowledge management is herein defined in terms of three main components: information, people, and information technology. The challenge is "to construct hybrid knowledge management environments in which we use both humans and machines in complementary ways" (Davenport & Prusak, 2000).

Advocates for a technology-centered approach need to accept that there are important aspects of human knowledge that cannot be encoded as information within current computer systems. On the other hand, proponents of a people-centered perspective need to understand that IT and its three fundamental information functions (storing, processing, and communicating) have played and will continue to play a critical role in the effective and efficient management of knowledge in modern organizations.

The need for cooperation between the people-centered and technology-centered perspectives has prompted one observer to note, "Knowledge management . . . embodies organizational processes that seek synergistic combination of the data and information-processing capacity of information technologies, and the creative and innovative capacity of human beings" (Malhotra, 2000). In the following section, we seek to better understand how individual humans manage knowledge and compare their methods with the management of knowledge in small and large organizations.

THE KNOWLEDGE MANAGEMENT CYCLE—
AT THE INDIVIDUAL LEVEL

For humans, the process of transforming data and information into knowledge is a cycle that is as natural and continuous as breathing. Figure 11.4 depicts this knowledge management cycle as consisting of four fundamental steps that involve the storage, processing, and communication of information.

Daily, individuals are faced with information and data overload. To deal with this concern, they use personal memory, as well as notes, paper files, and other methods, to select and store information. Their brains, possibly with the aid of a calculator or a small computer system, process the information. As a result, communication of information is primarily interpersonal.

Individuals effectively observe and analyze information. We are also good at identifying problems that threaten our well-being and discovering opportunities that satisfy our needs. Using such information, individuals are able to generate theories of how the environment works. These theories lead to practical approaches and methods that can then be tested and applied so as to extract value from the original information provided by the environment.

The results of these applications range from dismal failure to great success. Regardless, we are able to consolidate into our knowledge base those theories and approaches that led to the success or failure. As individuals, we pride ourselves on our ability to learn from our triumphs and our defeats through effective integration of knowledge. In short, knowledge management is one of the primary characteristics that ensures survival in a complex world and yet is unique and personal to each of us.

As Figure 11.4 illustrates, knowledge generated at the end of one iteration through the cycle provides new information that can be used to stimulate yet another iteration. It is also important to note that certain aspects of this cycle are uniquely human in nature. Humans have an incredible ability to observe and recognize complex patterns in data and information. This is largely due to the massive amount of interrelated information that is available from the person's consolidated knowledge. In addition, theory generation is one of the human brain's most fascinating abilities, wherein recent observations along with one or more existing theories are combined to solve a problem or approach a new opportunity. Once again, there is a reliance on a vast array of common knowledge.

Figure 11.4 The Knowledge Management Cycle

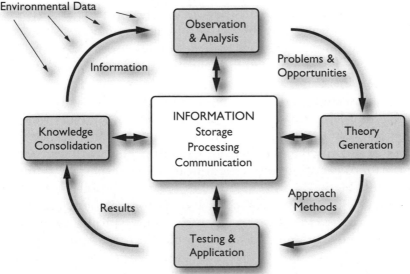

The testing of a new theory is something that most humans do quite well because the requirements are thoroughly understood. However, there tends to be more of a trial-and-error approach where a new theory is incrementally developed from one or more existing theories and tested. Fortunately, this can happen very rapidly in many cases, and errors tend to be minor due to the subtle change made in how the theories are tested.

Last, but certainly not least, is the consolidation of new information and knowledge into a common knowledge base. The ability to integrate a lifetime of observations and theories into a readily accessible collection of knowledge is most definitely a uniquely human capability (at least at the time of writing).

THE KNOWLEDGE MANAGEMENT CYCLE— AT THE ORGANIZATIONAL LEVEL

Small organizations, ranging from 3 to 20 persons, are able to emulate the knowledge management cycle of an individual with some degree of success. Such organizations receive requests and information from customers, partners, and the government. They then store portions of this information in their collective memories, in documents such as agreements, and within simple database systems. Information processing takes place in meetings where the strengths and weaknesses of the individuals are well understood, accepted, and used. In addition, various small computer systems and possibly a network server may be employed. Communication is primarily via ad hoc meetings augmented by telephone, fax, and e-mail messages when a person is traveling or at home.

Observation, analysis, and theory generation are accomplished on an individual basis and are communicated in working meetings or impromptu encounters. Many small organizations have well-defined and effectively communicated goals (written or unwritten) that lead to the identification of problems and opportunities. Methods and approaches for overcoming these challenges are typically created by those who will implement and track progress. Ideas are readily shared and typically critiqued in a constructive manner, balancing both short-term and long-term goals. The overlap of roles increases the probability that the methods are tested and applied in accordance with the requirements of each challenge.

Because the working group makes up a large portion of the organization, most individuals in the organization become aware of the successes and failures of the methods. Knowledge consolidation by each individual is facilitated by a collective effort to ensure that failure does not recur for the same reasons and that success can be repeated as often as possible. Consequently, small organizations are said to be efficient, creative, and able to move quickly to meet a changing environment with a high degree of synergy, where the value derived from a project can often be greater than the sum of the individual efforts. A primary key to this success is the effective management of organizational knowledge made possible by the small numbers of individuals in the organization.

Large organizations of 20 people or more, on the other hand, have a difficult time emulating the knowledge management cycle of an individual. Large companies and institutions receive proposals, queries, and other forms of information from a multitude of customers, channels, partners, government agencies, and regulatory bodies. Information is stored in various formats such as policy documents and in various locations including internal process and product databases, as well as external customer and distribution databases, filing cabinets, microfiche, audiotapes, and videotapes.

Portions of the information inflow are processed by individuals, who can then be confounded by a multitude of meetings as employees assigned to various roles change from quarter to quarter. Communication is achieved via a cornucopia of LAN, Internet, voice, pager, cellular phone, and PDA (personal digital assistant) devices. Meetings that must be scheduled a week or more in advance for many executives and that may be canceled and rescheduled due to conflicts also provide means of communication in large organizations.

Large organizations typically have a difficult time managing knowledge. Observation and analysis are the responsibility of domain specialists, who can often miss looming problems and lucrative opportunities because of a narrow perspective of organizational goals and capabilities. Bureaucracy, politics, and "buy-in" meetings stifle theory generation, which can lead to creative new approaches and methods.

When a new strategy does make it to testing and application, these tasks are often undertaken by someone other than the creator, so aspects of the strategy are lost between conception and execution. Ultimately, it may be uncertain as to whether the execution was correct but the concept was flawed, or the concept was correct but the execution was poor.

Increasingly, projects adversely affect the bottom line, not because they fail to meet original requirements but because they fail to keep pace with requirements that change during the project. As well, knowledge from previous undertakings or current activities is often not shared with the team, and the project stays on its original course, only to be marked a failure. Failure of a single project in a large organization would not be so bad if learning could take place. Unfortunately, this is not always the case.

Larger organizations also have a difficult time communicating relevant information for consolidation within the minds of team members. Although many organizations have policies and standards that specify actions such as project post-mortems and exit interviews, most organizations do a poor job of implementing them. Knowledge gained at the end of a product cycle is often lost, and for this reason, failure can recur and success is not repeated as often as it could be. Consequently, large organizations are said to be lethargic, to lack creativity, and to be slow to react to meet a changing environment.

Chaos runs rampant in many such organizations, and the value derived from a project can be far less than the sum of the individual efforts. This chaos is largely due to the ineffective management of organizational knowledge. Based on the differences between how individuals and how organizations manage knowledge, how can organizations work to improve their knowledge management?

IMPORTANT AREAS FOR RESEARCH IN KNOWLEDGE MANAGEMENT

A number of areas of research within knowledge management are of great importance to organizations, particularly large organizations. Figure 11.5 suggests research topics organized by each of the four steps of the knowledge management cycle. These research areas include the following:

Retrieval and Filtering of Data/Information

The rate of data and information inflow to organizations by way of card readers, automated telemetry, telephone calls and, most notably, the Internet is overwhelming. Most companies struggle every day to find effective methods of retrieving data and filtering out the salient information. Important topics for research include an examination of the relative strengths and weaknesses of systematic approaches to information retrieval and filtering in the workplace; a cataloging of library science research skills; the development of intelligent user interfaces that can learn the profile of a user's interests and filter information based on that profile; and an enhancement of advanced methods of Knowledge Query and Manipulation Language, or KQML (Finin & Wiederhold, 1993). Integrated with content management systems and the Internet, these technologies will provide very powerful observation tools.

Enabling Access to Salient Environmental Data

Although much of an organization's data is encoded into electronic form for ease of communications and analysis, other important information is not. For example, in hospitals, much patient information is recorded on paper; on the manufacturing floor, important data are communicated verbally; and information surrounding important interactions with customers is rarely communicated beyond the sales staff and their managers. Internet, groupware, and portal technologies can be used to assist with these problems; however, in most organizations the need exists for cultural change to encourage the capture of salient environmental data.

Sharing Organizational Goals and Objectives

Large organizations suffer greatly from a lack of sharing and caring about organization goals and objectives. Clear and repeated communication of company goals and objectives to all employees provides an environment in which knowledge can be better managed. Methods of sharing organizational goals and objectives and bringing them in line with individual goals are important areas of research.

Elimination of "Silo" Processing and Reinvention

Some authors suggest that an ideal organization is composed of organic networked teams, such that knowledge is able to flow freely across disciplines and departmental boundaries. Such organizations require dynamic management methods and career development approaches that consider individual and organizational objectives, as well as rewarding trusting relationships at every opportunity.

Fostering Knowledge Creation Through Small Teams

Work teams of small numbers of people who share common goals are highly innovative environments. Having members of an organization passing along best-practice methods as they move between these groups is very important, yet it can often be disruptive. However, technologies such as electronic mail, corporate intranets, portals, and collaborative software (such as IBM Lotus Notes® messaging and collaboration software) can be very helpful in creating and enabling small teams. Research and application of new management methods and technologies is needed.

Reduction of Bureaucracy and Formal Meetings

Moving from four levels of management bureaucracy to delegated authority and responsibility has been one of the most difficult transitions for modern organizations. The traditional hierarchy fosters a climate of presentations, proposals, and meetings versus strong analysis and decisive action. A healthy knowledge management environment is one in which people wish to share information for the common good and not one in which they must share information in order to proceed with projects or business plans. This having been said, legal and fiscal responsibility requires a formal chain of command within organizations.

Resolving this conflict continues to be an important area of research in business administration. Technologies such as message passing, groupware, and document management systems can facilitate a more efficient and effective movement of paperwork within the office and across the globe. Standard protocols and languages for interoperability between systems, such as the Extensible Markup Language (XML), is an active area of research.

Enabling Start-to-Finish Development and Deployment

Too often in large organizations, design engineers or business strategists are not involved in the testing of final products or the implementation of tactical operations. This can lead to a false sense of accomplishment on the part of the engineer or strategist and a poor opinion of upper management and technical authority on the part of frontline employees. Methods of feedback between designer and user need to be created to ensure better communication of success and failure with a minimum investment of both parties' time. Solutions can include people-centered approaches such as education of frontline workers, practical job shadowing by designer engineers, and the involvement of designers, testers, and frontline workers from the start of design to implementation and deployment.

Effective Measurement of Business Processes and Knowledge Assets

Marketing through data mining and customer relationship management is really the first area of business administration outside of finance to employ rigorous mathematical methods widely. This has many management researchers excited about the use of measures and mathematics in other areas (Sveiby, 1997). Further work is needed in measuring the quality and value of business processes and intangible knowledge assets. In particular, methods of measuring success due to knowledge creation and knowledge transfer are needed.

Management of Changing Requirements

The pressures affecting modern organizations ensure that change will always occur. Tried and proven methods of managing change within projects and product cycles are needed. Project management research has turned to engineering methodologies that have established methods of change management. Innovative new methods of managing projects, products, and services have also been developed that take iterative, incremental approaches that can more easily incorporate change (for example, the Unified Software Development Process used in software engineering).

Methods of Collective Reflection

Unlike an individual, an organization rarely takes the time to reflect on successes and failures. Surprisingly, when it does do so, the event is often recognized as a hallmark, a defining moment in the life of the business. Most typically, these occasions take place off-site, in seclusion. They happen annually at best and often only at points of crisis. Why? There must be better ways to reflect regularly on successes and failures and share in the consolidation of new knowledge.

Building Trust for the Dissemination of Knowledge

Success factors within most organizations are closely guarded secrets. From an intellectual property perspective, this makes a great deal of sense. However, secrets among departments, work units, or project teams within the same organization are counterproductive. As Sveiby (1997) suggests, "trust is the bandwidth of communication." Without trust between people, there cannot be a productive sharing of information that results in knowledge transfer.

Organizations must generate a trusting environment that extends from the top to the grass roots. Authors such as Sveiby (2001) and Malhotra (2000) suggest that trust-building activities like team social events, induction programs, job rotation, milestone celebrations, impromptu lunches, and face-to-face communications be encouraged in organizations.

Retaining Knowledge When Employees Leave

The loss of organizational knowledge when an employee leaves is a very serious problem. Methods of retaining knowledge can be divided into proactive and reactive categories. Proactive methods include personnel rotation programs, master/apprentice schemes, and the recording of information (such as sales techniques) from internal experts. Reactive methods include exit interviews and aftermath peer discussion sessions. Further research is required to find better methods of retaining organizational knowledge.

Figure 11.5 Important Areas of Research in Knowledge Management

Observation & Analysis	• Retrieval and filtering of data/information
	• Enabling access to salient environmental data
	• Sharing organizational goals and objectives
Theory Generation	• Elimination of "silo" processing and reinvention
	• Fostering knowledge creation through small teams
	• Reduction of bureaucracy and formal meetings
Testing & Application	• Enabling start-to-finish development and deployment
	• Effective measurement of business processes and knowledge assets
	• Management of changing requirements
Knowledge Consolidation	• Methods of collective reflection
	• Building trust for the dissemination of knowledge
	• Retaining knowledge when employees leave

SUMMARY

Throughout this chapter, an important distinction has been made among data, information, and knowledge that recognizes that knowledge is a complex internal representation of information that is unique to human minds. Information can be stored, processed, and communicated by information technology, but current IT does not have the same capabilities with knowledge. This limitation emphasizes the people-centered approach to knowledge management but also demonstrates that effective and efficient knowledge management will necessarily involve and promote IT methods. An integration of the technology-centered and people-centered perspectives on knowledge management is encouraged so as to develop a richer strategy for managing organizational knowledge.

In addition, the knowledge management cycle has been introduced and the four major steps in the cycle have been explored within the context of an individual, a small organization, and a large organization. Based on differences between how individuals and how organizations manage knowledge, the chapter has presented 12 major challenges of which CI professionals, organizational theorists, and information technology specialists need to be aware. Overall, we conclude that the two most exciting and important areas of research are (1) fostering environments of trust that encourage knowledge sharing and (2) developing intelligence systems that learn user profiles and actively retrieve and filter salient information based on those profiles.

Much of the work in knowledge management is yet to be done. Researchers, practitioners, and other professionals are encouraged to discover more about the subject and to contribute to this emerging field through discussion with colleagues and the sharing of new ideas in articles and conference presentations.

SECTION

Web-Based CI in Corporate and Academic Classrooms

The Role of CI in Academia[1]

JOHN PRESCOTT

The integration of organizational theory and Web-based analysis is both novel and critical to incorporating CI into the mainstream of academic research and teaching. Professor Vibert's Web-based approach is novel in that there have been few, if any, attempts to link organizational theory to real-time strategic analysis. Using the Web as a source of data to explore strategic questions that can be directly linked to underlying theoretical positions brings life to what are often abstract concepts. Students will be able to explore the underlying assumptions of a theory, how the theory helps to explain organizational behavior, the limitations of a particular theory, and how managers struggle with incomplete and often conflicting data. Students exposed to Professor Vibert's approach will immediately see the link between the quality of competitive intelligence and their ability to draw conclusions and implications regarding organizational issues. Organizational theorists and the models that they develop need to be subjected to tests in the business world.

Competitive intelligence as a field of study challenges organizational theorists not only to construct models that explain firm behavior but also to modify their models as empirical data challenge their assumptions, boundaries, and conclusions. In essence, Professor Vibert's approach will encourage students to become organizational theorists. As students explore the variety of organizational models and hopefully develop models of their own, they will do so with an understanding of the symbiotic relationship between CI and organizational theory.

---

[1]John Prescott—The University of Pittsburgh

Academics who do not incorporate CI into their teaching and research run the risk of becoming increasingly irrelevant. In academia, CI is often criticized for being descriptive as opposed to theory-based. That is, the primary criterion applied to descriptive research is the extent to which it accurately mirrors the competitive domain one is trying to understand. For example, a typical descriptive CI research question is the following: In what way do a firm's intelligence processes accurately describe why, when, and how a competitor will introduce a new product? While academics view these types of questions as interesting, they prefer to begin by developing elegant models of product introduction and then sometimes to test them using "scientific methods." However, as Dubin so eloquently points out:

> I am . . . urging that the research stance towards theory building among behavioral scientists be that of constant alertness to the descriptive knowledge of the domain about which they wish to theorize. It is the facts against which the adequacy of the theory is always tested. Indeed, in the first place it is from facts that theory is developed. (Dubin, 1978, p. 230)

Professor Dubin is clearly advocating a synergistic relationship between descriptive research and hypothesis testing.

To further explore my assertion, it is essential to provide a brief historical perspective on the organizational theories articulated in this book. One of the more important yet subtle aspects of examining a variety of organizational theories is how they vary in their epistemological stance. In its simplest form, the field of epistemology asks the question, What constitutes warranted knowledge? (Johnson & Duberley, 2000, p. 5). Most of the theories in this book have epistemological foundations based on the belief that it is possible to model the business world objectively. For example, when two or more teams of students collect and analyze data related to an exercise involving game theory, it is assumed that their conclusions are not overly influenced by the values the students bring to the exercise. This is the traditional and most accepted view of epistemological foundations in management. However, there are several theories presented in the book that put forth an alternative epistemological foundation.

Perspectives such as postmodernism and critical theory are built on the foundation that there are no objective standards for assessing knowledge since all interpretations are value- and theory-laden. Thus, these perspectives embrace alternative interpretations and assert that there are no objective standards for preferring one interpretation over another. For students, it is important to recognize these differences as they work through their Web-based exercises.

One of the strengths of this book is that Professor Vibert provides a wide range of theories that differ in their epistemological foundation. Regardless of the epistemological foundations underlying each of the theories, organizational theorists increasingly view management as a social process. Students will be challenged to interpret their results in light of the social processes that surround all organizations.

Within the context outlined above, CI plays three roles in academia. First, the core processes of the intelligence cycle are ideally suited to be taught in academia. The intelligence cycle involves five activities: understanding an intelligence request, designing and implementing an information collection plan, analyzing information to create intelligence, disseminating intelligence to users, and assisting in the implementation of intelligence recommendations. In a previous article (Prescott, 1999), I articulated a way for academic institutions to design a program of study in competitive intelligence. I will not repeat those points here except to say that no one school within a university has all of the courses and skills to deliver quality intelligence training. Rather, the development of an interdisciplinary approach to a CI curriculum is already in place and needs only to be coordinated by a few broad-minded faculties. I also outlined eight different ways in which other academics and I have designed CI courses. Professor Vibert's approach is unique and would be a ninth method.

Professor Vibert's pedagogy is ideally suited to teach most, if not all, aspects of the intelligence cycle in real time. This is an important contribution to the teaching role of CI. This book also provides a tried-and-true method for teaching CI that other faculty can easily use. The integration of organizational theory with CI will go a long way toward addressing the concern that CI is a descriptive field of study. Students can develop and test CI hypotheses based on theory. Thus, we do not necessarily need to develop the "theory of CI." Rather, we can test CI hypotheses by applying existing theories.

The second role of CI in academia is research. For the reasons outlined above, there are only a handful of CI scholars in academia. In recent years there has been a growing interest in CI research, as evidenced by the number of CI dissertations. My perspective is a little different from those of most of my academic colleagues in the Society of Competitive Intelligence Professionals (*http://www.scip.org*). I believe there is a wealth of existing research that informs the field of CI. One example is sufficient to demonstrate my point.

The ultimate objective of any CI program is to provide timely and functional intelligence for managers as an input into their decision-making process. Given this objective, it seems wise to understand how and why managers use information. The vast decision-making literature is replete with articles focusing on the ways in which managers value and use information. CI researchers need to draw on this literature.

One simple way for CI researchers to make a significant impact would be to reframe much of the existing literature in CI terms. That is, what are the key findings of the decision-making literature that CI professionals can leverage in their daily activities? This process would also reveal important areas for future research. Conjectures and hypotheses can then be developed and tested using the set of theories outlined in this book. Since we have established that organizational theories are grounded in different epistemological foundations, researchers from a variety of disciplines and countries can provide rich and varied perspectives on the CI dialogue.

There is one other activity that I would encourage my research colleagues to consider. Researchers are rewarded for publishing in high-quality peer-reviewed journals. If these same researchers would also rewrite their articles for practitioner journals using CI terms and implications, their research impact would increase considerably.

The third role of CI in academia is that of service to our communities. In our increasingly globally connected and competitive world, it is imperative that managers have a fundamental understanding of the role of CI. Managers need to learn what CI is and is not, as well as to discover what it can and cannot do to improve decision making. This book fulfills this service by training the next generation of managers in how organizational theory, CI, and Web-based analysis are interrelated. As increasing numbers of students are exposed to the integration of theory and practice through processes such as the one Professor Vibert has developed, our impact in the service dimension will exponentially increase.

I am extremely excited about the future of CI in academia. There are so many opportunities to make an impact. My hope is that as students increasingly recognize the vital role that organizational theory plays in identifying, formulating, and implementing business issues, they will also appreciate how CI is the foundation of high-quality decision making.

13

CI Corporate Training Ideas From the Classroom[1]

CONOR VIBERT

For almost three decades, a number of different teaching modes have dominated North American business schools and have proven effective in molding a generation of corporate leaders. These modes of delivery have contributed directly to the development of a highly successful global management consulting industry, the legitimization of numerous nascent professions, and the institutionalization of business schools as significant contributors to local communities, academia, and society at large. Indirectly, these initiatives have also formed the underlying application base of many professional training programs, especially those related to competitive intelligence.

Unfortunately, competitive intelligence is a subject that has not yet been widely adopted for instruction in most business schools. Aside from inertial forces of resistance within the schools themselves, some authors suggest that academic institutions, by nature, may simply be poorly equipped to deliver effective CI instruction. One scholar questions the relevance of classic academic research techniques that continue to be offered to many undergraduate business students (Merritt, 1999) and suggests the result is a typical graduate ill prepared for the realities of the competitive business environment.

A second critique is far more forceful but may be representative of a significant body of opinion not normally found among supporters of management programs. The author goes as far as to question the existence of business schools, labeling them "acting schools which train experts in abstract methods to pretend

---

[1]From "Leveraging technology: CI in an electronic classroom teaching environment," by C. Vibert, 2001, *Competitive Intelligence Review* 12(1), pp. 48–58. Copyright 2001 by C. Vibert. Adapted with permission.

they are capitalists." The same critic also poses an intriguing question: "Is there any indication—practical, statistical, philosophical or financial—that training of business leaders in specialized management schools has benefited business or the economy?" (Saul, 1994, pp. 50–51). Although overly pessimistic, this query does suggest a need to look closely at how business students are trained at the undergraduate and graduate levels.

These arguments aside, the result has been the development of a growing industry of companies that specialize in offering competitive intelligence training to the public, private, and not-for-profit sectors. Despite their success and profitability, training firms and academic institutions alike face a similar challenge: figuring out the most effective means to deliver instructional material to students or clients.

One suggested course of action is to deliver content through a number of commonly accepted traditional teaching modes that include lecture, case, and independent study formats. In other traditional methods, the majority of the insight is gained through project work, the completion of practical exercises, or the comprehension of content found in a structured set of readings. Sadly, each of these methods alone is at best incomplete. The traditional case method of teaching offers but one example of why this is so.

IMPROVING THE CASE METHOD WITH TECHNOLOGY

Traditional case teaching typically involves an instructor or trainer choosing a case from a textbook or case-writing service and guiding a class of trainees or learners through a series of challenges toward the discovery of a business solution that is hidden and not obvious. Unfortunately, this style of teaching can be hindered by the instructor's limited knowledge of the case material, his or her personal teaching effectiveness, and the availability of meaningful sources of evidence. Given the uncertainty and rapid transformation of the contemporary business environment, traditional written cases themselves have an important weakness: their shelf life is becoming increasingly shorter and shorter.

Limitations such as these, coupled with improvements in Internet, communication, and educational technologies, suggest a need to develop new approaches for content delivery. Fortunately, this call has not been ignored and has led to the development of innovative teaching platforms, including collaborative software for distance learning, virtual learning environments (Follows, 1999), and electronic classrooms. Of interest to this discussion is the latter. An electronic classroom includes laptop docking stations, overhead projection, large-screen data projectors, video and audio capabilities, and power and data connections for each student. In this environment, each student is connected to the Internet using his or her notebook computer.

Competitive intelligence is particularly well suited to an electronic classroom instructional environment, as it offers instructors, among other benefits, an opportunity to introduce the concept of real-time case analysis, or online research missions. As compared to the process of traditional case development, during which case writers may spend weeks, even months, preparing material for publication and use, online research missions minimize preparation time but maximize the options available to trainees when conducting their analysis. Whereas a dated, purchased teaching case may comprise 15 to 20 pages of text plus appendices, an online research mission, customized by a trainer for a specific course, may consist of no more than a series of brief questions, as noted earlier, that address concerns relevant to specific organizations, industries, or settings. The method alters the manner in which students learn and clearly reinforces the notion of personal accountability for knowledge acquisition.

Why might corporate trainers consider electronic classrooms to be attractive forums for professional development? Four compelling reasons might be suggested:

First, when used creatively, these classrooms become practice fields or learning laboratories that simulate the complexity faced by CI professionals seeking to make sense of often bewildering competitive environments.

Second, the effectiveness of such practice fields can be assessed fairly easily. Success in this context refers to the development of analysts capable of resolving important business concerns. These trainees both acquire this skill and improve their interpretive abilities by applying theoretical or analytical frameworks using relevant online information sources such as those found in earlier chapters (Vibert, 2000).

Third, when coupled with real-time approaches to business case resolution, electronic classrooms allow traditional management insight to serve as a platform for training students in the practice of CI.

Fourth, electronic classrooms offer a compelling rationale for investment in physical classroom settings as opposed to options such as self-guided virtual learning environments or online tele-conferencing distance programs.

A NEW FORM OF TRAINING

So, how may electronic classrooms be used to deliver CI-related training? One approach, developed at Acadia University in Wolfville, Nova Scotia, is described in the following paragraphs. It underpins the development of the online research missions illustrated in earlier chapters.

Students work in teams. They adopt a publicly traded (U.S.) firm that files annually with the U.S. Securities and Exchange Commission and track it over time. For analytical purposes, an ideal firm is one whose shares have traded publicly for more than a year. This ensures that both a 10-K Annual Report and a DEF 14A Proxy Statement are available to online researchers. Early in the course, specific search techniques are taught, and important online information sources are identified and illustrated. Prior to each class, students are given a series of questions regarding a specific industry or company and asked to construct a case presentation in response. These are the research missions. No written case is provided.

In class, a group of students gives a multimedia presentation of their research mission, using online evidence to support their claims. The presentation is submitted 24 hours in advance and hosted in an online database, allowing classmates to access it ahead of time. While the presentation is being made, a second group of students constructs a multimedia critique while collaborating in a virtual team using ICQ instant messaging software. Shortly after the presentation, this group presents its appraisal. During each in-class presentation, groups of classmates search the Web for information that the presenting groups may have omitted.

To further simulate a real-world operating environment, the two groups delivering and critiquing the presentation Webcast their work using video streaming software. Members of other student teams are dispersed, with half viewing the presentation in the classroom while the others watch it on their laptops from a second on-campus location. Again using ICQ and working in virtual teams, audience members discuss the Web-based evidence and then collaborate online to write and submit a one-page group critique.

An open-ended discussion begins, guided by the professor. Students are challenged to present online evidence to support or counter the claims of the presenting or critiquing group. A customized software program, entitled "ICU," enables student laptop screens to be projected instantly onto the overhead screen at the front of the class. The professor's role includes accepting the presentation critiques of the audience teams, which are submitted using ICQ software. These are assessed later.

A SIMULATION OF THE REAL WORLD

But what is it that this training model simulates? Imagine the challenges faced by employees in geographically dispersed virtual teams working to project deadlines. For instance, suppose a team of analysts, working for a major investment bank, is responsible for delivering to clients a report of a major speech given in New York. The analysts are variously based in Los Angeles, Toronto, and London. They view the presentation via Webcast and communicate in real time using ICQ software to gather their thoughts. To assess the relevance and accuracy of the speaker's insights, team members use their own practical and theoretical knowledge, while searching the Internet to verify key points. They then work collaboratively online to create a report on the speech within an hour and distribute it via mass e-mail to clients.

SKILLS

Aside from specific CI-related knowledge, what skills should a student who has completed Web-based CI training in an electronic classroom have acquired? Reasonably, he or she would be expected to conduct laptop-based multimedia presentations, undertake Web-based financial and strategic analysis, work in virtual teams, work comfortably with the standard Microsoft® Office suite of software products, and seamlessly share documents using tools such as IBM Lotus Notes® messaging and collaboration software, ICQ software, or Microsoft® Outlook® messaging and collaboration client.

CHALLENGES

Competitive intelligence is not a new concept. Its military origins are well documented (Chussil, 1996). Its formalization as a topic that can be developed and presented in a training or higher education setting is, however, quite a recent occurrence (Prescott, 1999). Even more recent is the availability to educators and trainers of enabling technologies that allow CI concepts and applications to be delivered in ways that mirror contemporary operating environments. However, providing training in the form of Web-based CI practices has not been without challenges. Several are described in the following paragraphs:

- **Reliability of information sources.** How much of the information available through the World Wide Web is accurate?
- **Discrepancies in information sources.** How should an analyst deal with two or more online sources that offer contradictory data?
- **Capturing and incorporating changes to online information sources, search technologies, and intelligent software agents.** Which search engine or intelligent software agent is ahead this month in its ability to retrieve meaningful and accurate information from the Web?
- **Access to database aggregators such as Factiva or Lexis-Nexis upon completion of the training course.** If the client organization cannot afford a tool, then why use it in the training session?
- **Network connectivity and stability.** Effective Web-based CI training requires stable online connectivity.
- **Ongoing course content development.** One cannot be an island of technology. Trainers must continually monitor the field for discipline-related developments and incorporate them into the teaching environment. Course content will change from session to session as the online world of information changes
- **Complexities of in-class or training room technology.** Real-time e-mail, collaborative software, Webcasting software, presentation software, Internet service providers, and laptops don't always function smoothly despite glossy advertisements. How should they be incorporated into the course offering?
- **Time commitment.** Does the trainer shut off the laptop before or after midnight as he or she seeks to keep pace with changes in Web-based CI?

As technology and pedagogy evolve, so, too, do efforts to overcome these challenges. In the approach used at Acadia University described earlier in the chapter, student feedback was taken seriously, and suggestions for improvements were implemented when feasible. An example of one improvement driven by student feedback was to have the instructor accept in class presentation critiques submitted through ICQ, as opposed to having an assistant accept the material while situated in another location. This allowed online communication interruptions to be addressed immediately.

TEACHING TIPS

These challenges should also suggest the obvious: teaching CI is a skill in itself. In the case of the author, this skill was mastered through learning by doing. What advice might be offered to educators and trainers seeking to make use of a similar teaching environment? A partial list is as follows:

- Develop a level of personal comfort with the educational and communication technologies as course content is being developed.
- Develop a level of personal comfort with the online information sources, Net monitoring software, and database aggregation tools to be used throughout the course.
- In class, walk learners through the use of key online information sources, the Net monitoring software, and the database aggregation programs. Demonstrate their applicability to CI-related concerns.
- Ensure that an in-class technology assistant is available to help trainees overcome technical anxieties or challenges as they may arise.
- Never assume that online information sources will remain static or even available for use. Prior to each training session, review the Web sites or data to be used for instructional purposes.
- Put in place a flexible system to capture, as the course proceeds, learning related to new applications of technology or online information sources.
- Develop a level of personal comfort with in-class failures of technology and Web-based applications.

Using Web CI
to Understand the
Online Music Business:
A Case Example[1]

CONOR VIBERT

Imagine this. You are 42 years old. You have just been named CEO of a Fortune 1000 company. Five thousand employees now refer to you as "Boss." Fifty thousand individuals and entities own stock in your corporation. Thousands of analysts, academics, journalists, and market watchers now care about what you say. Suddenly into your mind pop a number of questions. To whom do you really report? How will your performance be judged? What rules or regulations should guide your behavior? What does success mean in your case? These are issues that many of us might ponder if we were faced with a similar predicament. They are also issues addressed by one explanatory concept discussed earlier—the agency perspective.

This chapter presents an alternative approach for using established managerial thinking when practicing Web CI. Corporate trainers and academics will find it of interest for three reasons. First, we present a case that highlights why CI analysts should explore the use of different explanatory perspectives such as agency theory when seeking to make sense of complex competitive issues. Second, a case example demonstrates how online information can be quickly organized in a coherent fashion to

[1]From "Mixing theory with real time analysis: a look at an online music distributor," by C. Vibert, 2001, *Competitive Intelligence Review* 12(3), pp. 10–20. Copyright 2001 by C. Vibert. Adapted with permission.

effectively argue a point. Third, the information sources used are freely available on the Internet.

Three assumptions underlie this case example. First, the entities under study are publicly traded corporations regulated by the U.S. Securities and Exchange Commission (SEC). Second, these corporations file yearly 10-K Annual Reports and DEF 14A Proxy Statements with the SEC, and these documents are publicly available on the EDGAR database. Third, in this instance, agency theory is useful for illuminating the contractual relationship that links corporate executives to shareholders.

To begin, let's consider agency theory. How might it be explained?

> Using the metaphor of the contract, agency theory addresses the agency issue in which one party (the principal) delegates work to another (the agent), who performs that work. Agency theory is concerned with resolving two problems that can occur in agency relationships. The first is the agency problem that arises when the desires or goals of the principal and agent conflict and when it is difficult or expensive for the principal to verify what the agent is actually doing. The second is the problem of risk sharing that arises when the principal and the agent may prefer different actions because of the different risk preferences. In the corporate world, an agency relationship exists between a firm's outside stockholders and its managers to the extent that stockholders delegate the day-to day management of their investments to those managers. (Jensen & Meckling, 1976)

This relationship can be effective as long as managers make investment decisions that are consistent with stockholders' interests (Jensen & Murphy, 1990). Thus, if stockholders are interested in maximizing the rate of return on their investments in a firm, and if managers make their investment decisions with that objective, then stockholders will have few concerns about delegating the day-to-day management of their investments to managers (Jensen & Meckling, 1976).

Unfortunately, in numerous situations the interests of the firm's outside stockholders and those of its managers do not coincide. From a financial perspective, there are two primary sources of agency costs. The first is when managers decide to take some of a firm's capital and invest it in perquisites that do not add economic value to the firm but directly benefit those managers.

A second source of agency costs is the risk profile of the managers. According to this line of thinking, stockholders lose out when managers are more risk-averse in their decision making than stockholders would prefer them to be. From an organizational view, agents might not adequately pursue the interests of principals for two reasons, termed *moral hazard* and *adverse selection*. Moral hazard refers to a lack of effort on the part of managers. Adverse selection means that agents misrepresented their abilities when hired. So how do theorists respond to these concerns?

Principal-agent theory seeks to determine the optimal or most efficient contract considering varying levels of outcome uncertainty, risk aversion, information, and other factors (Fama, 1980). Essentially, the question asked is whether behavior-oriented contracts (e.g., hierarchical governance) are more efficient than outcome-oriented contracts (e.g., transfer of property rights or market governance).

According to one version of this perspective, principals have either complete or incomplete information regarding agents. When information is complete, principals will make use of behavioral contracts to monitor agents. When information is incomplete, principals must deal with the agency problem because of the fear of opportunistic behavior in the form of moral hazard or adverse selection on the part of agents.

In this situation, principals are thought to have two options for monitoring agents: through hierarchy-related investments in information systems (such as budgeting systems, reporting procedures, boards of directors, or separate layers of management) or through market-related contracts based on the outcomes of the agents' behavior. This latter option in turn serves to transfer risk to the agents. Thus, when seeking to manage worrisome agents, diligent principals or shareholders will seek to match specific contract features to specific information contexts.

MP3.com—A Case for Web-Based CI

How might these ideas be applied? Let's consider the case of MP3.com.

We won't touch a .Com.

How things have changed. In the span of only a few years, the attractiveness of dot-com firms has gone from high to low in the eyes of many an investor and venture capitalist. Gone are the heady days of seemingly perpetual share price increases. They have been replaced by a stone-cold attitude of "show me the profits before I hand over the money." In these days of caution, shareholders and potential investors are far more diligent in their efforts to understand corporate activities and are no longer quite as willing to believe extravagant tales of future prosperity. Increasingly, these stakeholders are returning to tried-and-true protective practices as they seek to make sense of, and assess, complex opportunities.

One useful example of how established thinking can be used by corporate trainers to teach Web-based CI is illustrated in the following case, which highlights the relationship of a chief executive officer with his employer, MP3.com. Excerpts of online information sources are highlighted to demonstrate their role in building an argument for or against the effectiveness of an incumbent executive and how they might be positioned in a case write-up.

PROLOGUE

Where might a case write-up on agency theory begin? This writer suggests a catchy opening paragraph to grab the reader's attention. A good example is a story found on the CNET News.com Web site dated January 28, 2000. In this instance, MP3.com was portrayed as a successful yet controversial company.

The article begins by situating MP3.com in the minds of readers as a David fighting for survival against Goliath. The masses are rooting for David. The author puts a twist on this analogy by suggesting that the music industry may not necessarily be the only villain. Perhaps it is MP3.com that is not playing by the rules. Using quotes from leading industry experts, this article (Macavinta, 2000) convincingly creates a sense of drama for this case by making one important point. While it may have every right to bring the sounds of new and unknown singers and songwriters into the homes of listeners, MP3.com may not be on sound legal ground bringing the same service for more well known artists.

THE COMPANY

Following this introduction, MP3.com itself might be described briefly. One source of useful information is the company Web site. In most instances, an overview of the company can be found on the site itself or in one of its press releases.

In a search conducted May 14, 1999, on the MP3.com Web site, a press release was found containing a one paragraph synopsis of the company. It described the activities of the company, its innovative nature, the forms of technology used, and key suppliers as well as customers. It also described how customers might transact with MP3.com. It offered an approximation of the number of artists or suppliers whose music was available to consumers as well as the number of songs in the MP3.com catalog.

Like many modern corporations, MP3.com touted its business model as advantageous to its future. Details of this operating philosophy were available to CI professionals from MP3.com's SEC filings. Using keywords such as *business model*, we found the 10K Wizard Web site to be extremely useful in digging up information such as this:

> Our unique business model provides the following advantages for artists and consumers:
>
> - creates an easy and convenient way for consumers to listen to, download and purchase music;
> - dramatically lowers costs for artists to promote and distribute their music;
> - enables artists to reach a large number of consumers worldwide;
> - enables consumers to discover local and lesser-known artists in ways they cannot through traditional music retailers; and
> - facilitates direct communication between fans and artists. (MP3.com Form S-1/A, 1999)

THE CANDIDATE

Following the company description and a discussion of its business model, we chose to profile the chief executive officer, highlighting his previous accomplishments and work experience. At the time of our research, one source for this information was MP3.com's most recent DEF 14A Proxy Statement filed with the SEC. An excerpt follows:

> Michael L. Robertson founded MP3.com and has served as our Chief Executive Officer and Chairman of the Board since March 1998. From September 1995 to March 1998,

Mr. Robertson operated several web sites that focused on merging search technologies with commerce. From September 1995 to September 1996, Mr. Robertson was President and Chief Executive Officer of Mounds, Inc., a developer of digital picture software. From January 1994 to August 1995, Mr. Robertson was President and Chief Executive Officer of Muc Software, a developer of networking and security tools. Mr. Robertson received his Bachelor of Arts from the University of North Carolina. (MP3.com Form DEF 14A, 2000)

According to a Hoover's Online Company Capsule (now the Fact Sheet feature), Michael Robertson also owned 37 percent of the outstanding common stock of MP3.com (*Company Capsule for MP3.com*, n.d.).

THE CONTEXT

Next, the operating environment of MP3.com was introduced, highlighting aspects of the industry within which it competes. One source was the Industry Profiles catalog available through WetFeet (*Internet*, n.d.). In which industry did MP3.com compete? A glance at its WetFeet company profile suggested a category.

Which industry is home to MP3.com? One argument is that it belongs in the Internet industry. According to one description of this industry found in late 2000, on the WetFeet Web site (*Internet*, 2000), participants reinvent existing activities. They seek out distinct niches by taking advantage of the Internet's ability to link people, share information, and transact anywhere in the world almost instantly. More specifically, the Profile suggests some of the activities that these firms sought to reinvent. These include the distribution of food and books, information sharing about matters related to personal health, and the online delivery of education.

Along with a basic overview of the industry, the WetFeet Industry Profile also suggested major trends that impacted firms competing in this arena, as well as organizational types.

A Fall 2000 glance at the trends noted on the WetFeet Industry Profile (*Internet*, 2000) suggested insight that was novel at that time. First, Internet companies had a problem. They needed content but did not possess it. Media companies did. Second, for some odd reason, analysts, whose role was to value these companies, were placing more importance on the market capitalization of these firms than their cash positions. Third, traditional incentives such as coupons, sweepstakes, and frequent flier points were now being used to overcome privacy concerns related to Internet usage and entice visits to Web sites.

The industry as defined by WetFeet was broad. MP3.com faced competition from other organizational types, including online publications, aggregators, portals, online communities, and Internet service providers.

THE CONCERN

With a general understanding of the company, its CEO, and its competitive environment, we returned to the idea raised at the beginning of this case example—that MP3.com was a somewhat controversial entity. Aside from news articles like the one cited above, a most obvious place to identify concerns facing shareholders and stakeholders of this young company was its S-1 form and associated amendments. Even leaving aside the section labeled "Risk Factors," a keyword search, again using 10K Wizard and the term *business model*, yielded information on a number of issues that, in hindsight, would worry even the most optimistic of investors. An excerpt from a May 1999 S-1/A filing suggested caution:

> Our model for conducting business and generating revenues is new and unproven. Our business model depends upon our ability to generate revenue streams from multiple sources through our website, including:
>
> – website advertising fees from third parties;
> – online sales of CDs and music-related merchandise;
> – promotional activity fees; and
> – leveraging our aggregated artist and consumer information. (MP3.com Form S-1/A, 1999)

Two months later, excerpts from a 424B4 filing from MP3.com suggested panic:

> It is uncertain whether a music-based website that relies on attracting people to learn about, listen to and download music, mostly from lesser-known artists, can generate sufficient revenues to survive. We cannot assure you that this business model will succeed or will be sustainable as our business grows.

In order for our business to be successful, we must not only develop services that directly generate revenue, but also provide content and services that attract consumers to our website frequently. We will need to develop new offerings as consumer preferences change and new competitors emerge. We cannot assure you that we will be able to provide consumers with an acceptable blend of products, services, and informational and community offerings that will attract consumers to our website frequently. We provide many of our products and services without charge, and we may not be able to generate sufficient revenue to pay for these products and services. Accordingly, we are not certain that our business model will be successful or that we can sustain revenue growth or be profitable. (MP3.com Form 424B4, 1999)

THE CONTRACT

Clearly, shareholders and stakeholders of MP3.com had reason to watch its performance with great attention. With this in mind, how might they have acted to protect their investment? One approach was to structure an employment contract with the CEO in a manner that encouraged this individual to act in their best interests. In this instance, an employment contract was found at the FindLaw Web site.

The employment agreement between Michael Robertson and MP3.com was dated May 13, 1999, and contained a number of points of interest. It listed Mr. Robertson's salary as $150,000 for the years 1999 through 2002 and his eligibility to receive annual bonuses of up to $50,000 per year based on the recommendation of the Board of Directors of MP3.com. It also stated that his salary could be altered as needed and suggested his role in managing the company was subject to the wishes of the Board of Directors and the company bylaws.

Was the contract binding Michael Robertson to MP3.com outcome-based or behaviorally oriented? The open-ended nature of the request in the employment agreement for Mr. Robertson to manage the company as required by the Board of Directors and according to MP3.com's bylaws suggest an outcome-based orientation.

THE COMPARISON

So how does Michael Robertson's compensation stack up to that of his competition?

CEO Compensation

How might one describe the pay of MP3.com's CEO in 1999? The company's April 28, 2000, DEF 14A Proxy Statement suggests that it was quite equitable. A search using the keywords *executive compensation* on 10K Wizard disclosed that, in 1999, Robertson received $158,626 in salary, $148,500 in bonus payments, and $4,850 towards a car lease. This was an increase from a salary of $70,833. Was Robertson's compensation comparable to that of his competition? Using two competitors listed at Hoover's Online as a base, we found that Robertson's compensation compared favorably, as the most directly competing CEO received $162,500 in base salary along with stock options (*Company Capsules for ARTISTdirect, Inc.*, n.d.; *Launch Media, Inc.*, n.d.; *MP3.com*, n.d.).

Corporate Performance

So what does this tell us? MP3.com did not do so well in 1999. It lost $42.5 million on revenues of $22 million. If we think in terms of the competition, however, MP3.com did not do so badly after all. According to Hoover's Online Company Capsules, its two most direct competitors lost $57.8 million and $37.5 million on sales of $10.3 million and $16.6 million, respectively (*Company Capsules for ARTISTdirect, Inc.*, n.d.; *Launch Media, Inc.*, n.d.; *MP3.com*, n.d.). In terms of share price performance (*Stock chart*, n.d.), the results were not outstanding either. From an initial IPO priced above $60 per share, stockholders ended 1999 with shares worth half that amount. This was in line with the performance of MP3.com's major competitor, whose initial price of $35 per share melted away to $20 per share at year-end.

CONCLUSION

How might we interpret these results in light of agency theory? MP3.com shareholders chose to use an outcome-based contract to hire Michael Robertson. During MP3.com's first year as a publicly traded company, its stock lost a significant amount of its value. But Robertson was not overcompensated in terms of salary and benefits. On the contrary, his salary and benefits were quite modest in comparison to those of other CEOs. Robertson did not profit from the decrease in share equity. In fact, as a shareholder himself, holding 37 percent of the company's shares, he too felt its effect. Despite the mixed financial performance, the interests of shareholders actually were fairly well protected.

Michael Robertson appeared to be working in the best interests of shareholders. How credible are the information sources used to make this assessment? Very credible. The bulk of information used to build the case for or against this executive originated with SEC regulatory documents. Sources with more inherent biases, such as company Web sites, independent news stories, and commercial industry overviews, were used primarily to add interest and context.

In conclusion, the advent of the Internet and growth of the World Wide Web have revolutionized the manner by which analysts and CI professionals monitor competitive environments and assess complex business relationships and concerns. This has enabled corporate trainers to continue to play a pivotal role in helping people learn and manage knowledge (Vibert, 2000). Web-based CI has also allowed proponents of powerful, yet traditional, explanatory models such as agency theory to offer further evidence of their relevance and rigor. This chapter has described this perspective and has provided an illustrated case supported by online evidence to help corporate trainers develop the next generation of CI analysts.

15

Conclusion

CONOR VIBERT

In Chapter 12, John Prescott suggests that academic theory can inform the practice of competitive intelligence. Why connect CI with management thought and the Internet? Fleisher and Bensoussan implicitly answer this question as follows:

> The formula for placing CI analysis in context is [that] an understanding of the business situation . . . determines the type of analysis which determines the type of data needed which in turn determines the data collection process. (Fleisher & Bensoussan, 2003, p. 9)

Academic insight—in this instance, organization theory— enhances understanding of business situations. In turn, the Internet offers analysts access to relevant data. Our underlying argument is that researchers, CI practitioners, managers, analysts, academics, and students may combine ideas from current management thought with the resources of the Internet to improve business analysis. Organizational theory offers insight to explain business situations.

How does this book fit in the larger context of competitive intelligence knowledge? We thought to answer this question by exploring issues that are currently being considered by CI writers. We asked the opinions of the editors of two leading CI publications, Bonnie Hohhof and Ian Smith. Each was asked, "What are CI authors writing about these days?" Their thoughts are discussed in the following paragraphs and summarized in Figure 15.1.

Ian Smith is the editor of *Competia Magazine* (*http://www. competia.com*), an online magazine published monthly by Competia.com. When asked about popular writing topics, he suggested the following:

Readers would like easier access to sources of industry-specific information. They seek to bypass the search engines and get to the content. Readers are less concerned with theories behind the analytical tools. They want to know how to apply the tools via templates and step-by-step frameworks. Increasingly prevalent are discussions regarding the tools of the trade that enable the non-CI professional to practice CI to make better business decisions. With budgets being cut, professionals are looking for frameworks to assess their efforts to establish their raison d'être of their units. Finally, software applications are making life easier for professionals to search and track information. (C. Vibert, personal communication with I. Smith, March 25, 2003)

This desire for easier access to information appears to be shared by corporate executives. A March 2003 online survey of North American corporate executives, sponsored by Forbes.com and GartnerG2 (*http://www.forbes.com/fdc/dayinlife.pdf*), suggests that executives have also caught the Internet bug (Forbes.com & GartnerG2, 2003). Surprisingly, they are quite proactive at undertaking their own online research when seeking to understand their operating environments.

Hohhof's thoughts were somewhat different. The editor of *Competitive Intelligence Magazine*, published monthly by SCIP (*http://www.scip.org*), she suggested the following:

There has been an increase in real analysis articles and books. Some of this is due to an increased need for knowledge of how to use and apply analysis. The number of analysts coming out of government and making an impact on companies (either as employees or as consultants) has increased dramatically. The major consulting firms are becoming more serious about CI. One high-profile CI practitioner is now with Deloitte and Touche. Many firms that have spent time and money developing or acquiring knowledge management software have been disappointed. In many cases, these firms are turning to CI as an alternative or a complement to existing systems. (C. Vibert, personal communication with B. Hohhof, March 25, 2003)

The thoughts of Hohhof and Smith present a strong case for *Competitive Intelligence: A Framework for Web-Based Analysis & Decision Making*. This book addresses how theoretical frameworks and knowledge of specific Web site or information portal content can be integrated to support competent analytical efforts to resolve important business concerns. As we explored this subject, two themes were pursued: competitive intelligence in an online world and linking management thought and analysis with an online world.

With respect to the first theme, readers were informed of the role of competitive intelligence, the challenges of online research, the questionable reliability of many online information sources, and strategies for protecting organizations from Web-based CI. Building upon this knowledge, we then turned our attention to the second theme, highlighting the importance of analysis as well as offering an overview of the different perspectives of organization theory.

Subsequently, a number of research missions were set forth. These missions demonstrated the usefulness of contemporary management insight when online information is incorporated. They were followed by a series of case examples. Finally, the link with knowledge management was explored.

Figure 15.1 Writing Trends in CI

	COMPETIA MAGAZINE IAN SMITH	COMPETITIVE INTELLIGENCE MAGAZINE BONNIE HOHHOF
Current Subjects of Interest	• Information sources • Practical side of analysis • Practical side of CI • Measuring CI efforts • Timesaving tools	• Real analysis • Use and application of analysis • Impact of government-trained CI analysts on companies • Acceptance of CI by major consulting firms • Replacement of knowledge management (KM) software by CI software
Changes	• Link to strategy • Influence of end products • Level of analysis • Technology • Availability of information	• Increase in number of CI books • Increase in number of CI courses in graduate programs and continuing education • External information software linked to KM systems • Middle and senior managers' acceptance of Internet and intranets for information retrieval and use

So where is CI headed? If Bonnie Hohhof is right, the future will see far more use of the Internet by executives and much more sophisticated software that integrates internal and externally derived data and insight:

> Software companies, particularly those who in the past have defined "business intelligence" as data warehousing (internal information organization and analysis) are turning their software capabilities to managing external information in conjunction with that internal information for a more "holistic" approach to competitive information. This is not entirely successful as of yet, but the increase in software applications that integrate the two (internal and external) is a strong indication that they see a need or market for such software. A corollary is that companies which have invested all that money in internal information "mining" software, but are not getting the return they wanted, are looking at external information and its integration with internal information as a way to save that investment and to "remain relevant" to decision makers. Finally, middle-level and senior managers are increasingly accepting of technology and the internet/intranet as a vehicle for obtaining information and using it. They are able to make a distinction between information on the internet, and information via the internet. (C. Vibert, personal communication with B. Hohhof, March 25, 2003)

Chapter Notes

Chapter 1 Introduction

Dodge, B. (1999). The WebQuest page. Accessed August 22, 2003, at *http://webquest.sdsu.edu.*

Metayer, E. (1999). Demystifying competitive intelligence. *Ivey Business Journal, 64*(2), 70–74.

Vibert, C. (2000). *Web-based analysis for competitive intelligence.* Westport, CT: Quorum Books.

Vibert, C. (2001). Staying smart: Competitive intelligence isn't just for the high and mighty anymore. *Atlantic Progress, 8*(8), 190–195.

What is CI? (2001). Accessed May 5, 2001, at *http://www.scip.org.*

Chapter 2 A Primer on Competitive Intelligence

Best Practices, LLC. (2002). *Managing the competition: Turning competitive intelligence into strategy.* Chapel Hill, NC: Author.

Blake, K. J. (2002). Targeting for success: How the Michigan Economic Development Corporation targets companies to attract investment. In *Proceedings of Strategic Intelligence & Knowledge Management for Growth and Competitiveness, Competia Public Service Symposium.* Retrieved March 2002 from *http://www.competia.com/symposium/ottawa/home.html.*

Brantford Educational Services. (2001). Understanding search engines. Retrieved March 2002 from *http://www.kerrvance.com/html/lesson36.htm.*

Campbell, D. (2002). Estimate made from review of online newspapers at *http://www.onlinenewspapers.com.* Unpublished raw data.

Cappel, J. J., & Boone, J. P. (1995). A look at the link between competitive intelligence and performance. *Competitive Intelligence Review, 6*(2), 15–23.

Corporate CI "eagles." (1998, January). *Competitive Intelligence Magazine.* Retrieved March 2002 from *http://www.scip.org.*

F-H expands competitive intelligence offering via alliance. (2001, November 14). *The Holmes Report.* Retrieved November 2001 from *http://www.holmesreport.com.*

Fuld & Company. (2000). *Intelligence software report 2000.* Retrieved March 2002 from *http://www.fuld.com.*

Fuller, M. B. (1993). Business as war. *Fast Company, 1*(1), 44–50.

Google's total indexed sites. (2001, April 12). Retrieved March 2002 from *http://www.fuld.com/softwareguidetest.*

The laws that govern the securities industry. (2003, June 27). Retrieved July 30, 2003, from *http://www.sec.gov.*

Membership survey, Society of Competitive Intelligence Professionals. (2001). Retrieved March 2002 from *http://www.scip.org.*

Miller, S. (2001). Competitive intelligence: An overview. Society of Competitive Intelligence Professionals. Retrieved May 8, 2001, from *http://www.scip.org.*

Monitor Company/Decision Architects. (1998). *Monitor Company/Decision Architects: Competitive simulation white paper.* Retrieved May 10, 2001, from *http://www.decisionarc.com/cs_wpaper.PDF.*

Outsell, Inc. (2001, September 7). *Information About Information Briefing, 4*(40). Burlingame, CA: Author.

P&G brushes with infamy in spy case. (2001, November 2). *Brand Strategy.* Retrieved March 2002 from *http://www.hoovers.com.*

Peters, T. (1986). Getting to know your competitor. Retrieved March 2002 from *http://www.tompeters.com.*

SCIP code of ethics for CI professionals. (2002). Retrieved March 2002 from *http://www.scip.org.*

Search engine watch. Retrieved March 2002 from *http://www.searchenginewatch.com.*

ShiftCentral Inc. (2002). Retrieved March 2002 from *http://www.shiftcentral.com.*

Vibert, C. (2000). *Web-based analysis for competitive intelligence.* Westport, CT: Quorum Books.

What is CI? (2003). Retrieved August 25, 2003, from *http://www.scip.org.*

Chapter 3 Strategically Searching the Web

Bergman, M. K. (2000). *The deep Web: surfacing hidden value.* Retrieved August 22, 2003, from *http://www.brightplanet.com/technology/deepweb.asp.*

Brethour, P. (2001, March). Bill comes due for Web freebies. *The Globe and Mail,* B1–B4.

Bushko, D. (2001). The metatag edge: Hidden tools for cyber-marketing. *Consulting to Management, 12*(3), 4–5.

FAQ. (2003). Accessed September 4, 2003, at *http://vivisimo.com/faq/Overview.html.*

George, W. (1999, August 23). Piracy against Apple: It's a cultural thing. *The Mac Observer.* Retrieved March 2002 from *www.macobserver.com/columns/appletrader.*

Green, D. (2000). The evolution of web searching. *Online Information Review, 242,* 124–137.

Harris, G. (2001). Find articles online. *Information Highways, 86,* 27.

Hock, R., & Berinstein, P. (1999). *The extreme searcher's guide to Web search engines: A handbook for the serious searcher.* Medford, NJ: Information Today Inc.

Kassel, A. (1999). NTIS on the Web: Northern Light versus Dialog et al. *Searcher: The Magazine for Database Professionals, 78,* 10–18.

Kassler, H. (2000). CI on the Internet: Going for the gold. *Information Outlook, 42, 37–42.*

Kiernan, V. (1999). Open Archives Project promises alternative to costly journals. *The Chronicle of Higher Education, 46*(15), A43–A44.

Lanza, S. R. (2001). The end of an era: Online world 2000. *Searcher, 9*(1), 18–22.

McGonagle, J., & Vella, C. (1999). *The Internet age of competitive intelligence.* Westport, CT: Quorum Books.

Notess, G. (1999). Search engines in the Internet age. *Online, 233,* 20–22.

Novack, D. (2001). Web sites hidden from view. *Link-Up, 185,* 26–27.

Price, G. (2002, June 26 update). Direct Search. Accessed August 21, 2003, at *http://www.freepint.com/gary/direct.htm.*

Sherman, C. (1999). The future of web search. *Online, 233,* 54–61.

Sherman, C. (2001a, July 11). Power searching with SurfWax. *Search Day,* 48, 1–5. Retrieved August 25, 2003, from *http://www.searchenginewatch.com/searchday.*

Sherman, C. (2001b, August 27). Keeping up with search engine patents. *Search Day,* 27, 1–2. Retrieved August 25, 2003, from *http://www.searchenginewatch.com/searchday.*

Sherman, C. (2001c, October 31). Google unveils more of the invisible web. *Search Day,* 128, 1–6. Retrieved August 25, 2003, from *http://www.searchenginewatch.com/searchday.*

Sullivan, D. (2001a, October 2). Google may get personal. *Search Engine Report,* 591, 1–2. Retrieved August 25, 2003, from *http://www.searchenginewatch.com/sereport.*

Sullivan, D. (2001b, November 5). Is AltaVista's stale index the last blow? *Search Engine Report, 602,* 1–13. Retrieved August 25, 2003, from *http://www.searchenginewatch.com/sereport.*

Weiss, A. (2001). Knowledge counts in large amounts. *Information World Review, 168,* 14–15.

Zelnick, N. (2000). The post-spider world: Developing peer-to-peer and metadata alternatives to spidering. *Internet World 72,* 1.

Chapter 4 Differentiating Good Online Information From Bad

Anhang, A., & Coffman, S. (2002). The great reference debate. *American Libraries, 33*(3), 50–54.

Berland, G. K., Elliott, M. N., Morales, L. S., Algazy, J. I., Kravitz, R. L., Broder, M. S., Kanouse, D. E., et al. (2001). Health information on the Internet: Accessibility, quality, and readability in English and Spanish. *JAMA, 285*(20), 2612–2621.

Fogg, B. J., Swani, P., Treinen, M., Marshall, J., Laraki, O., Ospipovich, A., et al. (2001). What makes Web sites credible? A report on a large quantitative study. *Proceedings of the SIGCHI conference on human factors in computing systems* (pp. 61–68). New York: ACM Press.

McLellan, F. (2001). 1996 and all that—When is a literature search done? *The Lancet, 358*(9282), 646–647.

Quist, D., & Chapela, I. H. (2001). Transgenic DNA introgressed into traditional maize landraces in Oaxaca, Mexico. *Nature, 414*(6863), 541–543.

Chapter 5 Protecting Your Company From Web-Based Competitive Intelligence

Kassel, A. (2001). *Super searchers on Wall Street: Top investment professionals share their online research secrets.* Medford, NJ: Cyber-Age Books.

Lang, E. A., & Tudor, J. D. (2001). *Best Websites for financial professionals, business appraisers, and accountants.* New York: John Wiley & Sons.

McGonagle, J. J., & Vella, C. M. (1998). *Protecting your company against competitive intelligence.* Westport, CT: Greenwood Group.

McGonagle, J. J., & Vella, C. M. (1999). *The Internet age of competitive intelligence.* Westport, CT: Greenwood Group.

Silverman, R. E. (2002). Internet recruiters' tricks of the trade: A how-to manual for headhunting online. Retrieved March 2002 from *http://www.careerjournal.com/recruiters.*

Vella, C. M., & McGonagle, J. J. (2000). Profiling in competitive analysis. *Competitive Intelligence Review, 11*(2), 20–30.

Vibert, C. (2000). *Web-based analysis for competitive intelligence.* Westport, CT: Quorum Books.

Weiss, A., & England, S. (2000, June 22). Internet intelligence— Analysing web-sites for competitive intelligence. *Free Pint,* 65. Retrieved March 2002 from *http://www.freepint.com/issues.*

Chapter 6 Analysis: Why It Is Important

American Productivity & Quality Center (2000). *Developing a successful CI program: Enabling action, realizing results.* Houston, TX: Author.

Cartwright, R. (2001). *Mastering the business environment.* Hampshire, UK: Palgrave.

Commission on the Roles and Capabilities of the United States Intelligence Community. (1996, March 1). *Preparing for the 21st century: An appraisal of U.S. intelligence.* Retrieved August 22, 2003, from *http://www.fas.org/irp/offdocs/report.html.*

Fahey, L. (1999). *Outwitting, outmaneuvering and outperforming competitors.* New York: John Wiley & Sons.

Fleisher, C. (2001). Analysis in CI: Process, progress and pitfalls. In C. Fleisher & D. Blenkhorn, *Managing frontiers in competitive intelligence.* Westport, CT: Quorum Books, 77–89.

Fleisher, C. S., & Bensoussan, B. (2002). *Strategic and competitive analysis: Methods and techniques for analyzing business competition.* Upper Saddle River, NJ: Prentice Hall.

Gannon, J. (1996, November 18). *Intelligence analysis for the 21st century.* Excerpt from address delivered to the Fletcher School at Tufts University, Medford, MA.

Gilad, B. (1998). What is intelligence analysis? Part II. *Competitive Intelligence Magazine, 13,* 29–31.

Godson, R. (1987). Intelligence: An American view. In K. Robertson (Ed.), *British and American approaches to intelligence* (p. 19). London: Macmillan Press for Royal United Services Institute.

Herring, J. (1999). Key intelligence topics: A process to identify and define intelligence needs. *Competitive Intelligence Review, 102,* 4–14.

Lackman, C., Saban, K., & Lanasa, J. (2000). Organizing the competitive intelligence function: A benchmarking study. *Competitive Intelligence Review, 111,* 17–27.

Langley, A. (1995). Between paralysis by analysis and extinction by instinct. *Sloan Management Review, 363,* 63–76.

Prescott, J., Herring, J., & Panefly, P. (1998). Leveraging information for action: A look into the Competitive and Business Intelligence Consortium benchmarking study. *Competitive Intelligence Review, 91,* 4–12.

Vibert, C. (2001). Leveraging technology: CI in an electronic classroom teaching environment. *Competitive Intelligence Review, 12*(1), 48–58.

Werther, G. (2001). Building an "analysis age" for competitive intelligence in the 21st century. *Competitive Intelligence Review, 121,* 41–47.

Chapter 7 Management Thought: The Connection With CI

Barney, J. B. (1991). Firm resources and sustained competitive advantage. *Journal of Management, 17,* 99–120.

Fleisher, C. S. (2003). Are competitive intelligence practitioners professionals? In C. S. Fleisher & D. L. Blenkhorn (Eds.), *Controversies in competitive intelligence: The enduring issues* (pp. 29–44). Westport, CT: Praeger.

Fleisher, C. S., & Bensoussan, B. (2003). *Strategic and competitive analysis: Methods and techniques for analyzing business competition.* Upper Saddle River, NJ: Prentice Hall.

Gergen, K. J. (1985). The social constructionist movement in modern psychology. *American Psychologist, 40*(3), 266–275.

Gilad, B., & Herring, J. P. (2001). CI certification: Do we need it? *Competitive Intelligence Review, 4*(2), 28–31.

Gioia, D. A., & Pitre, E. (1990). Multiparadigm perspectives on theory building. *Academy of Management Review 15*(4), 584–602.

Grant, R. M. (1996). Toward a knowledge-based theory of the firm. *Strategic Management Journal, 17,* 109–122.

Hall, R. H. (1996). *Organizations: Structures, processes and outcomes.* Englewood Cliffs, NJ: Prentice Hall.

Kuhn, T. (1962). *The structure of scientific revolutions.* Chicago: University of Chicago Press.

Langley, A. (1995). Between paralysis by analysis and extinction by instinct. *Sloan Management Review, 36*(3), 63–76.

Machlup, F. (1980). *Knowledge: Its creation, distribution and economic significance: Vol. 1.* Princeton, NJ: Princeton University Press.

Prescott, J. E. (1999). Debunking the "academic abstinence" myth of competitive intelligence. *Competitive Intelligence Review, 2*(4), 22–27.

Prescott, J. E., & the Society of Competitive Intelligence Professionals. (2000). *Developing a successful competitive intelligence program: Enabling action, realizing results.* Consortium Benchmarking Study, Best Practices Report, Executive Summary, American Productivity & Quality Center. Houston, TX: American Productivity & Quality Center.

Smith, M. J. (1998). *Social science in question.* London: SAGE Publications.

Vibert, C. (2001). Staying smart: Competitive intelligence isn't just for the high and mighty anymore. *Atlantic Progress, 8*(8), 190–195.

Vibert, C. (2003). Why should theory matter to competitive intelligence practitioners? In C. S. Fleisher & D. L. Blenkhorn (Eds.), *Controversies in competitive intelligence: The enduring issues* (pp. 133–144). Westport, CT: Praeger.

Windle, G. (2003). How can competitive intelligence practitioners avoid relying on the Internet? In C. S. Fleisher & D. L. Blenkhorn (Eds.), *Controversies in competitive intelligence: The enduring issues* (pp. 85–97). Westport, CT: Praeger.

Chapter 8 Management Thought: Ideas That Can Improve CI

Bain, J. S. (1968). *Industrial organization.* New York: John Wiley & Sons.

Barney, J. (1996). *Gaining and sustaining competitive advantage.* Reading, MA: Addison-Wesley.

Chandler, A. (1962). *Strategy and structure.* Cambridge, MA: The MIT Press.

Child, J. (1972). Organization structure, environment, and performance: The role of strategic choice. *Sociology, 6,* 1–22.

Clegg, S. (1990). *Modern organizations.* London: SAGE Publications.

Clegg, S. R. (1992). Postmodern management. *Journal of Organizational Change Management, 52,* 31–49.

Conner, K. R. (1991). A historical comparison of resource based theory and five schools of thought within industrial organization economics: Do we have a new theory of the firm? *Journal of Management, 17,* 121–154.

Cooper, R., & Burrell, G. (1988). Modernism, postmodernism and organizational analysis: An introduction. *Organization Studies, 91,* 91–112.

Cyert, R. M., & March, J. G. (1963). *A behavioral theory of the firm.* Englewood Cliffs, NJ: Prentice Hall.

Donaldson, L. (1995). *American anti-management theories of organization: A critique of paradigm proliferation.* Cambridge: Cambridge University Press.

Eisenhardt, K. (1989). Agency theory: An assessment and review. *Academy of Management Review, 14,* 57–74.

Freeman, R. E. (1984). *Strategic management: A stakeholder approach.* Boston: Pitman.

Gergen, K. J. (1991). Organization theory in the postmodern era. In M. Reed & M. Hughes (Eds.), *New directions in organization theory and analysis* (pp. 207–226). London: SAGE Publications.

Grant, R. M. (1996). Toward a knowledge-based theory of the firm. *Strategic Management Journal, 17,* 109–122.

Hannan, M. T., & Freeman, J. H. (1976). The population ecology of organizations. *American Journal of Sociology, 82,* 929–964.

Hannan, M. T., & Freeman, J. H. (1984). Structural inertia and organizational change. *American Sociological Review, 49,* 149–164.

Hart. S. (1995). A natural resource-based view of the firm. *Academy of Management Review, 204,* 996–1014.

Helms Mills, J. C., & Mills, A. J. (2000). Rules, sensemaking, formative contexts and discourse in the gendering of organizational culture. In N. Ashkanasy, C. Wilderom, & M. Peterson (Eds.), *Handbook of organizational climate and culture* (55–70). Thousand Oaks, CA: SAGE Publications.

Hinings, C. R., & Greenwood, R. (1988). *The dynamics of strategic change.* New York: Basil Blackwell.

Jensen, M. C., & Meckling, W. H. (1976, October). Theory of the firm: Managerial behavior, agency costs and ownership structure. *Journal of Financial Economics, 3,* 305–360.

Jones, G. R. (1995). *Organizational theory: Text and cases.* Reading, MA: Addison-Wesley.

Jones, T. M. (1995). Instrumental stakeholder theory: A synthesis of ethics and economics. *Academy of Management Review, 202,* 404–437.

Kogut, B., & Zander, U. (1992). Knowledge of the firm, combinative capabilities and the replication of technology. *Organization Studies, 3,* 383–397.

Levy, D. (1994). Chaos theory and strategy: Theory, application and managerial implications. *Strategic Management Journal, 15,* 167–178.

Lorenz, M. (1963). Deterministic non-periodic flow. *Journal of the Atmospheric Sciences, 20,* 130–141.

Mason, E. S. (1939). Price and production policies of large-scale enterprises. *American Economic Review, 29,* 61–74.

Miles, R. E., & Snow, C. C. (1978). *Organizational structure, strategy and process.* New York: McGraw-Hill.

Miller, D. (1986). Configurations of strategy and structure. *Strategic Management Journal, 7,* 233–249.

Miller D., & Friesen, P. H. (1978). Archetypes of strategy formulation. *Management Science, 24,* 921–933.

Mills, A. J., & Murgatroyd, S. J. (1991). *Organizational rules: A framework for understanding organizations.* Milton Keynes, UK: Open University Press.

Mintzberg, H. (1979). *The structuring of organizations.* Englewood Cliffs, NJ: Prentice Hall.

Montagna, P. (1992). *Post modernism and the management of large professional service firms.* Paper presented at the Conference on Professional Service Firms, University of Alberta, Edmonton, Alberta, Canada.

Nelson R. R., & Winter, S. G. (1982). *An evolutionary theory of economic change.* Cambridge, MA: Harvard University Press.

Oliver, C. (1997). Sustainable competitive advantage: Combining institutional and resource-based views. *Strategic Management Journal, 18*(9), 697–713.

Parker, M. (1992). Post-modern organization or post-modern organization theory? *Organization Studies, 131,* 1–17.

Pettigrew, A. M., & Fenton, E. M. (2000). *The innovating organization.* London: SAGE Publications.

Pfeffer, J. (1982). *Organizations and organization theory.* Chicago: Pitman.

Pfeffer, J., & Salancik, G. R. (1978). *The external control of organizations: A resource dependence perspective.* Chicago: Harper and Row.

Porter, M. E. (1980). *Competitive Strategy.* New York: Free Press.

Powell, W. W., & Dimaggio, P. J. (1991). *The new institutionalism in organizational analysis.* Chicago: University of Chicago Press.

Schreyogg, G. (1980). Contingency and choice in organization. *Organization Studies, 4,* 304–326.

Spender, J. C., & Grant, R. M. (1996). Knowledge and the firm. *Strategic Management Journal, 17,* 5–9.

Stigler, G. J. (1957). Perfect competition, historically contemplated. *Journal of Political Economy, 65,* 1–17.

Stigler, G. J. (1961). The economics of information. *Journal of Political Economy, 69*(3), 213–225.

Tawney, R. H. (1958). Foreword. In M. Weber, *The Protestant work ethic and the spirit of capitalism* (T. Parsons, Trans.). New York: Scribner's and Sons.

Teece, D. J. (1985). Economic analysis and strategic management. In J. M. Pennings (Ed.), *Organizational strategy and change* (pp. 45–64). San Francisco: Jossey-Bass.

Thietart, R. A., & Forgues, B. (1995). Chaos theory and organization. *Organization Science, 6,* 19–31.

Weber, M. (1947). *The theories of social and economic organizations* (A. M. Henderson & T. Parsons, Trans.). New York: Free Press.

Chapter 9 Web-Based Research Missions: Incorporating the Internet Into Analysis

Bain, J. S. (1956). *Barriers to competition.* Cambridge, MA: Harvard University Press.

Chandler, A. (1962). *Strategy and structure.* Cambridge, MA: The MIT Press.

Child, J. (1972). Organization structure, environment and performance: The role of strategic choice. *Sociology, 6,* 1–22.

Cohen, M. D., March, J. G., & Olsen, J. P. (1972). A garbage can model of organizational choice. *Administrative Science Quarterly 17*(1), 1–25.

Dodge, B. (1999). The WebQuest page. Accessed August 22, 2003, at *http://webquest.sdsu.edu.*

Donaldson, T., & Preston, L. E. (1995). The stakeholder theory of the corporation: Concepts, evidence and implications. *Academy of Management Review, 20*(1), 65–91.

Eisenhardt, K. (1989). Agency theory: An assessment and review. *Academy of Management Review, 14,* 57–74.

Gilad, B., & Herring, J. P. (2001). CI certification: Do we need it? *Competitive Intelligence Review, 4*(2), 28–31.

Hannan, M. T., & Freeman, J. H. (1976). The population ecology of organizations. *American Journal of Sociology, 82,* 929–964.

Hickson, D. J., Hinings, C. R., Lee, C. A., Schneck, R. E., & Pennings, J. M. (1971). A strategic contingencies theory of intra-organizational power. *Administrative Science Quarterly, 16*(2), 216–229.

Jensen, M. C., & Meckling, W. H. (1976). Theory of the firm: Managerial behavior, agency costs and ownership structure. *Journal of Financial Economics, 3,* 305–360.

Liebeskind, J. P. (1996). Knowledge, strategy and the theory of the firm. *Strategic Management Journal, 17,* 93–107.

Marx, K. (1859). *Contribution to a critique of political economy.* Moscow: Progress Publishers.

Morgan, G. (1980). Paradigms, metaphors and puzzle solving in organizational theory. *Administrative Science Quarterly, 25,* 605–622.

Novack, D. (2001). Web sites hidden from view. *Link-Up, 185,* 26–27.

Pfeffer, J. (1982). *Organizations and organization theory.* Chicago: Pitman.

Pfeffer, J., and Salancik, G. R. (1978). *The external control of organizations: A resource dependence perspective.* Chicago: Harper & Row.

Porter, M. E. (2001, March). Strategy and the Internet. *Harvard Business Review, 79*(3), 63–78.

Price, G. (2002, June 26 update). Direct Search. Accessed August 21, 2003, at *http://www.freepint.com/gary/direct.htm.*

Strebel, P. (1992). *Breakpoints: How managers exploit radical business change.* Cambridge, MA: Harvard Business School Press.

Suchman, M. C. (1995). Managing legitimacy: Strategic and institutional approaches. *Academy of Management Review, 20*(3), 571–610.

Teece, D. J. (1985). Economic analysis and strategic management. In J. M. Pennings (Ed.), *Organizational strategy and change.* San Francisco: Jossey-Bass.

Vibert, C. (2000a). Real time business analysis: How CI practitioners can assess internal competitor power structures. *Competitive Intelligence Review, 11*(1), 28–36.

Vibert, C. (2000b). *Web-based analysis for competitive intelligence.* Westport, CT: Quorum Books.

Vibert C. (2001). Mixing theory with real time analysis: A look at an online music distributor. *Competitive Intelligence Review, 12*(3), 10–20.

Vibert, C. (2003). Why should theory matter to competitive intelligence practitioners? In C. S. Fleisher & D. L. Blenkhorn (Eds.), *Controversies in competitive intelligence: The enduring issues* (pp. 133–144). Westport, CT: Praeger.

Williamson, O. E. (1976). *Markets and hierarchies: Analysis and anti trust implications.* New York: The Free Press.

Chapter 10 Analysis: Web-Enhanced Case Studies in Real Time

AOL Time Warner Form DEF 14A. (2001 filing). U.S. Securities and Exchange Commission. Retrieved February 2002 from *http://www.sec.gov.*

Company capsule for ARTISTdirect, Inc. (n.d.). Retrieved November 20, 2000, from *http://www.hoovers.com.*

Company capsule for Launch Media, Inc. (n.d.). Retrieved November 20, 2000, from *http://www.hoovers.com.*

Company capsule for MP3.com. (n.d.). Retrieved November 20, 2000, from *http://www.hoovers.com.*

Company capsule for The Walt Disney Company. (2002). Retrieved February 2002 from *http://www.hoovers.com.*

Company capsule: "Media" Industry Snapshot. (2002). Retrieved February 2002 from *http://www.hoovers.com.*

Echostar chided by FCC, settles with Disney. (2002, April 5). *Denver Business Journal.* Retrieved September 4, 2003, from *http://denver.bizjournals.com/denver/.*

Employment agreement by and between MP3.com and Michael L. Robertson. (1999, May 13). Retrieved November 20, 2000, from *http://www. findlaw.com.*

Fox Family Network Form S-1. (1998 filing). U.S Securities and Exchange Commission. Retrieved February 2002 from *http://www.sec.gov.*

InfoSpace, Inc., Form S-1. (2001 filing). U.S Securities and Exchange Commission. Retrieved February 2002 from *http://www.sec.gov.*

MP3.com Form DEF 14A. (2000, April 28 filing). U.S. Securities and Exchange Commission. Retrieved July 2000 from *http://www.sec.gov.*

MP3.com Form 424B4. (1999, June 21, filing). U.S. Securities and Exchange Commission. Retrieved July 2000 from *http://www.10kwizard.com.*

MP3.com Form S-1/A. (1999, May 24 filing). U.S. Securities and Exchange Commission. Retrieved May 5, 2001, from *http://www.10kwizard.com.*

Multimedia industry. (n.d.). Retrieved February 2002 from *http://www.competia.com/express.*

Stock chart for MP3.com and competitors. (n.d.). Retrieved November 20, 2000, from *http://www.bigcharts.com.*

Viacom Inc. Form DEF 14A. (2001 filing). U.S Securities and Exchange Commission. Retrieved February 2002 from *http://www.sec.gov.*

Vibert, C. (2001). Mixing theory with real time analysis: A look at an online music distributor. *Competitive Intelligence Review,* *12*(3), 10–20.

Wagner, H. J. (2002, January 25). Disney pooh-poohs family's claim. Retrieved March 15, 2002, from *http://www.hive4media.com.*

The Walt Disney Company Form DEF 14A. (2001 filing). U.S. Securities and Exchange Commission. Retrieved February 2002 from *http://www.sec.gov.*

Weinstein, H. (2002, February 21). Studios may have the most to lose. *Los Angeles Times.* Retrieved March 15, 2002, from *http://www.latimes.com.*

Yahoo! Form 10-K. (2000 filing). U.S. Securities and Exchange Commission. Retrieved February 2002 from *http://www.sec.gov.*

Chapter 11 The Knowledge Management Cycle

Davenport, T., & Prusak, L. (2000). *Working knowledge: How organizations manage what they know.* Cambridge, MA: Harvard Business School Press.

Finin, T., & Wiederhold, G. (1993). An overview of KQML: A knowledge query and manipulation language. Department of Computer Science, Stanford University.

Malhotra, Y. (2000). Knowledge management for e-business performance: Advancing information strategy to Internet time. *Executive's Journal, 16*(4), 5–16.

Manasco, B. (2001). The knowledge imperative: Leverage it or lose it. *Knowledge Inc.* Retrieved August 20, 2003, from *http://www.webcom.com/quantera/empires5.html.*

Maturana, H., & Varela, F. (1980). *Autopoeisis and cognition: The realization of the living.* London: Riedl.

Newell, A. (1982). The knowledge level. *Artificial Intelligence, 18,* 87–127.

Saint-Onge, H. (1996). Tacit knowledge: The key to the strategic alignment of intellectual capital. *Strategy and Leadership, 24*(2), 10–14.

Schrage, M. (2000, July/August). The things about management that will never change. *Across the Board, 37*(7), 67–69.

Sveiby, K. (1997). *The new organizational wealth: Managing and measuring knowledge-based assets.* San Francisco: Berrett-Koehler.

Sveiby, K. E. (2000, April). *A knowledge-based theory of the firm to guide strategy formulation.* Paper presented at the ANZAM Conference, Macquarie University, Sydney.

Sveiby, K. E. (2001). A knowledge-based theory of the firm to guide in strategy formulation. *Journal of Intellectual Capital, 2*(4), 344–358.

Thorp, J. (1998). *The information paradox: Realizing the business benefits of information technology.* Toronto: McGraw-Hill Ryerson.

Chapter 12 The Role of CI in Academia

Dubin, R. (1978). *Theory building.* New York: The Free Press.

Johnson, P., & Duberley, J. (2000). *Understanding management research: An introduction to epistemology.* Thousand Oaks, CA: SAGE Publications.

Prescott, J. E. (1999). Debunking the "academic abstinence" myth of competitive intelligence. *Competitive Intelligence Review, 2*(4), 22–27.

Chapter 13 CI Corporate Training Ideas From the Classroom

Chussil, M. J. (1996). Competitive intelligence goes to war: CI, the War College, and competitive success. *Competitive Intelligence Review, 7*(3), 1–7.

Follows, S. (1999). Virtual learning environments. *Technological Horizons in Education Journal, 27*(4), 100–106.

Merrit, C. (1999, October–December). Competitive intelligence and the higher education dilemma. *Competitive Intelligence Magazine, 2*(4), 19–21.

Prescott, J. E. (1999). Debunking the "academic abstinence" myth of competitive intelligence. *Competitive Intelligence Review, 2*(4), 22–27.

Saul, J. R. (1994). *The doubter's companion: A dictionary of aggressive common sense.* Toronto: Viking Penguin.

Vibert, C. (2000). *Web-based analysis for competitive intelligence.* Westport, CT: Quorum Books.

Chapter 14 Using Web CI to Understand the Online Music Business: A Case Example

Company capsule for ARTISTdirect, Inc. (n.d.). Retrieved November 20, 2000, from *http://www.hoovers.com.*

Company capsule for Launch Media, Inc. (n.d.). Retrieved November 20, 2000, from *http://www.hoovers.com.*

Company capsule for MP3.com. (n.d.). Retrieved November 20, 2000, from *http://www.hoovers.com.*

Employment agreement by and between MP3.com and Michael L. Robertson. (1999, May 13). Retrieved November 20, 2000, from *http://www.findlaw.com.*

Fama, E. (1980). Agency problems and the theory of the firm. *Journal of Political Economy, 88*(21), 288–307.

Internet and new media: Industry overview. (n.d.). Retrieved November 20, 2000, from *http://www.wetfeet.com.*

Jensen, M. C., & Meckling, W. H. (1976, October). Theory of the firm: Managerial behavior, agency costs and ownership structure. *Journal of Financial Economics, 3,* 305–360.

Jensen, M. C., & Murphy, K. J. (1990, May–June). CEO incentives—It's not how much you pay, but how. *Harvard Business Review, 3,* 138–153.

Macavinta, C. (2000, January 28). MP3.com's move to copy CDs stirs debate. CNET News.com. Retrieved August 21, 2003, from *http://news.com.com.*

MP3.com Form DEF 14A. (2000, April 28 filing). U.S. Securities and Exchange Commission. Retrieved July 2000 from *http://www.sec.gov.*

MP3.com Form 424B4. (1999, July 21 filing). U.S. Securities and Exchange Commission. Retrieved July 2000 from *http://www.10kwizard.com.*

MP3.com Form S-1/A. (1999, May 24 filing). U.S. Securities and Exchange Commission. Retrieved May 5, 2001, from *http://www.10kwizard.com.*

MP3.com, Inc. (1999, May 14). MP3.com, Inc. announces filing of registration statement with SEC for initial public offering of common stock [Press release]. Retrieved August 21, 2003, from *http://www.mp3.com.*

Stock chart for MP3.com and competitors. (n.d.). Retrieved November 20, 2000, from *http://www.bigcharts.com.*

Vibert, C. (2000). *Web-based analysis for competitive intelligence.* Westport, CT: Quorum Books.

Chapter 15 Conclusion

Fleisher, C. S., & Bensoussan, B. (2003). *Strategic and competitive analysis: Methods and techniques for analyzing business competition.* Upper Saddle River, NJ: Prentice Hall.

Forbes.com & GartnerG2. (2003, March). *Forbes.com research studies on C-level executives.* Retrieved September 26, 2003, from *http://www.forbes.com/fdc/dayinlife.pdf.*

Recommended Readings

Aldrich, H. (1979). *Organizations and environments.* Englewood Cliffs, NJ: Prentice Hall.

Alvesson, M. (1985). A critical framework of organizational studies. *Organizational Studies, 6*(2), 117–138.

Alvesson, M., & Berg, P. O. (1992). *Corporate culture and organizational symbolism.* Berlin/New York: de Gruyter.

Ansoff, H. I. (1984). *Implanting strategic management.* Englewood Cliffs, NJ: Prentice Hall International.

Ashkenas, R., Ulrich, D., Jick, T., & Kerr, S. (1995). *The boundaryless organization: Breaking the chains of organizational structure.* San Francisco: Jossey Bass.

Axelrod, R. (1987). *The evolution of cooperation.* New York: Penguin Books.

Babel Fish Translation. (n.d.). Accessed September 27, 2003, at *http://babelfish.altavista.com.*

Barney, J. (1986). Types of competition and the theory of strategy. Toward an integrative framework. *Academy of Management Review, 11,* 791–800.

Bacharach, S. B. (1989). Organizational theories: Some criteria for evaluation. *Academy of Management Review, 14*(4), 496–515.

Becker, G. S. (1964). *Human capital.* New York: Columbia.

Block, M. (2002). Gullible's travels. *Library Journal Net Connect, 127*(7), 12–14.

Calof, J. (1997). For king and country and company. *Business Quarterly, 61*(3), 32–39.

Campbell, A., Goold, M., & Alexander, M. (1995). The value of the parent company. *California Management Review, 38*(1), 79–97.

Caves, R. (1982). *Economic analysis and multinational enterprises.* Cambridge, UK: Cambridge University Press.

Chadwick, K., Franz, D., & Laverty, B. (2001, May). Assessing the reliability of information obtained through the Internet. *The CPA Journal,* 54–57.

Clegg, S. (1975). *Power, rule and domination.* London: Routledge and Kegan Paul.

Collis, D. J., & Montgomery, C. (1995). Competing on resources: Strategy in the 1990s. *Harvard Business Review, 73*(4), 118–128.

Commons, J. R. (1950). *The economics of collective action.* New York: MacMillan.

Company capsule for AOL Time Warner. (2002). Retrieved February 2002 from *http://www.hoovers.com.*

Company capsule for Viacom Inc. (2002). Retrieved February 2002 from *http://www.hoovers.com.*

Conner, K. R. (1991). A historical comparison of resource based theory and five schools of thought within industrial organizational economics: Do we have a new theory of the firm? *Journal of Management, 17,* 121–154.

Copeland, T., Koller, T., & Murrin, J. (1990). *Valuation: Measuring and managing the value of companies.* New York: John Wiley and Sons.

Cvitkovic, E. (1989, May–June). Profiling your competitors. *Planning Review,* 28–30.

Dance, S. X. (1967). *Human communications.* New York: Holt, Rinehart and Winston

Day, G., & Reibstein, D. (1997). *Wharton on dynamic competitive strategy.* New York: John Wiley and Sons.

Day, G. S., & Shoemaker, P. (Eds.). (2000). *Wharton on managing emerging technologies.* New York: John Wiley and Sons Ltd.

Dewitt, M. (1997). *Competitive intelligence: Competitive advantage.* Grand Rapids, MI: Abacus.

Doty, D. H., Glick, W. H., & Huber, G. P. (1993, December). Fit, equifinality, and organizational effectiveness: A test of two configurational theories. *Academy of Management Journal, 36*(6), 1196–1250.

Dublin Core Metadata Initiative. (2001). Accessed March 2002 at *http://dublincore.org.*

Dunphy, D., & Stace, D. (1994). *Beyond the boundaries.* Sydney: John Wiley and Sons.

Economic Espionage Act of 1996. Public Law 104-294. 104th Cong., 2nd Sess. (Oct. 11, 1996 - 110 Stat. 3488). Adding section 1831–1839 to USC Title 18 (1996).

Eisenhardt, K. M. (1989). Agency theory: An assessment and review. *Academy of Management Review, 14*(1), 57–73.

Euske E. J., & Player, R. S. (1996). Leveraging management improvement techniques. *Sloan Management Review, 38*(1), 69–79.

Fahey, L. (1999). *Competitors.* New York: John Wiley and Sons.

Filings & forms (EDGAR). (n.d.). Accessed March 2002 at *http://www.sec.gov.*

Fleisher, C. S., & Bensoussan, B. E. (2002). *Strategic and competitive analysis: Methods and techniques for analyzing business competition.* Upper Saddle River, NJ: Prentice Hall.

Fleisher, C. S., & Blenkhorn, D. L. (2001). *Managing frontiers in competitive intelligence.* Westport, CT: Quorum Books

Foucault, M. (1980). *Power/knowledge.* New York: Pantheon.

Ghemawat, P. (1999). *Strategy and the business landscape.* Cambridge, MA: Harvard Business School Publishing.

Ghoshal, S., & Bartlett, C. (1996). Rebuilding behavioral context. *Sloan Management Review, 37*(2), 23–36.

Gioia, E., & Pitre, D. A. (1990). Multiparadigm perspectives on theory building. *Academy of Management Review, 15*(4), 588–589.

Goffee, R., & Jones, G. (1996, November–December). What holds the modern company together? *Harvard Business Review,* 133–148.

Google Groups. (n.d.). Accessed March 2002 at *http://groups.google.com.*

Grant, R. M. (1991). The resource-based theory of competitive advantage. *California Management Review, 33*(3), 114–135.

Grant, R. M. (1996). Toward a knowledge-based theory of the firm. *Strategic Management Journal, 17,* 109–122.

Green, T. (2001). Teaching students to critically evaluate Web pages. *The Clearing House, 75*(1), 32–34.

Greenwood, R., Hinings, C. R., & Brown, J. (1990). The P2 form of strategic management. *Academy of Management Journal, 33*(4), 725–755.

Gulati, R. (1995). Does familiarity breed trust? The implications of repeated ties for contractual choice in alliances. *Academy of Management Journal, 2,* 85–105.

Hardy, C. (1990). *Retrenchment and turnaround.* Berlin: de Gruyter.

Harmon, H. H. (1967). *Modern factor analysis.* Chicago: University of Chicago Press.

Harrigan, K. R. (1985). *Strategies for joint ventures.* Lexington, MA: D.C. Heath and Company.

Harrigan, K. R. (1988). Strategic alliances and partner asymmetries. In F. J. Contractor & P. Lorange (Eds.), *Cooperative strategies in international business.* Lexington, MA: Lexington Books.

Herring, J. (1998). What is intelligence analysis? *Competitive Intelligence Magazine, 12,* 13–16.

Hinings, C. R., & Greenwood, R. (1988). *The dynamics of strategic change.* London: Basil Blackwell.

Hitt, M. A., Freeman, R. E., & Harrison, J. S. (2001). *The Blackwell handbook of strategic management.* Oxford, UK: Blackwell Publishers Ltd.

International Data Corporation. (n.d.). Accessed November 2001 at *http://www.idc.com.*

Jarillo, J. C. (1988). On strategic networks. *Strategic Management Journal, 9*(31), 31–41.

Jemison, D. B., & Sitkin, S. B. (1986). Corporate acquisitions: A process perspective. *Academy of Management Review, 11*(1), 145–163.

Kogut, B. (1988). Joint ventures: Theoretical and empirical perspectives. *Strategic Management Journal, 9,* 319–332.

Kogut, B., & Zander, U. (1992). Knowledge of the firm, combinative capabilities and the replication of technology. *Organization Studies, 3,* 383–397.

Lorange, P., & Roos, J. (1992). *Strategic alliances: Formation, implementation and evolution.* Cambridge, MA: Blackwell.

Lynch. R. P. (1990). *The practical guide to joint ventures and corporate alliances.* New York: John Wiley and Sons.

Macaulay, S. (1963). Non-contractual relations in business: A preliminary study. *American Sociological Review, 28,* 55–67.

Machlup, F. (1980). *Knowledge: Its creation, distribution and economic significance: Vol. 1. Knowledge and knowledge production.* Princeton, NJ: Princeton University Press.

March, J.G., & Simon, H. A. (1958). *Organizations.* New York: John Wiley and Sons.

Marx, K. (1859). *Contribution to a critique of political economy.* Moscow: Progress Publishers.

McGonagle, J. J., & Vella, C. M. (1998). *Protecting your company against competitive intelligence.* Westport, CT: Quorum Books.

McGonagle, J. J., & Vella, C.M. (1999). *The Internet age of competitive intelligence.* Westport CT: Quorum Books.

McGonagle, J. J., & Vella, C. M. (2000). Protecting your competitive advantage. Web-based course accessible at *http://www.cipher-sys.com.*

Meyerson, D., & Martin, J. (1988). Cultural change: An integration of three different views. *Journal of Management Studies, 24,* 623–648.

Miles, R., Coleman, H., Jr., & Creed, D. (1995). Keys to success in corporate redesign. *California Management Review, 37*(3), 128–145.

Miles, R. E., & Snow, C. C. (1986). Organizations: New concepts for new forms. *California Management Review, 28*(3), 62–73.

Miles, R. E., & Snow, C. C. (1992). Causes of failure in network organization. *California Management Review, 34*(4), 53–72.

Miller, D. (1990). *The Icarus paradox: How exceptional companies bring about their own downfall.* New York: Harper Collins.

Miller, D., & Friesen, P. H. (1984). *Organizations: A quantum view.* Englewood Cliffs, N.J.: Prentice Hall.

Mintzberg, H. (1998). *Strategy safari: A guided tour through the wilds of strategic management.* New York: The Free Press.

Morgan, G. (1986). *Images of organizations.* Los Angeles: SAGE Publications.

Noordhaven, N. G. (1992). The problem of contract enforcement in economic organization theory. *Organization Studies, 13*(2), 229–243.

Nystrom, P. C., & Starbuck, W. H. (1984). To avoid crises, unlearn. *Organizational Dynamics, 12*(4), 53–65.

Open Archives Initiative. (n.d.). Accessed March 2002 at *http://www.openarchives.org.*

Osterfelt, S. (2001). The facts… and nothing but the facts! *DM Review, 11*(8), 16–20.

Pant, P. N., & Starbuck, W. H. (1990). Innocents in the forest: Forecasting and research methods. *Journal of Management, 16*(2), 433–460.

Parkhe, A. (1993). Strategic alliance structuring: A game theoretic and transaction cost examination of interfirm cooperation. *Academy of Management Journal, 36*(4), 794–829.

Pearson, C., & Mitroff, I. (1993). From crisis prone to crisis prepared: A framework for crisis management. *Academy of Management Executive, 7*(1), 48–59.

Perrow, C. (1986). *Complex organizations: A critical essay* (3rd ed.). New York: Random House.

Pettigrew, A., Thomas, H., & Whittington, R. (2002). *Handbook of strategy and management.* London: SAGE Publications.

Pettigrew, A. M. (1990). Longitudinal field research on change: Theory and practice. *Organizational Science, 1*(3), 267–292.

Porter, M. (1987, May–June). From competitive advantage to corporate strategy. *Harvard Business Review,* 43–59.

Porter, M. E. (1993, March–April). How competitive forces shape strategy. *Harvard Business Review,* 137–145.

Porter, M. E. (2001, March). Strategy and the Internet. *Harvard Business Review,* 63–78.

Powell, W. (1987). Hybrid organizational arrangements: New forms or transitional development. *California Management Review, (30)*1, 67–87.

Powell, W. W. (1990). Neither market nor hierarchy: Network forms of organization. *Research in Organizational Behavior, 12,* 295–336.

Prahalad, C. K., & Hamel, G. (1990, May–June). The core competence of the corporation. *Harvard Business Review,* 80–91.

Prescott, J. E. (1999). Debunking the "academic abstinence" myth of competitive intelligence. *Competitive Intelligence Review, 2*(4), 2–4.

Radcliff, D. (2002, April 1). Guarding the Gates. *Computerworld.* Retrieved August 25, 2003, from *http://www.computerworld.com/securitytopics/security/story/0,108 01,69658,00.html.*

Radcliff, D. (2002, April 1). Watch those partner links. *Computerworld.* Retrieved August 25, 2003, from *http://www. computerworld.com/securitytopics/security/story/0,10801,69637, 00.html.*

Ring, P. S., & Van de Ven, A. H. (1992). Structuring cooperative relationships between organizations. *Strategic Management Journal, 13,* 483–492.

Rousseau, D. M., & Parks, J. M. (1993). The contracts of individuals and organizations. *Research in Organizational Behavior, 15,* 1–43.

Sapia, A., & Tancer, R. S. (1998). Navigating through the legal/ethical gray zone. *Competitive Intelligence Magazine, 1*(1), 22–31.

Saul, J. R. (1994). *The doubter's companion: A dictionary of aggressive common sense.* Toronto: Viking Penguin.

Scherer, F. M. (1980). *Industrial market structure and economic performance.* Chicago: Rand McNally College Publishing Company.

Scholarly Articles Research Alerting from Taylor & Francis. (n.d.). Accessed March 2002 at *http://www.tandf.co.uk/sara.*

Shoemaker, P. (1995). Scenario planning: A tool for strategic thinking. *Sloan Management Review, 36*(2), 25–40.

SCIP code of ethics for CI professionals. (n.d.). Retrieved March 2002 from *http://www.scip.org.*

Simon, H. A. (1961). *The new science of management decision.* New York: Harper.

Sitkin, S. B., & Pablo, A. L. (1992). Reconceptualizing the determinants of risk behavior. *Academy of Management Review, 17*(1), 9–38.

Stinchcombe, A. L (1990). *Information and organization.* Berkeley, CA: University of California Press.

Stopford, J. M., & Wells, L. T. (1972). *Managing the multinational enterprise.* New York: Basic Books.

Sullivan, D. (2001, February 6). The end for search engines? *Search Engine Report,* 511, 1–7. Retrieved August 25, 2003, from *http://www.searchenginewatch.com/sereport.*

Thompson, J. D. (1967). *Organizations in action.* New York: McGraw-Hill.

Tomer, J. F. (1987). *Organizational capital: The path to higher productivity and well-being.* New York: Praeger.

Ulrich, D., & Lake, D. (1990). *Organizational capability: Competing from the inside out.* Toronto: John Wiley and Sons.

Vibert, C. (2000). *Web-based analysis for competitive intelligence.* Westport, CT: Quorum Books

Vibert, C. (2001). Leveraging technology: CI in an electronic classroom teaching environment. *Competitive Intelligence Review, 12*(1), 48–58.

Watson, G. H. (1997). Understanding the essentials of strategic benchmarking. In G. H. Watson, *Strategic benchmarking: How to rate your company's performance against the world's best* (pp. 39–79). New York: John Wiley and Sons.

Weick, K. (1989). Theory construction as discipline imagination. *Academy of Management Review, 14*(4), 516–531.

Zahra, S., & Chaples, S. (1993). Blind spots in competitive analysis. *Harvard Business Review, 7*(2) 7–28.

List of Information Portals

Title	URL
1Jump	*http://www.1jump.com*
10K Wizard	*http://www.10kwizard.com*
724 Solutions	*http://www.spyonit.com*
About.com	*http://www.about.com*
Alert IPO	*http://www.alert-ipo.com*
AlltheWeb.com	*http://www.alltheweb.com*
AltaVista	*http://www.altavista.com*
American Federation of State, County and Municipal Employees	*http://www.afscme.org*
American Society of Association Executives	*http://www.asaenet.org*
Anonymizer	*http://www.anonymizer.com*
AOL Search	*http://search.aol.com*
Arthur J. Morris Law Library—University of Virginia School of Law	*http://www.law.virginia.edu/home2002/html/librarysite/library.htm*
Ask Jeeves	*http://www.ask.com*
BestCalls.com	*http://www.bestcalls.com*
BigCharts	*http://www.bigcharts.com*
bizjournals.com (American City Business Journals)	*http://www.bizjournals.com*
Business.com	*http://www.business.com*
BusinessWeek Online	*http://www.businessweek.com*
Business Wire	*http://www.businesswire.com*
CEOExpress	*http://www.ceoexpress.com*
CI Resource Index	*http://www.bidigital.com/ci*
CNN.com	*http://www.cnn.com*
CNN/Money	*http://money.cnn.com*
Competia.com	*http://www.competia.com*
Copernic	*http://www.copernic.com*
CorporateInformation.com	*http://www.corporateinformation.com*
Corporate Watch	*http://www.corporatewatch.org*
CorpWatch	*http://www.corpwatch.org*
Delphion	*http://www.delphion.com*
Direct Search	*http://www.freepint.com/gary/direct.htm*

Epinions	*http://www.epinions.com*
Factiva	*http://www.factiva.com*
Fast Company Magazine	*http://www.fastcompany.com*
FindArticles.com	*http://www.findarticles.com*
FindLaw	*http://www.findlaw.com*
Fortune.com	*http://www.fortune.com*
FreeEDGAR	*http://www.freeedgar.com*
FT.com	*http://news.ft.com*
Global Unions	*http://www.global-unions.org*
Google	*http://www.google.com*
Hoover's Online	*http://www.hoovers.com*
Hoover's Online IPO Central	*http://www.hoovers.com/global/ipoc*
HotBot®	*http://www.hotbot.com*
HotJobs	*http://hotjobs.yahoo.com*
InfoSpace	*http://www.infospace.com*
Ingenta	*http://www.ingenta.com*
Intelliseek	*http://www.intelliseek.com*
International Association of Broadcasting Manufacturers	*http://www.theiabm.org*
Internet Archive	*http://www.archive.org*
Invisible-web.net	*http://www.invisible-web.net*
IPO Express	*http://www.edgar-online.com/ipoexpress*
iWon	*http://home.iwon.com*
LookSmart	*http://www.looksmart.com*
Lycos®	*http://www.lycos.com*
Monster.com	*http://www.monster.com*
The Motley Fool	*http://www.fool.com*
MSN® Search	*http://search.msn.com*
Multex Investor	*http://www.multexinvestor.com*
National Association of Broadcasters	*http://www.nab.org*
National Pollutant Release Inventory—Environment Canada	*http://www.ec.gc.ca/pdb/npri*
National Venture Capital Association	*http://www.nvca.com*
Negotech—Human Resources Development Canada	*http://206.191.16.138/gol*
Netscape Search	*http://channels.netscape.com/ns/search*
NewsAlert	*http://www.newsalert.com*
NewsEdge	*http://www.newsedge.com*
NewsHub	*http://www.newshub.com*
NewsLink	*http://www.newslink.org*

NewsNow	*http://www.newsnow.co.uk*
Newsweek Front Page	*http://www.msnbc.com/news/ NW-front_Front.asp*
The New York Times on the Web	*http://www.nytimes.com*
Northern Light	*http://www.northernlight.com*
Office.com	*http://www.office.com*
ON24	*http://news.on24.com*
Open Directory Project	*http://dmoz.org*
Patent Alert	*http://www.patentalert.com*
Polson Enterprises	*http://www.virtualpet.com*
ProFusion	*http://www.profusion.com*
PR Newswire	*http://www.prnewswire.com*
Quicken.com	*http://www.quicken.com*
Red Herring	*http://www.herring.com*
The Right-to-Know Network	*http://www.rtknet.org*
RocketNews	*http://www.rocketnews.com*
Safe Web	*http://www.safeweb.com*
Scholarly Articles Research Alerting (SARA)	*http://www.tandf.co.uk/sara*
Search Engine Report	*http://www.searchenginewatch.com/sereport*
Search Engine Showdown	*http://www.searchengineshowdown.com*
Search Engine Watch	*http://www.searchenginewatch.com*
Search Systems—Public Record Locator	*http://www.searchsystems.net*
SEDAR	*http://www.sedar.com*
ShiftCentral	*http://www.shiftcentral.com*
Society of Competitive Intelligence Professionals	*http://www.scip.org*
Statistics Canada	*http://www.statcan.ca*
Strategis	*http://strategis.ic.gc.ca*
SurfWax	*http://www.surfwax.com*
Teoma	*http://www.teoma.com*
Thomas Register	*http://www.thomasregister.com*
TIME.com	*http://www.time.com*
U.S. Bureau of Labor Statistics	*http://www.bls.gov*
U.S. Consumer Product Safety Commission	*http://www.cpsc.gov*
U.S. Environmental Protection Agency	*http://www.epa.gov*
U.S. Federal Communications Commission	*http://www.fcc.gov*
U.S. Federal Trade Commission	*http://www.ftc.gov*

U.S. Occupational Safety and Health Administration	*http://www.osha.gov*
U.S. Patent and Trademark Office	*http://www.uspto.gov*
U.S. Securities and Exchange Commission	*http://www.sec.gov*
USATODAY.com	*http://www.usatoday.com*
USC's Marshall School of Business	*http://www.marshall.usc.edu*
Vault.com	*http://www.vault.com*
vFinance.com	*http://www.vfinance.com*
The Virtual Chase	*http://www.virtualchase.com*
Vivísimo	*http://www.vivisimo.com*
Wall Street Net	*http://wsn.doremus.com*
WetFeet	*http://www.wetfeet.com*
WiseNut	*http://www.wisenut.com*
Yahoo!	*http://www.yahoo.com*
Yahoo! Finance	*http://finance.yahoo.com*

INDEX

W

War Gaming, 32
Web, 201
  developers, 48
  Evaluation Sites, 58
  search, 21, 49, 64
  Site, 76
  surveillance software, 22

Web-based
  evidence, 196
  marketing project, 71
  tools, 22
WebQuests, 5
WetFeet, 47

About the Author and Contributors

ABOUT THE PRINCIPAL AUTHOR

Conor Vibert, Ph.D., is an associate professor of business strategy at the Fred C. Manning School of Business of Acadia University in Wolfville, Nova Scotia. Conor is the author of *Web-Based Analysis for Competitive Intelligence*, published by Quorum Books. He has presented his work at conferences of the Academy of Management, the American Psychological Association, the Administrative Sciences Association of Canada, and the Atlantic Schools of Business and has published in *Competitive Intelligence Review, Education and Information Technology*, and the *Journal of Business Strategy*. At Acadia University, Conor teaches business policy, change management, and organization theory, while his current research interests focus on the management of higher-risk alliance partners and the application of the Internet to contemporary business issues. He is a member of the Society of Competitive Intelligence Professionals (SCIP) and may be reached at *conor.vibert@acadiau.ca*.

ABOUT THE CHAPTER AUTHORS

John Prescott, Ph.D., is the author of Chapter 12. He is a professor of business administration at the Katz Graduate School of Business at the University of Pittsburgh. John has been teaching, researching, and consulting in the area of competitive intelligence for more than 18 years. He is the executive editor of *Competitive Intelligence Review*, subject matter expert for the American Productivity & Quality Center, international advisor to the Society of Competitive Intelligence Professionals in China, winner of a meritorious award from SCIP, and instructor for the first Web-based CI course. He consults internationally in the area of designing and managing CI processes. He can be reached at *Prescott@katz.pitt.edu*.

David Campbell is the author of Chapter 2. He is vice president of research and CI services with ShiftCentral and is responsible for the ongoing development of its competitive intelligence services, including methodology development, dissemination tools, and Web-based CI portals. David also writes monthly CI briefings and in-depth research reports in several key verticals, including e-learning/training, telecom, government, oil and gas, and portals. Before joining ShiftCentral, he spent more than ten years in business- and industry-related research activities with the Greater Moncton Economic Commission, Aliant (NBTel), and the New Brunswick Department of Economic Development. David has an undergraduate degree in business administration as well as an MBA. He has also completed postgraduate work in economics and economic development. He may be contacted at *david@shiftcentral.com* or through ShiftCentral's Web site, *http://www.shiftcentral.com.*

Tanja Harrison, MLIS, is the author of Chapter 3. She is an academic librarian at the Vaughan Memorial Library of Acadia University. She is responsible for research and instruction to the Faculty of Professional Studies (which includes the Schools of Business, Education, and Recreation Management and Kinesiology). She is active in the Canadian Library Association and is the new director of information/publicity and Web manager for the Nova Scotia Library Association. Her current research interests extend to all aspects of the search engine industry, digital reference initiatives, and the effects of technology on information literacy. Tanja can be reached at *tanja.harrison@acadiau.ca.*

Jennifer Richard, MLIS, is the author of Chapter 4. She is an academic librarian at the Vaughan Memorial Library, Acadia University. She is responsible for research and instruction to the Faculty of Pure and Applied Sciences and coordinates digital initiatives at the library. She is a councillor at large on the Canadian Library Association's Executive Council, as well as chair of the Local Arrangements Committee for the Canadian Library Association and Atlantic Provinces Library Association 2002 Joint Conference. Her current research interests include digitizing the holdings of E. C. Smith Herbarium, the impact of consortial e-journals on small academic libraries, and the creation of an electronic thesis project at Acadia University. Jennifer can be reached at *jennifer.richard@acadiau.ca.*

Carolyn M. Vella is founding partner and **John J. McGonagle** is managing partner of the Helicon Group. Helicon has been providing consulting, research, and training in competitive and strategic analysis since 1980. Carolyn is the recipient of the 2003 Meritorious Award from the Society of Competitive Intelligence Professionals (SCIP). Carolyn and John are the authors of Chapter 5 and prolific writers on competitive intelligence and related subjects, having coauthored seven books on competitive intelligence. The newest, *Bottom Line Competitive Intelligence*, was released in the fall of 2002 by the Greenwood Group. They are also coauthors of *How to Use a Consultant in Your Company: A Managers' and Executives' Guide* (John Wiley & Sons, 2001). They may be reached at *jjm@helicongroup.com* or through their Web site, *http://www.helicongroup.com.*

Craig Fleisher, Ph.D., is the author of Chapter 6. He is the Odette research chair in business and professor of business strategy and entrepreneurship at the Odette School of Business of the University of Windsor. Canada's only fellow of the Society of Competitive Intelligence Professionals (SCIP), he founded the Canadian Technology Triangle Chapter. He has been on the graduate faculties of Wilfrid Laurier University and the Universities of Calgary, New Brunswick, Pittsburgh, Sydney, and Waikato. He has also held industry positions in mortgage banking management and strategy consulting. His Ph.D. in strategy, environment, and organization was from the Katz Graduate School of Business (University of Pittsburgh), and his MBA was from Vanderbilt's Owen Graduate School of Management. The author of more than 100 articles and book chapters, Craig is a frequent keynote or plenary speaker to corporate, government, and industry association groups around Australasia, Europe, and the Americas. He has also advised leading global organizations such as Bell Canada, Chrysler, the Canadian Imperial Bank of Commerce (CIBC), EDS, Esso, IBM, Johnson & Johnson, Labatt, Levi Strauss, Merck, Noranda, Novo Nordisk, Philip Morris, Shell, State Farm, and Telstra. Craig can be reached at *fleisher@uwindsor.ca.*

Daniel Silver, Ph.D., is the author of Chapter 11. He an assistant professor in the Jodrey School of Computer Science at Acadia University, where he lectures and undertakes research in the areas of machine learning, data mining, intelligent agents, and e-knowledge management. Before coming to Acadia, Danny was a member of the Faculty of Management of Dalhousie University, where he was active in the areas of knowledge discovery, data warehousing, and data mining as a junior chair in business informatics. Danny continues to lecture at Dalhousie through the executive MBA program. He is also the founder and president of

CogNova Technologies, a consultancy specializing in knowledge discovery management methods and data mining technologies. Danny may be reached at *danny.silver@acadiau.ca.*